Poetry and the Feminine from Behn to Cowper

Poetry and the Feminine from Behn to Cowper

Jennifer Keith

Newark: University of Delaware Press

© 2005 by Rosemont Publishing & Printing Corp.

All rights reserved. Authorization to photocopy items for internal or personal use, or the internal or personal use of specific clients, is granted by the copyright owner, provided that a base fee of $10.00, plus eight cents per page, per copy is paid directly to the Copyright Clearance Center, 222 Rosewood Drive, Danvers, Massachusetts 01923. [0-87413-891-4/05 $10.00 + 8¢ pp, pc.]

Other than as indicated in the foregoing, this book may not be reproduced, in whole or in part, in any form (except as permitted by Sections 107 and 108 of the U.S. Copyright Law, and except for brief quotes appearing in reviews in the public press).

Associated University Presses
2010 Eastpark Boulevard
Cranbury, NJ 08512

The paper used in this publication meets the requirements of the American National Standard for Permanence of Paper for Printed Library Materials Z39.48-1984.

Library of Congress Cataloging-in-Publication Data

Keith, Jennifer
  Poetry and the Feminine from Behn to Cowper / Jennifer Keith.
    v. cm.
  Includes bibliographical references and index.
  Contents: Dryden, Pope, and the transformation of the muse—Speaking objects : women poets and the muse—Gender and order in the prospect—The voice of nature and the poet's labor—The nightingale's breast against the thorn : sensibility and the sublime.
  ISBN 0-87413-891-4 (alk. paper)
  1. English poetry—18th century—History and criticism. 2. English poetry—Early modern, 1500-1700—History and criticism. 3. English poetry—Women authors—History and criticism. 4. Women—Great Britain—Intellectual life. 5. Women and literature—Great Britain. 6. Authorship—Sex differences. 7. Femininity in literature. 8. Sex role in literature. I. Title.

PR555.W6K45 2005
821'.509353—dc22
                              2005001445

PRINTED IN THE UNITED STATES OF AMERICA

Contents

Introduction 11

1. Dryden, Pope, and the Transformation of the Muse 30
2. Speaking Objects: Women Poets and the Muse 51
3. Gender and Order in the Prospect 80
4. The Voice of Nature and the Poet's Labor 111
5. The Nightingale's Breast against the Thorn:
   Sensibility and the Sublime 140

Notes 167
Bibliography 205
Index 221

Acknowledgments

For his patient and thoughtful reading of the manuscript in its earlier and later stages I am indebted to John Sitter. Nancy Myers gave me vigorous encouragement over the years and excellent advice on several chapters. I thank Gail McDonald and Russ McDonald for their support and for generously reading nearly every chapter of this book: their suggestions significantly improved it. Denise Baker, David Fairer, Claudia Thomas Kairoff, Kathryn King, David B. Morris, Laura Runge, and Charles Tisdale gave wise comments on portions of the manuscript. I thank Rachael Mann, Melissa Bailes, and Thomas Christopher for editing and proofreading portions of the book. With gratitude I acknowledge the long-lived encouragement given by Janet Hampton, Peter Janssens, Helen Keith, Kent Keith, and Laura Nazareth. Finally, I thank Christine Retz for her good nature and patience in overseeing the production of the book.

A Summer Research Excellence Award from the University of North Carolina at Greensboro helped support my work on this book. Portions of chapters 2 and 5 are reprinted, with permission, from *SEL: Studies in English Literature 1500–1900* 38, 3 (Summer 1998). A portion of chapter 4 is reprinted, with permission, from *Études Écossaises*, No. 3 (1995), published by Éditions littéraires et linguistiques de l'université de Grenoble. I am grateful to the Wellesley College Special Collections for permission to reprint material from Anne Finch's "Wellesley Manuscript."

Poetry and
the Feminine
from Behn to Cowper

Introduction

In the last decades we have seen increasing attention to women poets of the Restoration and eighteenth century, with names such as Katherine Philips, Anne Finch, Mary Leapor, and Ann Yearsley now familiar to students of the era. But few larger frameworks have been provided to see their work next to each other and, still rarer, next to that of Dryden, Pope, and Gray, among others.[1] In his 1994 study of Anne Finch's poetic achievements, Charles H. Hinnant reminded us that most studies of women poets up to that point had "failed to undertake any fundamental revaluation of the relative position of individual women poets vis-à-vis the canon."[2] One of the recent exceptions is David Fairer's study of eighteenth-century poetry, which extensively integrates a range of poets as he traces poetic developments through categories such as politeness, pastoral and georgic, and the rediscovery of native traditions—all of which render the usual trajectory from "Augustan" to "Romantic" obsolete.[3] My particular focus is on how poetry by women has shaped the course of English poetry. To develop frameworks for these poets, this study revisits the foundations of literary representation and value and returns to the contributions of men poets that have defined Restoration and eighteenth-century periodization. But questions of literary value are notoriously difficult, not least because we have inherited standards of evaluation that emerged in part to exclude women writers, and therefore we must listen carefully to what women poets have to say about alternative approaches to poetic authority, representation, and value.

Accustomed to hearing of women writers' material exclusions, we rarely attend to their poetic responses to inherited rhetorical exclusions. Material exclusions against women were daunting, including illiteracy and the hazards to a woman's sexual reputation if she entered the literary marketplace. In fact, the excellent studies in the last decades of the material conditions of the eighteenth-century marketplace have unintentionally diverted attention from a more overtly evaluative criticism that would examine the poetic goals of these writers.[4] We continue to trivialize women's poetic accomplishments when we ignore their complex responses to a tradition of rhetorical conventions and aesthetic norms that assumed a male poet-subject. In other words, to engage thoughtfully in poetic discourse the best women poets had to develop alternatives to the most basic elements of establishing poetic value. There are few other sources for this analysis than the poems themselves.

Poetry made specific demands on women writers that other genres did not. Although on one level poetry had a chaster reputation than the novel or drama, its elite status made it more forbidding than other genres to women writers. Even well into the eighteenth century, the expectation that the poet be educated in the classics continued to nurture poetry's elite status, which could thus exclude women and men from lower ranks. The training ground for poets was usually the translation and imitation of classical poetry—exercises available to a select few. The sense of hierarchy within poetry further established its privileges: women might attempt the lower rungs such as pastoral and song, but fewer considered writing an ode or epic. Compounding this was the expectation that women not exhibit artfulness, should they attempt poetry: but in adopting a simple style with few formal pyrotechnics women often received the damning compliment that they lacked art. The most important obstacle to women poets, however, was poetry's increasing attention to a speaker or narrator. In constructing characters for a play or novel, a writer could distribute and veil her agency, observation, and judgment among several characters, including male characters, or in a narrator. But women poets entered the scene in greater numbers at a time when men poets were especially focused on developing an authoritative voice (often most authoritative when the poetic self seemed to disappear) in relation to increasingly complex notions of subjectivity. Their methods for achieving authority would rely heavily on rhetorical structures where the subject was male and the object female. This structure would be the greatest challenge for women poets and they responded to it by changing the course of English poetry.

Thus, while throughout I highlight what could have been rhetorical obstacles for women writing poetry, I do so to emphasize the extraordinary inventiveness and success of their responses to such structures. This is not an account of women poets' defeat (what Sandra Gilbert and Susan Gubar once described as the "profoundly debilitating" anxiety of authorship for women), but rather it demonstrates their successful techniques.[5] These techniques ultimately help us reconsider aesthetic standards for women and men poets. Astute readers and critics of a largely male-authored tradition, women poets altered the conventions that had rhetorically excluded them as writers.[6] They did so by fundamentally questioning the divisions between subjects and objects of representation, by exploiting the theme of friendship as a model for an intersubjective mimesis, by elevating lower poetic kinds and in turn speeding the collapse of the hierarchy of poetic kinds, by questioning "objective" empirical representations of nature, by introducing sensibility as a value long before the middle of the eighteenth century, and by inquiring into whether language *can* represent. To adapt what Claudia Thomas Kairoff has said of Pope's women readers: many women poets of this era provide a "model of fearless critical reading."[7]

Integrating the work of men and women poets, I seek to balance previous studies on *what* has been represented with equal attention to *how* it has been represented. In considering less familiar techniques of representation I explore how we may conceive alternative aesthetic standards. To understand more completely women's and men's aesthetic achievements in this era I underscore the following: (1) the adoption of or changes to representation as a gendered structure, where the object is typically feminized; (2) inquiries into the nature of representation itself, which may result in formal irregularities, tonal and generic shifts, simplicity instead of ornament, obscurity rather than clarity; and (3) the construction of "poetical character," or in today's parlance "subject effects" that define aesthetic and ethical achievements.

I

Fundamental to my examination of how women and men worked with the medium of poetry is my argument that they relied on a rhetorical structure where feminine figures authorized the poet and characterized the quality of representation. This gendered structure inheres in the era's familiar dictum that the goal of Art is the imitation of Nature. In imitating Nature both men and women poets persistently figure Nature as feminine.[8] To represent, then, is to enter into, and usually revise, a structure wherein the subject is conventionally figured as male, the object female. As has been repeatedly shown by feminist critics, this representational structure presents obvious challenges to women writers who would imitate Nature, the object of art, from their own positions as female subject-speakers occupying a range of social strata.[9]

For poets of the Restoration and eighteenth century, to imitate Nature is to imitate an ordering principle. Not simply the world of flora and fauna, *Nature* infinitely expands to include orders of being and knowing. Nature is a complex notion of form that defines the object of representation, the act of representation, and the subject of representation, as the following chapters will show. Such a focus exposes how complex and transformative are the poets' approaches to imitation, invoking a range of identifications between the subject and object of representation. *Imitation*, or *mimesis*, was of course never a simple notion of copying. Arne Melberg describes the dialectic that accounts for its range: "*never* a homogeneous term, . . . if its basic movement is towards similarity it is *always* open to the opposite. Perhaps, modern theorists have become modern by emphasizing the differential movements and possibilities of what earlier was called *mimesis*."[10] In the period I examine here, writers' attention to the transforming function of mimesis relies on this dialectic of similarity and difference. This transformative function can apply both to the subject who imitates and the object imitated. Central to the possibilities of mimesis is the era's increasing assertion that Nature *is* form, a dynamic entity whose order is so complex that it may even appear formless. "Nature," argues Raymond Williams, "is perhaps the most complex word in the language."[11] Arthur O. Lovejoy analyzed the numerous senses of Nature in the eighteenth century in his essay "'Nature' as Aesthetic Norm."[12] Lovejoy's definitions include Nature as platonic form, the structure of human psychology, and the ordered external realm. Nature can signify deep form, "the cosmical order as a whole, or a half-personified power."[13] For the poets, Nature as "half-personified power" was always feminine.

My study argues the necessity of recognizing feminine Nature as an infinitely expandable category of form—its elasticity allows poets to redefine poetry. The poet's increased attention to *being* poetic, I argue, depends on emulating values ascribed to feminine Nature. Revisions of form are social acts of composition shared by men and women in their common work of transforming the goals and values of poetry.[14] Form—ranging from the medium of poetry to poetic kinds (such as the prospect poem) to internal structures (such as patterns of invocation and stanzaic forms) to modes (such as the sublime)—carries poetic value and revaluation. On a rhetorical level, feminine Nature is the form for self and other that these poets explore.

Yet some feminist critics have seen formal studies as inimical to the appreciation of women's writing, in part because formal studies have historically taken canonical works by men as their object. In rejecting the significance of form, however, these critics have inadvertently implied that women's writing has little formal and aesthetic value but only contributes to a narrative of contextual studies.[15] Attending to form does not exclude women poets; on the contrary, it serves as a lens for revealing their distinctive achievements. This explanatory function of form is especially clear if we are mindful of ways in which gender has organized form, requiring women to develop alternatives for poetic representation. Such an approach, then, does not separate text and context but rather exposes how they interact.[16]

The older literary historical narratives, based on what was a canon of Restoration and eighteenth-century poetry, will alter within the perspective I offer. The traditional story, in a thumbnail sketch, identifies an era often called Augustan (1660 to the 1740s), which develops a public, politically engaged poetry characterized by objective imitation of the world outside the "self." The Augustan style is "manly," sometimes reformulated as exuberant or energetic, excelling in the satiric mode. Following the Augustan period is one sometimes called preromantic, post-Augustan, or the Age of Sensibility (from the 1740s to the 1780s or 1790s), associated with a more private poetry that flees from history and politics, concerning itself, rather, with the world "within."[17] The post-Augustan matter and manner have at times been characterized as "feminine," showing a greater sensitivity to Nature and a devotion to feminine personifications. This poetry specializes in descriptive meditation and private versions of the ode. My crude sketch does not begin to convey the often nuanced and valuable characterizations of Restoration and eighteenth-century poetry, but I include it to recall the background against which we might develop another narrative about the poetic experiments and achievements in the long eighteenth century. Increasingly, recent studies have dismantled these divisions in Restoration and eighteenth-century literature, among them, the work of David Fairer cited above and that of Dustin Griffin.[18]

Some frameworks, however, have seemed to echo the "masculine" standards so persuasively authorized by the canonized poets, reproducing in eighteenth-century criticism an eighteenth-century ideology.[19] Although recent studies of individual poets have substantially overturned the stereotype of manliness that long informed the praise of eighteenth-century poetry, in some larger frameworks its masculine merits—at least implicitly—linger.[20] Eric Rothstein's insightful survey of Restoration and eighteenth-century poetry establishes thematic and stylistic categories for poetry that arise from masculine stereotypes of the poet. He outlines a three-part trajectory of Restoration and eighteenth-century poetry based on male figures from the rake, to the urbane gentleman whose aim is "interconnectedness," to the man of feeling.[21] Margaret Anne Doody's compelling analysis of the energy of canonical Augustan poetry uses stereotypes of masculine power to characterize writers such as Pope, who followed the imperative "'Rise, kill and eat.' They asserted their right to dominion over all creatures, all riches, all spaces, and all styles."[22] Doody, however, attends to feminine figures in her analysis of the element of "charivari" in Augustan poetry, which "often entails the strong presence of a feminine being, or even of feminine power(s), which may be officially mocked according to the daily regulations of customary life but which cannot readily be weakened or overcome."[23]

To include the work of women poets in this history is to dissolve such distinctions in chronology, characteristics, and values. Women poets' experiments with authority, language, and relations between self and other indicate qualities of Restoration and eighteenth-century poetry that have been misleadingly withheld until the discussion of Romantic poetry.[24] The work of women poets of the Restoration and eighteenth century does not, however, simply change the starting date for Romanticism, since these eighteenth-century women poets respond to problems of representation differently from their male successors in the Romantic era. Although the number of publications by women poets increases in the second half of the eighteenth century, we should not equate the significance of women's contributions to poetry with this increase in their numbers.[25] In the era that concerns me, poetic experimentation by women is at least as significant in what is labeled the Augustan era (1660 to the 1740s) as it is in that labeled pre-Romantic and Romantic (1740s to 1790s), when still more poetry by women was published.

II

The feminine not only occupies the position of the object represented, it performs a central figurative function. The use of feminine images permits the poet to evoke spiritual and mythological correspondences, cover gaps in argumentation, "simplify" public issues into literary conventions of sexual intimacy, and "universalize" English nationalism into sexual potency. To the poets of this period, the importance of the feminine lies not in absolute value but in its figurative function to transfer meaning and order onto something else. In the traditional canon, for example, Nature and universals are often "clarified" by being figured as feminine objects accessible to the male poet's authority. The feminine appears in many forms in this poetry—from feminized landscapes, to feminized personifications, to a diffusive sensibility associated with the cult of the feminine later in the century. The feminine, then, serves as the figure that seems not to figure as it enlists, enforces, or revises social codes for women's behavior. The range of values for the feminine enables it to trope poetic authority because these values draw on longstanding cultural paradigms in the histories of men and women. Laura

Brown acknowledges the range of figures of the feminine in her analysis of the tropes of female sexual autonomy. The function of these figures, she explains, can range from attacking the status quo, to shaping standards for heterosexual identity, to "enact-[ing] epistemological and political crises."[26] In a poetic era commonly considered the *least* metaphoric in English literature, we find a deep structure of gendered metaphors that conceal discursive gaps precisely because the categories of masculine and feminine were often used transparently. Ironically, part of the feminine's use in clarifying meaning lies in its association with the irrational. The feminine often conveys mythological associations that belie the poetry's empirical claims.[27] Canonical versions of the feminine remind us that myth is a more important mode of the Enlightenment than is often recognized, as Anthony Cascardi has argued.[28] In this mythopoeic function of the feminine lies its cultural-historical significance: its mythical inscriptions mask its power to mold conduct.

The feminine participates in the structure of gender difference that appears to simplify the complex act of representation. The structure of gender difference may reveal or obscure representation as both an aesthetic and ethical relation between subject and object, self and other. Troping virtually all of the canonical poetry's central ideas, from Nature and Science to Virtue and Dulness, the feminine allows the male poet to capitalize on a system of difference. Poetic authority is often demonstrated in narratives of seduction and conquest where the feminine resists but is ultimately controlled: the Daphne who may escape Apollo's arms is turned into a crown for great art. Thus, eighteenth-century canonical poets could use cultural figurations of women to assert their identities as manly poets who at times wish to remind their readers that poets should be men. As Mary Poovey has argued in another context, "sexual difference ... becomes the fundamental organizing dichotomy of a semantic system that produces distinctions," where "distinctions" correspond to aesthetic values.[29]

Roger Lonsdale has observed that as the eighteenth century wore on, Romantic poets asserted aesthetic criteria in part as a reaction to women poets' entrance as competitors: "superficially more democratic than Richard Steele's definition of the poet as 'a very well-bred Man,' Wordsworth's notion of the poet [as a 'man speaking to men'] may seem even more relentlessly masculine and, in the loftiness of his conception of poetic genius, even more exclusive.... If Steele's definition of the poet in 1712 might seem effectively to exclude women from a male preserve, Wordsworth's formulations may appear calculated rather to recover that territory from the women who had recently occupied it."[30] The aesthetics of Romantic genius, according to Christine Battersby, prescribed a "new rhetoric of exclusion that developed in the eighteenth century, and which gradually grew louder as the nineteenth century progressed. This rhetoric praised 'feminine' qualities in male creators . . . but claimed females could not—or should not—create."[31] This so-called exclusion in fact generated innovations in poetry by women and, in turn, men.

The expanding literary marketplace reshaped the community of poets and readers. These reconfigurations required poets to confront (1) a readership no longer limited to the more controlled network of manuscript circulation or of a highly educated elite, and (2) an extraordinary number of other poets who, like the amorphous print audience, did not belong to the elite circles of masculine privilege in the universities or government. The double-edged sword of these advantages has been noted by Shevelow: "many of the very agents that were enabling, even actively promoting, women's participation in print culture were also those engaged in containing it."[32] That is, in this expanding literary marketplace, men and women writers increasingly examined the grounds of their authority and the nature of representation whether or not they themselves were the interlopers in this arena of high culture. The response to the burgeoning print culture was to police it through the category of Taste, one of the functions, it will be remembered, of the essays of Addison and Steele.[33] As Laura Runge has argued, these standards of evaluation became increasingly inflected by stereotypes of gender that were often conflated with the gender of the writer.[34] In an age that was attempting to fix the standards of Taste, the feminine was the aesthetic quality that defied analysis—the "je ne sais quoi."[35]

III

In organizing this study, I often refer to the older subdivisions of this period to highlight how they no longer hold in the perspective that I offer. The structure of my chapters, and, by extension, of this alternative literary history, originates from my study of the feminized categories that women poets repeatedly revise in their experiments with authority and representation: the muse, Nature, personifications, and sensibility. Such an organization based on women's poetic experiments provides points of access that expose characteristics of the traditional male canon as well.

How do both men and women poets imitate the feminized order that they called *Nature*? I begin to answer this question by analyzing their uses of the muse, the foundational mythological feminine figure used to authorize representation. In revising the traditional relation to the muse, poets articulate the modern self through complex relations to alterity. Especially for men, these relations may range from a narrative of sexual conquest to one of emulation of or sympathy with the other. Thus the muse and other feminine objects may figure elusive aspects of the self: the spiritual, the irrational, the transcendent, the ineffable.

Chapter 1 considers the uses of the muse in defining the poetic authority and modes of representation typically called Augustan. The poet's relation to the muse can either engage or evade some of the most urgent problems of aesthetic, epistemological, sovereign, and sexual authority.[36] The figure of the muse serves as a mediator in these conflicts while allowing the poet to express the inexpressible. Great poetry is figured according to a range of romance paradigms that include a male poet's sexual-poetic procreation with a female muse or the poet's pose as a muse courting a male friend. Restoration and eighteenth-century poets most often read today saw that in revising the muse they could broaden their tonal and thematic range and renegotiate their relation to a new audience.

We might expect the gendered structure of representation, seen most obviously in the male poet's invocation of the female muse, to preempt women poets writing from the position of a female subject. While many women poets were at odds rhetorically with the muse or with other feminized figures whom, they argue, prefer men over women, many women poets approach this inhospitable gendered structure by reconceiving the grounds of authority and representation. For some, the poetic persona identifies with rhetorical characterizations of the feminine. This simple difference—where the poet's gender corresponds to the object of representation—requires women to reconstitute the conditions and nature of representation. Rather than serving as invisible cultural metaphors supporting ostensibly nongendered issues, gendered tropes in women's poetry define the speaker's relation to the poetic tradition. Such tropes point to a contemporary extraliterary world in which literary figurations of the feminine bear a striking resemblance to definitions of women's roles in a mercantile economy.[37]

Through the muse, women writers confront the paradox of speaking within a tradition that objectifies them, a paradox analyzed in chapter 2. Their exploration of the poet-subject demythologizes and humanizes the role of the feminine in English poetry. I use *subject* here to denote the effect of a subject in verbal representation, not to refer to an actual state of being. As Katherine Philips, Anne Killigrew, and Anne Finch inscribe their gender identities in many of their poems, they revise the conventions of poetic authority and value associated with the poet's relation to the muse. In their relations to the muse, women poets often depart from the mimetic norms of the canon, described by one critic as an "orientation which stresses the order of a universe outside the mind and the obligation of art to capture certain enduring truths within that universe."[38] In poems by Philips and Finch, for example, the poet's orientation is toward an order shared by the poet's mind and the universe outside it to the extent that divisions between self and object are effaced. Instead of conforming to either a canonical "Augustan" mimesis that represents the "world around" or an anticipatory "Romantic" mimesis that represents the "world within," Philips and Finch represent the conjunction of worlds within and without the writer.[39]

IV

Chapter 3 addresses the era's explicit representations of Nature in the prospect poem: here the function of the muse is redistributed in the landscape surveyed by the poet. In the eighteenth-century prospect, canonical poets retain a romance paradigm for inspiration by internalizing the muse's powers as their own or by dispersing the muse's characteristics onto the feminized landscape. Dryden, Pope, Addison, and Thomson, for example, establish their authority through centuries-old figures of gender inherent in ancient poetic representations of the landscape, but they revise the gendered landscape through an ostensibly empirical and mimetic relation to Nature. This *apparent* turn to the empirical is part of the era's shift toward an emphasis on sensory perception that nevertheless continues to be dominated by figures of gender. The prospect is one of the chief Augustan means of *asserting* poetic subjectivity as masculine, objective, disinterested, elite, and empirical. In the canon, the feminization of Nature helps to control and personalize through gendered narratives the varying notions of Nature entertained in the seventeenth and eighteenth centuries.

What Frederick Burwick describes about Romantic imitation applies as well to poems a century earlier: "the province and techniques of mimesis were being redefined.... Self-awareness, with its alert attention to the subjective apprehension of external reality, involved an attendant concern with the representation of the interior processes of perception."[40] In the act of imitating Nature, prospect poems expose imitation as a process of relatedness between poet and Nature, a relatedness that is often the poet's emulation of or identification with the other/object. The poet seeks to represent Nature as ordering principle, but we find that to convey the form of the object of representation, the poet typically strives for an ontological emulation of that form. This tendency appears as early as Sir John Denham's *Cooper's Hill* in the middle of the seventeenth century and is developed by Pope in *Windsor Forest* and *An Essay on Man*. Indeed, such a goal is consistent with earlier notions of Nature as an order that comprises the entire Chain of Being. While the prospect poem appears to epitomize the authoritative qualities of Augustan poetry sometimes characterized as political, ratiocinative, secular, public, and nationalistic, the poets' insistent gendering of the landscape destabilizes these labels.

For women poets, the prospect presents obvious dilemmas in its tropological structure, its tone of controlled disinterestedness, and what John Barrell calls its "equal, wide survey."[41] Women's prospect poetry typically does not "expatiate free" over Nature but instead observes a terrain of constraint. The moralized landscapes of Aphra Behn, Anne Finch, Lady Mary Wortley Montagu, and Jean Adams are usually based on the poet's identification with objectified feminine nature. Constructed from a position of intimacy or submission rather than control, these poems highlight the poet's gender and class identity and, in turn, reveal the poet's interest in the landscape as a subject and object. Women poets' uses of the prospect exhibit a wide range of approaches to creating a subject from "those 'unlivable' and 'uninhabitable' zones of social life which are nevertheless densely populated by those who do not enjoy the status of the subject."[42] In women poets' landscapes we see drastic reductions of space and abrupt shifts in tone—all of which might be deemed mimetically or technically incompetent according to the inherited standards of this era.

Women's poetry reminds us of an important feature of men's: its inscription of the modern self as riven by the polarities of subject and object, masculine and feminine, and embodiment and disembodiment.[43] Versions of the prospect show us that the poetic "self" and its functions do not aim for autonomous individuation but are always supported or bound by a relation to the other that often relies on gendered narratives. That the subject emerges, or is suppressed, in relation to gender is a familiar claim, as is the subject's reliance on the object to articulate itself. For men and women poets the subject is always a hybrid of subject and object. At times the poetic "self" may even aspire to the condition of the object. The poetic self becomes complex—that is, acquires deep interiority—by incorporating the feminine, which can be incorporated because it is an object and yet "contains" the unfathomable. As a figure, the feminine cannot be fixed; thus, to identify with or incorporate the feminine enables innumerable subject-object positions.

In the relations between the feminine object and masculine subject, poets can construct a deep resistance to the pressures of commodification of poet and poem in the burgeoning literary marketplace. Although Linda Zionkowski has argued that the eighteenth century "saw the emergence of a new 'stereotype of manliness' that took as its reference point the market rather than the court, the bourgeois or economic man rather than the gentleman or aristocrat," I argue that much of the poetry exposes a subject increasingly incorporating the feminine and resisting the commodification of poet and poem.[44] According to Zionkowski the commodification of poets in the literary marketplace initially threatened ideals of masculinity: precisely "by making their works public," men and their work "become a vehicle for the reader's pleasure, which undermines their autonomy and integrity as masculine subjects.... From the Restoration onward, this conception of the poet's compromised manhood was gradually challenged by the emergence of an alternative rhetoric: one which proposed the commercial market in texts as the arena where manhood and cultural authority are established."[45] But another kind of rhetoric also appears in the poems. By inscribing the poet-subject as incorporating more and more of "the feminine" and by focusing in greater detail on the object of representation as feminine, many men poets attempted to free both themselves and their work from commodification.

V

By examining Nature as *object* in the prospect we discover ways in which Nature becomes *subject* in this era. Key to the imitation of Nature is not only the intimacy between subject and object, but also the poet's projection of subjectivity onto the object. These divisions and recombinations of subject and object expose the inextricability of representation and ontology.[46] The turn from position of object to subject, and from representation to being, is achieved through the most characteristic trope of eighteenth-century poetry: personification. In the dynamic notion of Nature as form, form is able to "bite back" in this figure of the person.[47] Thus personification reminds us of Theodor Adorno's observation that "the unsolved antagonisms of reality return in artworks as immanent problems of form."[48] Nature is, of course, the fundamental personification of eighteenth-century poetry and poetics.[49] Animated by personifications, the landscape is the large body of female Nature that contains other bodies in the form of (usually feminine) personifications.

Using personification, a trope considered by M. H. Abrams *the* figure of poetic imagination in the eighteenth century, even of poetic exhibitionism, poets of this era explore the convergence of subject and object (e.g., Warton with Melancholy, Collins with Evening, Greville with Indifference).[50] Almost always figured as feminine, personifications are the revenants of the muse adapted to a culture that sees itself as postmythological. Nodes of subject-object relations, personifications can figure a range of ontological depths. This projection of the human, aligning itself with various abstract forces and entities, is the poet's demonstration of poesis, or making.[51] Endowed with the power to make and to speak, personifications can undo poetic authority, the stability of subject-object divisions, and the reliability of language itself. In personifying, then, many poets grapple with the problem of whether language can represent. Poems by Finch, Thomson, Gray, and Leapor show how the poetics of immanence sought through the use of personification begets an inquiry into language.

Chapter 4 examines how the use of personification destabilizes the model of Nature as property to be surveyed and owned, at least imaginatively. In elaborating on Nature as person/personification, the poet may assert the property—and, ironically, intangibility—of the self, buoyed and threatened by its complex mimetic relation to nature. Working the land poetically, then, involves another kind of labor, a labor of *being* rather than *doing*. For Finch this labor is primarily a perceptual one that frees the female subject from social, political, and psychological restraints. For Thomson this labor is an erotic and spiritual surrender based on his eroticization of material labor. In his *Elegy*, Gray redefines the plowman's labor as the labor of the self, the burden of being poetic, while in "On Winter" Leapor asserts the materiality of labor and its erosion of subjectivity and poetry.

VI

In contrast to numerous theoretical approaches to the subject as subjected, these eighteenth-century versions of the subject as object or object as subject may provide liberating models for early modern and modern contexts. Might there be another approach to the object that provides a foundation for (1) a liberating ontology, (2) an ethical inquiry into the grounds of representation, and (3) an alternative aesthetic pleasure founded in an ethical consciousness of subject-object relations? Tracing the increasing sympathy for, or identification with, the other entails its own aesthetic and ethical challenges.

In the varying identifications between subject and object we see the range of experiments with representation that too often have been polarized as Augustan and Romantic. Because of the complexity of identification that subtends representation, the "play of difference and similitude in self-other relations," we must attend to the ethical and aesthetic ramifications of identifying *with* an object.[52] For "how can the other," asks Diana Fuss, "be brought into the domain of the knowable without annihilating the other *as other*—as precisely that which cannot be known?" "*Every* identification," observes Fuss, "involves a degree of symbolic violence, a measure of temporary mastery and possession."[53] The aesthetic and ethical implications of these two kinds of identification are most relevant to this study of poetry by men and women. Much Restoration and eighteenth-century poetry offers us ample evidence of (1) the poets' complex understanding of the nature of representation as a relation between self and other or subject and object and, hence, (2) a struggle precisely with representation as ethical and aesthetic.[54]

In examining the uses of the muse, the prospect, and personification, we have already observed the overlapping goals of poetic representation and identification. Indeed, one of the achievements of eighteenth-century poetry lies in its transformation of the subject's domination of the object into the subject's convergence or sympathy with the object. In the vocabulary of aesthetics, these relations of convergence and sympathy may be understood as the sublime and sensibility, respectively. In repeatedly separating the sublime and sensibility, however, scholars have neglected eighteenth-century poets' concerns with the intersections of aesthetics and ethics.

We are accustomed to analyses of the sublime that mark it as masculine territory—only a male subject can heroically endure its terrors, achieving the highest aesthetic goal of sublime transcendence. The familiar scenario of the sublime—in which the subject is awed by an object but made stronger and more expansive, even imperialistic, by the confrontation—finds its most obvious examples in Romantic poetry. The sublime scenario just outlined derives from Longinus, Burke, and Kant. Recent critics, among them John G. Pipkin, Laura Runge, and Barbara Claire Freeman, have demonstrated how this scenario excluded women writers from an elite aesthetic territory and, consequently, from a sector of the literary marketplace. In the canonical sublime, the male subject's preservation requires the confrontation with and conquest of an obscure, threatening element identified with the unruly "feminine" imagination, or, alternatively, the unruly encroachments of women writers. In this narrative of the sublime, masculine reason consumes or absorbs feminine imagination.

David B. Morris has focused on the religious sublime to reestablish the sublime in the eighteenth century, but he dismisses an equally important version of the sublime, the sentimental sublime, where theories of sensibility and the sublime meet.[55] Eighteenth-century treatments of the sublime indicate a much more entangled relation between the sublime as it is conventionally defined and the discourses of sentiment and sensibility than is typically acknowledged. Indeed, in the relation between sensibility and the sublime we can best understand how women poets in the second half of the eighteenth century entered into these high aesthetic stakes. The sentimental sublime is seen in many eighteenth-century theories of the sublime, including those of John Baillie (1747), Alexander Gerard (1759), James Beattie (1783), and Hugh Blair (1763 and 1783). In his *Lectures on Rhetoric and Belles Lettres* (1783), Blair describes the "moral, or sentimental Sublime" as "arising from certain exertions of the human mind; from certain affections, and actions, of our fellow-creatures.... High virtue is the most natural and fertile source of this moral Sublimity."[56]

Understanding the eighteenth-century sublime in relation to both the suffering soul of the religious sublime (seen in poems such as Isaac Watts's "The Hurry of the Spirits . . ." or William Cowper's "[Hatred and Vengeance]") and the feeling self of the sentimental sublime can restore the relation between aesthetics and ethics in the period's poetry. Chapter 5 examines how women and men poets combine the discourses of sensibility and the sublime, especially in the later eighteenth century, to explore the subject's vulnerability rather than its preservation. In certain poems by Christian Carstairs, Thomas Gray, Anna Seward, and Ann Yearsley, their subjects brave the dangers but rarely transcend them, remaining irrecoverably decomposed or indifferent to transcending the threat. Typically, the subject of the sentimental sublime prefers material danger to psychological suffering.

In this forgotten sublime, eighteenth-century poets show us the isolated self *in extremis*—a condition in which the self explores, emulates, and even suffers, as fully as possible, the cultural values of what has been coded feminine and yet without conquering the feminine. William Collins, Anna Seward, and William Cowper, for example, develop relations between the subject and object of representation that offer "feminine" ideals of sensibility, interrelatedness, and self-abnegation. Gray, Cowper, and many women poets throughout the long eighteenth century dwell in the possibility of surrendering power to the other. Their surrender need not be seen as aesthetic incompetence but rather as a challenge to our notions of the ethics and pleasures of representation. This version of the sublime recalls not only the poetical character described by Keats but the words of an early eighteenth-century writer, the Earl of Shaftesbury, who "considered that in the conception and portrayal of his subject the poet is, ideally speaking, 'annihilated,' and is 'no certain man, nor has any certain or genuine character.'"[57]

VII

My attention to women writers and constructions of the feminine has been informed by the insights of early and more recent feminist criticism, but my focus is on the detailed formal experiments of women poets rather than on tracing comparisons and contrasts between their work and feminist theory. Such a reexamination of feminist theory is another study, perhaps better suited as a sequel to charting women's and men's writing in its more immediate dialogue with Restoration and eighteenth-century poetic contexts. While this study's division of writers into men and women poets is made precisely to investigate the nature of gendered identity in relation to the transformations of representation, such an investigation also shows the fluidity and transferability of gender as a mode of poetic self-characterization. Because of the overlapping of social codes for gender decorum and the recurrent function of these codes to figure the poetic prerogative in canonical poetry, the poet's gender identity frequently informs his or her approach to representation.[58] Rather than proposing an *écriture féminine* or an *écriture masculine*, I hope to show the relevance of analyzing poetic values in relation to the poet's inscription of gender in an era in which the poet's self-representation was allied with the authority to write.

A final word on my selection of poets: in charting this alternative narrative of Restoration and eighteenth-century poetry, I have included poets such as Dryden, Pope, Thomson, and Gray precisely to show how the traditional canon alters when the vantage point alters.[59] The selection of women poets stands on less familiar ground. Indeed, one of the challenges and pleasures of this study has been selecting poems by women for analysis through an evaluative lens, locating standards for poetic values in their thoughtful experiments with representation. Readers will undoubtedly think of other poems and poets that could have been included—to support or erode my claims.[60] I hope, however, that in necessarily selecting a small portion of these poems, my study shows much of what is useful about integrating poems by women and men. Still better, I hope to spur continued inquiries. Margaret J. M. Ezell has reminded us of the collaboration and community between men and women poets in the manuscript circles of the Restoration and eighteenth century.[61] For practical reasons I have had to limit my analysis to printed poems by women. Future studies that include the many poems by women and men that circulated only in manuscript will no doubt reshape the next literary histories.

1
Dryden, Pope, and the Transformation of the Muse

> Lute, harp, and lyre, muse, muses, and inspirations,
> Pegasus, Parnassus, and Hippocrene, were all an
> abomination to him. In fancy I can almost hear
> him now exclaiming, "Harp? Harp? Lyre?
> Pen and ink, boy, you mean! Muse, boy, Muse?
> Your Nurse's daughter, you mean!"
> —Coleridge, *Biographia Literaria*

THIS CHAPTER CONSIDERS THE USES OF THE MUSE IN DEFINING THE poetic authority and modes of representation that have been called Augustan. In the traditional Augustan canon, the authority to imitate Nature and clarify the complex is established through values coded as feminine: poets invoke or evoke these values by adapting the longstanding invocation of the muse. As a conventional part of the invocation, the muse helps defuse what Mark Conroy has called the audacity of beginning. "Beginnings are always scandalous," he argues, but by returning to a traditional source, a "sanctified origin," a "beginning that erupted in the remote past," a poet can confirm authority through lineage and precedent.[1] The figure of the muse served the poet to maintain *and* revise authority by placing the poet's endeavors against the valued background of classical literature: in this longstanding contract with a cultured audience, the poet's invocation of the muse acknowledges the reader's familiarity with the classical tradition so long as both reader and poet accept the fiction that this figure authorizes the poem and represents truth. By calling on the muse, the poet implies the merit of the verse, announces access to the highest kinds of poetry, especially the epic genre and the sublime mode, and identifies the reader as participating in this elite community.

Although Coleridge's teacher the Reverend James Boyer was attempting to dispense with the conventions of poetic authority at the end of the eighteenth century, demythologizing them into their components of pen, ink, and flesh, others had tried long before he did. Such conventions, however, had persisted for a very long time, with the muse in particular serving as "one of the 'concrete' formal constraints of the literary tradition."[2] Long before Boyer would decry the lingering muse, Thomas Hobbes had roundly condemned her. For the Earl of Shaftesbury, the invocations of the muse were already anachronistic by the early eighteenth century. Although he criticizes his contemporaries for clinging to the convention, he also acknowledges "what a mighty advantage" the muse must have been to the ancient poet: "to be thus orthodox, and by the help of his education, and a good will into the bargain, to work himself up to the belief of a divine presence and heavenly inspiration."[3] Indeed, Restoration and eighteenth-century poets (and their predecessors and successors) found in the muse a "mighty advantage." Although the figure would appear in other forms, poets would return again and again to *some* feminine entity that would signal their contact with the best poetry and that would allow them to shape a fit audience for their changing poetic objectives. The "Augustan" speaker, observes Clifford Siskin, "paradoxically asserts his presence by his absence": "Overt efforts at self-definition would only tend to undermine his claim to be a representative observer," and so he makes that claim indirectly by using "particular figures who function as surrogates."[4] These surrogates were typically feminine figures—the muse, feminine personifications, and feminine Nature.

In an era that saw a rapidly growing literary marketplace as well as, eventually, poetry's isolation from the center of political power, both men and women depended on the figurative values of the feminine to establish their authority to write poetry. Using feminine figures, poets legitimated their right to write and convinced the reader of the justness of their representations. I use *authority* and *representation* in both their poetic and political senses: authority in poetic claims is rarely unaccompanied by strategies of domination from within and without the text; *representation* is to be understood as both poetic imitation and as a proxy for an identity, constituency, or perspective. To establish poetic authority was necessarily to participate in the changing understanding of authority in the period. The nation faced obvious challenges to older models of political authority—from the beheading of its king and civil war to the emerging social contract theory that enabled the bloodless deposition of James II.

The debates over authority dominated the realm of poetry as thoroughly as they did that of government. "Augustan" poetry, often identified as beginning with the restoration of Charles II and ending with Pope's death (1744), participates in these various kinds of authority.[5] Steven Zwicker captures this distinctive confluence of political and poetic authorities: "the return of monarchy," he explains, "could be argued as a restoration not only of political forms but of 'culture' in our sense of the word; and the royalist conjoining of arts and empire forms a significant cultural claim in the decades to come."[6] At the same time, a series of events would conspire to put into question the king's authority and patriarchalism: Charles II's barren marriage and promiscuity threatened the succession, first in the Exclusion Crisis and then in the Glorious Revolution. Many literary historians base their characterizations of the Restoration and early eighteenth-century poetry on its yoking of poetic and political authority. In a typically public voice, the poet, such critics argue, saw *himself* living in a political and cultural era that recalled if not resembled some of the political stability, prosperity, and cultural development of Augustan Rome.[7] The authority often associated with this literature is based on the poet's assumption of a universal position from which *he* writes with objectivity and clarity.[8] Margaret Doody has described this strategy in her account of Augustan poetry's appetitive and imperialistic character.[9] Augustan style—clear, urbane, and expository—assumes an authority over what can be represented as well as what constitutes an artistically successful representation, asserting the truthfulness and universality of what is actually "contingent and partisan."[10]

The flexibility of the category of the feminine would enable poets to transform older notions of poetic authority and imitation into new notions.[11] But in analyzing their reliance on the feminine, we find different characteristics than have been previously attributed to "Augustan" poets. Legitimating one's authority is, of course, a fundamental gesture of writing: a writer typically uses rhetorical strategies to defend the very fact that to write is to usurp the authority of other writers and to demand the reader's attention.[12] The status of the author and the nature of authority became increasingly scrutinized as the expanding print culture created a different reader who needed convincing of the poet's authority and whose very literacy challenged poetry's elite place within the hierarchy of literary culture. By highlighting within a poem his authority to write poetry, the poet attempted to maintain the genre's privileged literary status in the face of its "devaluation": men and women of all classes had begun not only to write poetry but also to acquire public authority by having their work distributed through the booksellers. Indeed, rhetorical strategies of inscribing poetic authority allowed those without the appropriate social status to figure their access to the steeps of Parnassus. As the definition of a coherent notion of political authority became increasingly difficult, so did the definition of a coherent notion of poetic authority.

As a pagan figure, the muse had to be modernized in an era that wished to emphasize its freedom from a mythological past either through Christian doctrine or through Enlightenment empiricism and reason. Pagan mythology, which had still conveniently authorized claims to poetic privilege in Renaissance poetry, was by the middle of the seventeenth century in still greater conflict with the authority of both science and Christianity. With the development of empirical scientific authority, the "poetic gods," as Lawrence Lipking has described them, were being reexamined and in part rejected. The skeptical reconsideration of mythology was one reason why, although they valued the epic as the pinnacle of poetic achievement, poets of the age produced no great epic poem.[13] "Perhaps no earlier age," Lipking argues, "had found it so difficult to take poetic gods for granted."[14]

Born, in part, out of this partisan war over politicized poetic inspiration, Restoration and eighteenth-century poets would learn important lessons from both Milton and Cowley for establishing authority through the muse. Poets confronted the problems of authority, the conflicts between pagan mythology and Christianity, the threat of sedition with the national compromise made to absolute sovereignty, and the increasingly open poetic field that included women writers and the lower classes. The muse was particularly useful in "resolving" these problems of authority through sexual narratives involving the analogy of a male poet's sexual-poetic procreation with a female muse or the poet's identifying himself as a muse courting a male friend. Such narratives could transform or contain volatile political conflicts in an apparently less political context, especially by supplying gendered stereotypes to replace gaps in poets' claims to empirical vision and authoritative representation. Yet these sexual narratives could also represent another challenge to authority inextricable from the challenges to sovereignty. The authority of the husband over his wife , which had long been used and challenged as a figure of the monarch over his people, was facing still greater challenges in the seventeenth century.[15] Poetic authority figured through sexual narratives could imitate or revise (1) the monarch's authority over his people who were figured as his bride, (2) the authority of a husband over his wife, (3) and the scientist's authority over the conventionally feminized Nature. Harold Bloom has asserted the sexual valence of the poet-muse relationship as one in which the poet "must be self-begotten, he must engender himself upon the Muse his mother," who "has whored with many before him."[16]

The modernization of the muse would serve diverse purposes, from Dryden's purifying hermaphroditic sublime in his later years to Pope's homosocial dynamic in which epistolary conversation between men would be raised to great art. The poets most read today revised the muse's role to reformulate their tonal and thematic range, adjusting their relation to a new audience.[17] Thus the era's demotic spirit of expansion, like its maritime imperialistic ventures, found the strength to wander by leaning on elite frameworks, including rhetorical conventions such as the muse.[18] Revising the muse could authorize other kinds of representation and other objects of representation as the mythological muse's claims to mimetic authority and truth were applied to empirical epistemological modes.

I

Writers of the Commonwealth and the Restoration saw the claims to poetic inspiration as religiously, and, in turn, politically loaded. In Davenant's preface to *Gondibert*, Cowley's prefaces to his poems, and Hobbes's statements on poetry, for example, writers "were calling for the reformation of the politics and poetics of inspiration."[19] Insofar as poetry established its authority through the notion of inspiration, it could and often did align itself with religious and political sides. The politics of inspiration were heated because the associations of inspiration with divinity—whether the pagan muses or the Judeo-Christian God—brought religious-political partisanship directly into poetry. Zwicker argues that during the Commonwealth, royalist writers depicted poetic inspiration in ways that would wrest authority over sacred poetry from the Puritans.[20] By invoking and revising even the pagan divinity of the muse, poets negotiated their territory and conveyed royalist or republican sympathies.[21] Abraham Cowley's use of the muse in his pindaric odes provided his successors with a model of eroticism that figured inspiration. Milton's famous invocation of the "Heav'nly Muse" in *Paradise Lost* demonstrated to his successors how flexibility with categories of gender could figure complex representational strategies.

For the poetic and political programs of Cowley's interregnum *Poems* (1656), the royalist poet relies heavily on the muse to establish inspiration.[22] In the Pindaric imitations, his sexually suggestive relationship with "her" allows Cowley to explore themes of poetic greatness in a less politically charged religious context, but one that still invokes spiritual power. Cowley justifies the importance of the muse to his project not only in the poems but also in one of their headnotes: "the Reader must not be chocqued to hear him speak so often of his own Muse; for that is a Liberty which this kind of Poetry can hardly live without."[23]

In the Pindaric "Destinie" (1668), he fearlessly blends the muse's sexual and religious deeds in a remarkable spectacle:[24]

> Me from the *womb* the *Midwife Muse* did take:
> She cut my *Navel*, *washt me*, and mine *Head*
>   With her own *Hands* she *Fashioned*;
>   She did a *Covenant* with me make,
> And *circumcis'ed* my tender *Soul* . . .
>
> (33–37)

The poet, although of woman born, describes his proximity to divine poetic power at his very entrance into the world: it is the midwife muse who pulls him into the mortal realm. His relation with the muse begins as that with his mother ends, with the cutting of the umbilical cord. The muse provides a set of godlike functions that indicate the poet's spiritual purity (she washes him) and priority (his head fashioned with the personal attention only Adam received from the creator-God). The poet's creativity depends on what might have been the intangible, elusive site of his "tender Soul" had he not identified it as the penis, recipient of the muse's covenant in the act of circumcision. The foreskin provides the site, now absent, where, from covenant to circumcision, words become deeds. To our ears, the muse's roles as seventeenth-century midwife, lover, God, and rabbi sound incredible, but Cowley's depiction of a masculine poetic authority based on a connection with the feminine was a paradigm of authority that Restoration and eighteenth-century poets would appropriate and transpose in their worldly poems.[25] In this paradigm, where there is an explicit or implicit sexual narrative between the poet and some feminine entity (a muse or an abstraction, such as Nature), the feminine entity authorizes the poet's work, giving it spiritual or moral value in addition to poetic worth. The poet's success will be proven through qualities that demonstrate his manliness, where his penis takes on the attributes of soul.

Revising the muse was critical to the coherence of Milton's authority in *Paradise Lost*, where he explicitly engages several kinds of authority to justify God's sovereignty and to anchor his vision of the divine in the aftermath of royalist triumph. Although Milton's changes to the muse were complex enough to satisfy theological problems in *Paradise Lost*, they were too particular to be imitated by his successors; but Milton showed later poets how to exceed the limits of rational, worldly discourse by using the gender dynamics attendant on the figure of the muse.[26] More importantly, he reminded them of the usefulness of blending gender identities to legitimate poetic authority.

Milton's revision of the muse is profound because he exploits the mythic status and the sexuality borne out in references to the muse. As a figure of inspiration his muse complies with Christian doctrine; he tells the muse it is the "meaning, not the Name I call: for thou / Nor of the Muses nine, nor on the top / Of old *Olympus* dwell'st, but Heav'nly born" (7.5–7).[27] Milton's muse commands transcendental power but not one in competition with God's; she is Urania, one of the classical nine that in the seventeenth-century had become associated with the Christian epic (7.1).[28] Invoking the muse to identify the epic genre of his poem, he alters the muse's mythological identity to establish his epic as Christian.[29] While the first sentence of *Paradise Lost* includes the command, "Sing Heav'nly Muse" (1.6), Milton underscores that this is a Judeo-Christian heaven by "recounting" a Mosaic history of the muse (1.6–10). Having reformed the muse from a literary and religious perspective, Milton supplants this source of creativity with another, which he calls "spirit" (1.17–23). The substitution and transfer of the muse's powers will be a technique seen in much poetry after Milton. Here the muse's sexual attributes are transferred to the creating God—winged and fertile and at the same time impregnating the abyss, an abyss that, like the poet, is dark but capable of being informed. The winged God recalls the account in Genesis while incorporating the muse's flight. Milton's God can then impregnate a world and a poet whose gender fluctuates according to the requirements for inspiration.

In the most theologically demanding section of *Paradise Lost*, in which he must present God and His heavenly discourse, Milton calls on Light, not on the Muse: "Hail holy Light, offspring of Heav'n first-born, / Or of th' Eternal Coeternal beam / May I express thee unblam'd?" (3.1–3). In choosing the image of Light he makes his ultimate authority the sacred text of Genesis, and by identifying God as Light, he can, in turn, identify with the muse. Book 3, it will be recalled, opens with the narrator's self-portrait, which resembles both muse and fallen angel.[30] Putting on the muse's wings at the beginning of the passage, Milton then takes them off to figure himself as a forlorn lover who must wait for his visitor.[31] Quickly adopting and discarding one role after another, the poet exploits the narrative of courtship and changes his gender identity as needed—as his successors will.

II

The tone characteristic of Restoration and eighteenth-century poetry has been described by Bonamy Dobrée as a shift from the reader condescended to, to the reader regarded as privileged equal.[32] The revised muse connected contemporary worldly interests and the empirical mode to earlier poetic standards—linking the chaos of empirical sensory data with a standard of unified, universal truth and elevating the worldly. Poets such as Dryden and Pope recast a relation with the muse to enable generic and mimetic experimentation while asserting the poetic authority to do so. While it was commonplace for male writers to describe themselves as "courting the muse," they also used "the muse" or "my muse" as a way to describe themselves, thus, as James Winn has argued, "temporarily imagining some part of their creativity as female."[33]

Dryden's account of history and politics—what Mark Van Doren called Dryden's "poetry of statement"—asserts an objectivity free from the religious and political resonances of inspiration figured by the muse.[34] Categories such as friendship and patriarchy more overtly inform his politico-historical poetry. He asserts his reliance on "rational" discourse and observation, not the mysteries of the muse. This empirical posture is audible in such incontrovertible statements as that beginning *Mac Flecknoe*, "All humane things are subject to decay, / And, when Fate summons, Monarchs must obey" (1–2); or with the observation cum jingoism that opens *Annus Mirabilis*, "In thriving Arts long time had *Holland* grown, / Crouching at home, and cruel when abroad" (1-2).[35] In *Threnodia Augustalis: A Funeral-Pindarique Poem Sacred to the Happy Memory of King Charles II* (1685), Dryden invokes Clio, the muse of history, to affirm that his account derives from empirical observation rather than from mythic sources:

> Be true, O *Clio*, to thy Hero's Name!
>   But draw him strictly so
>   That all who view, the Piece may know;
> He needs no Trappings of fictitious Fame:
>   The Load's too weighty: Thou may'st chuse
>   Some Parts of Praise, and some refuse:
> Write, that his Annals may be thought more lavish than the Muse.
> (327–33)

Ironically, the mythological muse establishes the nonmythological, empirical authority of the poem.

Throughout his early poetry, Dryden uses the sexual narratives derived from the poet-muse relationship to unify his discourse and to authorize what cannot be justified or explained.

Dryden, as do many other writers in his era, "most commonly celebrates" the artistic imagination "with exuberant sexual imagery."[36] These sexual narratives function on at least two levels in his poetry: on the one hand, they assert his authority to represent, and on the other hand, they legitimate the political content—monarchical authority—that is the object of many of his poems from 1660 to the end of his tenure as poet laureate in 1688. Zwicker has demonstrated Dryden's repeated use of sexual narratives at the beginning of the 1660s to celebrate the restoration of the monarch and to yoke "personal and national fertility."[37] By the mid-1660s, however, the King's barren marriage had given such images of procreation a more troubled tone.[38] As poet laureate, Dryden's strategies for representing his poetic authority would be influenced by the issues of paternity and legitimacy besieging Charles's reign.

Most famously in *Absalom and Achitophel* (1681), the King's lack of legitimate progeny is blamed on "A Soyl ungratefull, to the Tiller's care" (12)—that is, a barren queen.[39] The King's extramarital sexual activities are defended by harkening back to an ancient Hebrew model:

> In pious times, e'r Priest-craft did begin,
> Before *Polygamy* was made a sin;
> When man, on many, multiply'd his kind,
> E'r one to one was, cursedly, confind.
>
> (1–4)

The conspiracy between Shaftesbury and the King's illegitimate son is also given its sexual valence, where Shaftesbury plays the role of Satan tempting an Eve-like Duke of Monmouth. The poem abounds in sexual narratives that sometimes explicitly and sometimes implicitly justify the King's authority. It is almost too obvious to state that this justification of the king is also a way for the poet to justify his own authority: the ease of the lines and the knowing winks shared between the manly writer and an ideal male reader yoke the assertion of the King's authority with the assertion of Dryden's poetic authority. In a tour-de-force of apparent objectivity, the poem impresses by the apparent absence of a poetic self, where the poet dexterously represents "truth" from a stance so ostensibly objective that no poetic subjectivity can be located, only inferred.

Dryden's elegies often delineate more explicitly his authorial subjectivity and poetic process. At times in the elegies the muse appears by name, to be remade according to the poetical and political program at hand. In *Threnodia Augustalis*, although Dryden presents the muse as inadequate to the emotional demands of his task, she steps in to help him establish James II's authority to succeed his brother. This is Dryden's only poem treating a male subject in which he makes more than a passing reference to the muse, and he complains that even his "audacious Muse" (71) cannot find the language "to adorn so vast a Woe" (73) as James feels at his brother's death. This muse is quite willing to perform but is outstripped by the greatness of Dryden's topics—James's grief and Charles's merits. The poet can only suggest the brother's grief by establishing James's relation to Charles—not as a brother but as a male friend:

> The grief of all the rest like subject-grief did show,
>   His like a Sovereign did transcend;
> No Wife, no Brother, such a Grief cou'd know,
>   Nor any name, but Friend.
>
> (74–77)

Dryden's shift in authorities impinges on the political hierarchy of England itself. By giving precedence to friendship between brothers, the poet ignores another blood relationship that had authorized the controversial succession, and so he establishes James's authority to succeed Charles. This emphasis allows Dryden to replace the contested value of patrilineal succession that emerged in the Exclusion Crisis with the value of fraternity and, more importantly, what appears to be *apolitical* and erotic friendship.

The erotic content of Dryden's reference to Nisus and Euryalus in the poem's epigraph has been analyzed by Winn: in comparing this "fortunate pair" with Charles and James, "Dryden evidently believed that his readers would interpret the epigraph as an appropriate, even heroic celebration of the intensity of their feelings for each other."[40] Dryden also, argues Winn, "gave both royal brothers some feminine features, most obviously when James weeps for his brother."[41] Elevating friendship and establishing his poetic authority over public politics by describing a system of relations between men, this eroticism conveys their intimacy and personal worth rather than their sexual behavior.

We find Dryden's most direct attention to the muse's powers in his elegies for women, specifically the Countess of Abingdon (Eleonora) and Anne Killigrew. That Dryden elevates the muse only in his elegies to women suggests a thematic connection between this classical source of poetic inspiration and the poetic and social roles of women: for Dryden, the use of the muse appears most developed in his focus on virtue, increasingly prescribed in the era as women's chief attribute.[42] The women remembered in these elegies, however, provide a model by which Dryden defines his poetic power as a moral condition—a notion of poetic character usually associated with the next generation of poets. "To the Pious Memory of the Accomplisht Young Lady Mrs Anne Killigrew . . . " (1685), which appeared with other poems that prefaced the posthumous edition of Killigrew's poetry, remembers the woman poet by putting her on the highest of pedestals, placing her in the starry heavens to function as Dryden's muse.[43] Thus he removes her from the role of poet. In turn, Dryden identifies himself as a "Mortal Muse" (16–22), making explicit his internalization of inspiration. Killigrew's function will be not to give the poet the right words but to atone for his and other poets' sins: she purifies rather than inspires in her role as moral conduit. Dryden thus redefines the muse, both historicizing this female personage and eliminating the need for further transcendental assistance following the sacrifice of Killigrew. In his poem, the death of Killigrew seems to establish for poets in the future an accord between the fallen and the divine at the expense of Killigrew's relation to the material world, a disjunction that Dryden seems to account for in the ambiguous praise he bestows on Killigrew's art.[44]

The tone of Dryden's poem has received a fair amount of critical attention. Some find a satirical streak in his praise of Killigrew's art.[45] Others defend the terms by which Dryden characterizes her: according to Winn, Dryden emphasizes Killigrew's natural talent rather than her learning to avoid associating her with those learned women so frequently and viciously satirized.[46] While praising Killigrew, Dryden's mortal muse (i.e., his poetic self) establishes the superiority of his sublunary intelligence to define and contain the very source of poetry. He performs this mortal service through the use of visual imagery that transforms Killigrew from a woman into parts of Renaissance cosmographical diagrams and baroque paintings, placing her in the cosmos (6–10).[47] At the end of the ode Killigrew appears "Among the *Pleiad's* a New-kindl'd Star" (175). He liberates himself from personal morality by offering Killigrew's virtue as proxy. Thus Killigrew's virtue allows Dryden the moral authority to fulfill sublime aspirations. In his elegies for both Killigrew and Eleonora, he establishes his authority based on his exaltation of feminine virtue.

Dryden defines the sublime of feminine virtue by transforming the muse in *Eleonora: A Panegyrical Poem Dedicated to the Memory of the Late Countess of Abingdon* (1692). The poet transforms Eleonora into inspiring abstractions that act as muses for his ambitious foray into the sublime.[48] In the title and in his prefatory epistle to *Eleonora*, Dryden exalts the poem in the hierarchy of poetic kinds, identifying it as a Pindaric ode. Signalling his sublime objectives, he invokes the notion of sublime transport in an epigraph from the *Aeneid*, where he professes the goal "to pass out to the upper air" ("Superas evadere ad auras, / Hoc opus, hic labor est").[49] Men may accomplish this feat by writing—women by dying.

Throughout his prefatory epistle Dryden explains the difficulty of representing the perfection of the deceased, a challenge increased by his "disadvantage," which was "never to have known, or seen my Lady."[50] This disadvantage is not crippling, however, because Dryden's goal transcends such particulars. He claims to have modeled the "panegyric" after the intention of Donne's *Anniversaries* (which ostensibly mourns the death of Elizabeth Drury): "to raise an Emulation in the living, to Copy out the Example of the dead."[51] "Pattern of Charity, Devotion, and Humility; of the best Wife, the best Mother, and the best of Friends," Eleonora functions as an abstraction.[52] The poem itself he "once intended to have call'd . . . 'The Pattern,'" an intention that corresponds to the mimetic challenge of representing perfection as well as the moral challenge of emulating feminine virtue.[53] He claims access to imitating this inimitable perfection by using the dead woman as a kind of inspiring muse figure. Although he calls on the muse to represent Eleonora's perfection, Dryden emphasizes visual imagery to explain the problem of representation:

1 / Dryden, Pope, and the Transformation of the Muse 43

> Muse, down again precipitate thy flight;
> For how can Mortal Eyes sustain Immortal Light!
> But as the Sun in Water we can bear,
> Yet not the Sun, but his Reflection there,
> So let us view her here, in what she was;
> And take her Image, in this watry Glass.
>
> (134–39)

His phrasing is ambiguous, with the address "Muse" applicable either to the classical source of truth or to the deceased. In the same breath claiming this access to the unrepresentable—"how can Mortal Eyes sustain Immortal Light!"—Dryden asserts the authenticity of his mimetic refraction: "So let us view her here, in what she was, / And take her Image, in this watry Glass" (138–39). The muse and the dead woman, who is the muse's historical analog, combine with an empirical attention to sight that allow Dryden to express spiritual perfection while having no empirical knowledge of Eleonora.

Abstracted from the exemplary Countess of Abingdon, this pattern of feminine virtue becomes a springboard to Dryden's artistic achievement. By using feminized abstractions the poet takes the mystery of the feminine and makes it conform, or appear to conform, to empirical discourse. That is, Dryden demythologizes the pagan elements only to create another mythology of abstractions that he *figures* as empirical observations:

> Yet look not ev'ry Lineament to see;
> Some will be cast in shades; and some will be
> So lamely drawn, you scarcely know, 'tis she.
> For where such various Vertues we recite,
> 'Tis like the Milky-Way, all over bright,
> But sown so thick with Stars, 'tis undistinguish'd Light.
>
> Her Vertue, not her Vertues let us call,
> For one Heroick comprehends 'em all:
> One, as a Constellation is but one;
> Though 'tis a Train of Stars, that, rolling on,
> Rise in their turn, and in the Zodiack run.
> Ever in Motion.
>
> (140–51)

As an abstraction, distilled in the poet's claim that she "was not Humble, but Humility" (96), Eleonora dead is little different from Eleonora alive (301–6).

Despite the usefulness of these feminized abstractions, when Dryden wrote of his own inspiration, which he claimed was never stronger than in the writing of this poem, he used another gender model as old as the muse:[54]

> We, who are Priests of *Apollo*, have not the Inspiration when we please; but must wait till the God comes rushing on us, and invades us with a fury, which we are not able to resist: which gives us double strength while the Fit continues, and leaves us languishing and spent, at its departure.

Dryden initially plays a passive, stereotypically feminine, role, notes Winn, which shifts to one of stereotypically masculine power and then concludes with spent sexual energy.[55] Taking the place of the priestesses who worshipped at the Delphic oracle, Dryden figures an eroticism more intense than his descriptions of his relation to the muse: in his "new fable of conception," Kramer observes, "the Poet who once 'layd about' with the Muse is transformed to the Priestess who opens herself up to penetration by 'the God.'"[56] In this passage from the prefatory epistle to the earl of Abingdon, Dryden articulates a stereotypically feminine submission to masculine authority, not just Apollo's but also the earl's material patronage—a gesture of humility that is developed still further by Pope.

III

Both Pope and Dryden transform the muse's role to authorize earthbound man-to-man discourse, but whereas Dryden accomplishes this most often by superseding the muse with other values, Pope appropriates and even plays the muse himself. Pope used the muse in nearly every kind of poem he wrote, but he consistently claimed its powers as his own, either transforming the figure to articulate masculine authority or identifying with the figure to claim access to the feminine.[57] The muse's epic connection made it an important figure for Pope, who saw himself following Virgil's progress toward the epic, and he used the muse in his nonepic poetry as a symbol of literary continuity and value.[58]

His delicacy in summoning the muse in nonepic contexts serves whatever tone he requires, from serious and sublime in "Messiah" to mocking in *The Rape of the Lock*. Pope reframes and reranks the hierarchy of poetic kinds by including the muse, just as he assiduously incorporates other literary conventions and generic signals. Through the muse he weakened this hierarchy and replaced it with poetic values in which the attributes of gender worked to establish poetic authority and justify a mode of representation less objective than it claimed to be. His use of the feminine attributes of the muse contributed to ways in which he "linguistically and aesthetically" exploited the political implications of representation "while mystifying or naturalizing the consequences of its operations in terms of power relationships."[59]

Most importantly, Pope not only invokes but emulates these feminine attributes. In his study of Pope's imagination, David Fairer demonstrates the importance of Pope's focus on female characters—Eloisa, Belinda, and Dulness—to his exploration of creative powers, positive and negative.[60] Helen Deutsch has analyzed in depth the rhetorical role of the feminine in his poetry.[61] Catherine Ingrassia has demonstrated the relation between gender and commerce in Pope's conception of poetry, especially in relation to his own "feminized" position.[62] And Valerie Rumbold has comprehensively analyzed his relation to women in his world.[63] We see Pope's identification with mysterious feminine power in his description of his imaginative relation to the world: "Like a witch, whose carcase lies motionless on the floor, while she keeps her airy sabbaths, and enjoys a thousand imaginary entertainments abroad, in this world, and in others, I seem to sleep in the midst of the hurry, even as you would swear a top stands still, when 'tis in the whirl of its giddy motion."[64]

The gender politics of Pope's authority appear early in his career in his pastorals. Although writing these poems to support the classical hierarchy and begin his trajectory that would culminate in the epic, he appropriates the muse to help unravel this hierarchy.[65] Pope's elevation of masculine conversation to the highest generic value required transforming the muse into the poet himself or his patron. In the *Pastorals* (1709) Pope announces his allegiance to men rather than to the muses. Each of the four pastorals is dedicated to a male patron, except for "Winter," which is dedicated "To the Memory of Mrs. Tempest."[66]

In notes to each of the pastorals, Pope elaborates on the support and inspiration received from these male mentors. The first pastoral, "Spring," claims privileged connections with the age's progenitors of culture, including "Mr. *Walsh*, Mr. *Wycherley*, G. *Granville*, afterwards Lord *Lansdown*, Sir *William Trumbal*, Dr. *Garth*, Lord *Halifax*, Lord *Somers*, Mr. *Mainwaring*, and others." "All these," Pope adds, "gave our Author the greatest encouragement, and particularly Mr. *Walsh*, (whom Mr. Dryden, in his Postscript to Virgil, calls the best critic of his age)."[67] Even though "Winter" is dedicated to Mrs. Tempest, Pope establishes the progenitor of the poem as one of the men mentioned above rather than the late Mrs. Tempest: "This Lady was of an ancient family in Yorkshire, and particularly admired by the Author's friend Mr. *Walsh*, who having celebrated her in a Pastoral Elegy, desired his friend to do the same."[68]

In constructing an identity between muse and man, Pope helped to redefine the gentleman in the eighteenth century to include feminine attributes. To introject particular feminine characteristics, especially feminine virtue, was for Pope to imitate Nature. The characteristics of the muse were assigned especially to a gentleman, a like-minded arbiter of culture who approved of Pope's poetry. The male patron could inspire Pope's endeavors, and, in turn, Pope could inspire his patron's endeavors. Making the muse mortal, whether the poet or the patron-addressee, Pope made human relationships the source of the highest poetry. Pope did not need the muse to jump the low hedge of pastoral, which is why his frequent references to the muse in his pastorals are all the more significant. Through his adroit handling of the figure, he subtly establishes the lines of authority that he maintained in his verse until his death. His renovations of the muse made it a figure to be associated with any discerning man of quality. For Pope and Dryden ideal relationships between men usually involved incorporating cultural notions of the feminine.

The *Pastorals* abound with examples of Pope's translation of the muse into men. In "Summer" Pope conflates himself with the muse but invokes Garth, poet and physician, to hear him: "Accept, O *Garth*, the Muse's early Lays, / That adds this Wreath of Ivy to thy Bays" (9–10). In "Autumn" Pope invokes Virgil's muses, "Ye *Mantuan* Nymphs" (5), but he also addresses William Wycherley as the writer inspired by the muses: "Thou, whom the

Nine with *Plautus*' Wit inspire, / The Art of *Terence*, and *Menander*'s Fire" (7–8). In "Spring," Pope wrings the muse inside out, dissolving the notion of who inspires whom. The muses are not invoked but depicted as already singing, choruslike, on the banks of the Thames ("Fair *Thames* flow gently from thy sacred Spring, / While on thy Banks *Sicilian* Muses sing" [3–4]). In the same poem he invokes Trumbal: "O let my Muse her slender Reed inspire, / 'Till in your Native Shades You tune the Lyre" (11–12). The pastoral poet conflates himself with the muse while he asks his patron Trumbal to inspire him. For Pope, his own judgment of virtue determines who is muse, and so he and any of his male companions may share in this role. Long before the appearance of the "cult of the feminine" associated with the culture of sensibility in the second half of the eighteenth century, the internalization of feminine virtue establishes the poetic character.

The most thorough demonstration of Pope's treatment of the muse as trope and his transformation of himself into muse appears in his poetic manifesto *An Essay on Criticism* (1711). Written early in his career, it shows his self-assurance in his poetic skill already mature. Pope includes the muse to remind the critic of the modern poets' ancient legacy and modern freedom with this legacy. By studying Homer's work, the critic may "trace the Muses *upward* to their *Spring*" (127). Pope charts the history of poetic progress from ancient Greece to modern England by following the trail of the muses: "But see! each *Muse*, in *Leo*'s Golden Days" (697); "But soon by Impious Arms from *Latium* chas'd, / Their *ancient Bounds* the banish'd Muses past" (709–10). Having followed the progress of poetry, Pope summarizes by referring again to the trope: "Such was the Muse, whose Rules and Practice tell, / *Nature's chief Master-piece is writing well*" (723–24).

Pope concludes the poem with attention to his own poetic progress, which depends on his use of the term *muse*. Using syntax parallel to the preceding couplet on the muse of the ancients, Pope replaces it with his modern muse, the man of sense: "Such was *Roscomon*—not more *learn'd* than *good*, / With Manners gen'rous as his Noble Blood" (725–26); likewise, "Such late was *Walsh*—the Muse's Judge and Friend, / Who justly knew to blame or to commend" (729–30). The poem's elegiac close includes Pope's characteristic use of the muse—its subordination to a male patron—when the poet affectionately salutes Walsh: "This Praise at least a grateful Muse may give! / The Muse, whose early Voice you taught to Sing, / Prescrib'd her Heights, and prun'd her tender Wing" (734–36). To strengthen his connection with the male patron Pope associates himself with the muse in a paradigm of intimacy, in which men take turns being muse, with the interchangeability of these roles essential to their function. Patricia Meyer Spacks describes the "exaggerated humility" of Pope's position in the poem as mirroring the "moral doctrine of this religion of art."[69] The poet's decision to figure himself as muse, argues Spacks, shows his personal commitment to enact the ideal of morality, criticism, and poetry he promotes in the poem.[70] In its frequent inclusion and transformation of the muse Pope's poetry shows the canon's most explicit turn from epic inspiration to urbane masculine conversation and its concomitant shift from supernatural to human understanding. Thanks to the muse, Pope can define the poetic quality of his relations with other men as worldly and social. Pope's rerouting of poetic authority here is not simply the flattery of an obsequious poet toward his patron: it is a fundamental reordering of tone and theme based on a dynamic relation with a feminine referent and ideal.

We see Pope's greatest transformation of the muse and the index of how central the feminine was to his control of art in the figure of Dulness. (Although Pope invokes the "Smithfield muses" to launch his attack on cultural entropy, they are minor heralds of the greater antimuse of Dulness.) Antimuse or muse of perverted culture and, ultimately, of social chaos, Dulness had to be a woman: his habitual incorporation of feminine virtue to define his poetic authority necessarily found its counterpart in this other extreme stereotype of negative feminine power.[71] Enchained at the base of her throne, the real muses languish:

> held in ten-fold bonds the *Muses* lie,
> Watch'd both by Envy's and by Flatt'ry's eye:
> There to her heart sad Tragedy addrest
> The dagger wont to pierce the Tyrant's breast;
> But sober History restrain'd her rage,
> And promis'd Vengeance on a barb'rous age.
> There sunk Thalia, nerveless, cold, and dead,
> Had not her Sister Satyr held her head. . . .
>
> (4.35–42)

1 / Dryden, Pope, and the Transformation of the Muse   49

Unlike Pope, who incorporates the feminine or takes on a role associated with feminine passivity, Cibber humiliates himself because the feminine appropriates *him*. Wrapped in this disordering feminine force, he lies in "Dulness' lap" (3.2).

IV

The poetry of Jonathan Swift profoundly critiques the convention of the muse in ways that suggest his debt to women poets. Swift enlists the muse as part of his larger agenda to demystify poetry and politics, a tendency that Ellen Pollak has described as calling "its own organizing structures into question, insistently making them the grounds of their own critique."[72] The muse as an elite source of authority becomes comically human in Swift's hands. Its humanization exposes the mortal grounds of poetic and political authority as well as the gender stereotypes that inform them. We find fairly conventional references to the muse in Swift's early poems such as the "Ode to the Athenian Society" and the "Ode to the Honourable Sir William Temple." But even in early poems such as "To Mr. Congreve" and "Occasioned by Sir William Temple's Late Illness and Recovery," Swift has already begun to experiment radically with poetic conventions as he exposes his culture's notions of gender decorum. In "To Mr. Congreve" Swift's muse reprimands rather than inspires the poet, and In "Sir William Temple's Late Illness," the muse instructs the poet to "Listen while the muse thus teaches thee to sing" (136).[73] Swift regularly emphasizes the muses' and Apollo's unwillingness to inspire him—a common complaint in women's poetry. In "Stella's Birthday (1723): A Great Bottle of Wine, Long Buried, being that Day Dug Up," Apollo and the muses have refused to help Swift write the annual tribute to Stella; finding an alternative source for inspiration becomes the poem's focus. Finally discovered, the bottle is suitably exalted as a source of inspiration:

> 'The god of winds and god of fire
> Did to its wondrous birth conspire;
> And Bacchus, for the poet's use,
> Poured in a strong inspiring juice:
> See! as you raise it from its tomb,
> It drags behind a spacious womb,

> And in the spacious womb contains
> A sovereign medicine for the brains.
>
> (63–70)

Swift's description of the bottle, now phallic, now womb-like, brilliantly mocks not only the mysterious ritual of invocation but also its submerged sexual narratives.

Although Swift at times refers to his muse as stand-in for himself, he is not concerned, as Pope is, with deepening his poetic self by acquiring feminine characteristics. (Indeed, like much of Aphra Behn's poetry, Swift's insists on the elusiveness of the self.) The muse is uncannily real, however, in one of his most dramatic and comic passages. She keeps the secret of whether Vanessa (Esther Vanhomrigh) succeeded in her pursuit of the Dean:[74]

> But what success Vanessa met,
> Is to the world a secret yet:
> Whether the nymph, to please her swain,
> Talks in a high romantic strain;
> Or whether he at last descends
> To like with less seraphic ends;
> Or, to compound the business, whether
> They temper love and books together;
> Must never to mankind be told,
> Nor shall the conscious muse unfold.
>
> (*Cadenus and Vanessa*, 826–35)

Clearly Swift's "conscious Muse" is a wry intervention where, ironically, a mythological character steps in to respect the social and sexual constraints on an eighteenth-century woman's reputation. However fundamentally Swift subverts the conventional muse, it is usually with a detachment that contrasts women poets' subversions of the figure, which as the next chapter shows explore the tragic, comic, and ontological dimensions of their relations to this figure of poetic power.

2
Speaking Objects: Women Poets and the Muse

IN POEMS BY MEN AND WOMEN WE SEE VARYING DEGREES OF THE speaker's identification with the muse. At times this identification is made superficially and briefly; at others it constitutes a complete reworking of authority and representation. Identifying with the muse suggests the internalization not only of inspiration but also of the object represented. That is, if the traditional poet-muse paradigm constitutes the subject-object relation of mimetic representation, then the revised poet-as-muse paradigm can constitute a post-mimetic representation, where imitator and imitated begin to converge.

The muse served several functions for women poets that it did not for their male contemporaries. Indeed, its frequent appearance in the work of some women poets can seem "awkwardly real," to use Dorothy Mermin's expression.[1] In using the muse, many women explored their most basic rhetorical conflict: how to perform the poet's usual role as speaker in a literary tradition in which women and the "feminine" functioned as objects of representation rather than as artists. In the canonical poetic tradition, the muses are given their presence and function by the poet: "without his words they are not, neither can they speak. Nor indeed, have they anything to say."[2] Women's alienation from the position of speaker and their identification with the position of object has been extensively explored.[3] Many women poets throughout the centuries have expressed this paradox in their use of the muse with different results.[4] Restoration and eighteenth-century women poets employ a range of relationships with women and feminine entities such as the muse to establish various grounds for representation. These poets reveal that in addition to the sociohistorical difficulties of women's lower levels of literacy, education, and cultural and legal authority in this era, there was also a felt rhetorical difficulty in which women struggled to take the role of speaker. In their treatments of the muse, women poets articulate their awareness that poetic authority is typically gendered—that the male poet imitates female Nature. What Charles Hinnant wrote of Anne Finch applies to several of the women poets in this chapter: "Her achievement . . . lies in taking over poetic forms and tropes that had hitherto largely been employed by men and giving those poetic forms and tropes an ironic and subversive twist by speaking through them as a woman."[5] Through the muse, women writers confront the paradox of speaking within a tradition that objectifies them, and in doing so they demythologize and humanize the role of the feminine in English poetry.

Often women poets show an ambivalent attitude toward the muse. For all of these poets, poetic authority is clearly connected to how they see their own gender allowing them to use or revise long established conventions of poetic authority. The most radical revision of the muse by women writers is to make the muse human. We have seen in chapter 1 how Pope made himself or his male friends into muses as a way of appropriating this source of poetic greatness. But when women poets make themselves or their female friends into muses, not only do they claim this mythological power as part of their human abilities, but they also claim their gender as an advantage in accessing poetic power.

In their range of approaches to the muse, women often depart from the mimetic objectives of the traditional canon, which have been described by one critic as an "orientation which stresses the order of a universe outside the mind and the obligation of art to capture certain enduring truths within that universe."[6] In poetry by women discussed in this chapter, the poet's mimetic orientation is often toward an order shared by the poet's mind and the universe outside it. Thus, divisions between self and object are effaced and another objective of representation is created. If one way of describing the movement from Restoration and early eighteenth-century poetics to Romantic poetics is a shift of the represented from the "world around" to the "world within" the writer, then the women poets studied here show a different course of eighteenth-century poetry.[7] They define poetic representation as a world within and without. Women poets of the Restoration and eighteenth century explore an identity between poetic self and the external world that allows the object of representation to maintain its place and identity. This mimesis entails (1) establishing the right or ability to represent based on a surrender of authority or a rejection of the category of authority altogether, (2) presenting a poet-subject that is often neither universal nor whole, but often diffusive and oriented toward the other and (3) at times engaging in a mode of representation founded on self-effacing friendship that serves as an analogy for an alternative mimesis, one that has profound ethical implications for the relations between self and other. Its ethics of relinquishing power over the other yields an approach to language that sets itself apart from the politics of mimesis described by Gunter Gebauer and Christian Wulf: "the history of mimesis is a history of disputes over the power to make symbolic worlds, that is, the power to represent the self and others and interpret the world."[8]

Many of the poets discussed here share social and political affinities in their connections with the Stuart court. It has been repeatedly observed that women poets of the Restoration and early eighteenth century are often aligned with Toryism and in some cases are actively involved in the Stuart court or cause. Katherine Philips, Anne Killigrew, Aphra Behn, and Anne Finch all supported the Stuart cause, with Killigrew and Finch serving as ladies in waiting to Mary of Modena, second wife of James the Duke of York, and later James II.[9] Catherine Gallagher has analyzed this convergence of Toryism and women's writing (specifically in the works of Margaret Cavendish and Mary Astell). According to Gallagher, "the ideology of absolute monarchy provides, in particular historical situations, a transition to an ideology of the absolute self" with a resulting "paradoxical connection between the *roi absolu* and the *moi absolu*."[10] In the poems that follow, however, I argue that the poetic subject is far from a *moi absolu*, to borrow Gallagher's phrase. Rather, we see an exploration of the self in relation to the community, which establishes an intersubjective approach to poetic and political representation.[11]

I focus less on the poets' relations to governmental politics and more on what they were attempting to do with the category of poetry itself, their medium of choice. In her use of female friends as muse figures, Katherine Philips developed a crucial analogy for defining poetry and poet. The muselike female friend created a like-minded audience as well as a relation of identity or sameness between poet and object of representation. Anne Killigrew's embattled relation to poetic authority and audience is borne out explicitly in her references to the muse, who in the figure of the queen is an approving source of poetic privilege but is ultimately powerless to help Killigrew negotiate her reception with her readers. Her ambitious poetry exposes the difficulties of a woman poet's relation to the muse: Killigrew's practice of what today we might call a *gynocentric* religious sublime in her poetry is hindered by the sexual politics that contaminate the reception of her poetry. In less overtly ambitious modes and kinds, women poets will avoid the tragic bid for poetic power that marks some of Killigrew's work. The poetry of Anne Finch, Countess of Winchilsea, shows the greatest range of poetic modes and the greatest versatility and ingenuity in solving problems of poetic authority through the muse. Finch establishes different standards for representation that develop the notions of identity and similarity seen in Philips's use of the dynamic of friendship. One of this era's most daring poets—man or woman—Finch offers a comprehensive alternative model for mimesis, subjectivity, and reader.

I

The strategy of humanizing the muse was, as we have seen in chapter 1, used by Dryden and Pope to establish a more worldly, conversational authority and to elevate the powers and status of the poet. Pope in particular used the relation of friendship to reformulate the poet's relation to the muse as a symbol of poetic power and to reformulate his relation to his audience. Women writers' concerns with the nature of friendship was motivated not only by their desire to establish a more receptive community for their poetry, but also by their desire to construct alternative relations between subject and object. Friendship allowed women to figure their authority and their relation to the reader as a private act that valued private virtues. In their uses of women friends as muses, women poets claimed a humbler poetic authority than they would have claimed in summoning the classical muses.

Scholars have acknowledged Katherine Philips's (1632–64) role for other women writers as a model of "humble" authority. But what has not been sufficiently appreciated are Philips's changes to the grounds of representation itself. Her approach to representation is based on a dynamic of transcendence through female friendship, where affinity and sameness define representation. In numerous poems addressed to female friends, Philips, or "The Matchless Orinda," attributes to a female friend all the properties of a muse to establish her authority to write. In "To my Excellent Lucasia, on our Friendship," Philips describes Lucasia as possessing a soul "Which now inspires, cures and supplies, / And guides my darkned Breast" (13–14, p. 105).[12] Philips's use of female friends as muses provides her with a remarkably liberating approach to representation based on the connection between poet and addressee, between artist and object of representation. Her ideal of female friendship relies on a commingling of like-minded souls that instead of authoritatively asserting a poetic self, seeks to lose this self through the virtue of friendship:

> I did not live untill this time
> Crown'd my felicity,
> When I could say without a crime,
> I am not thine, but Thee.
>
> (1–4)

Philips makes clear that the notion of friendship on which her poetic community is based is not defined through possession, subordination, or sacrifice but through a profound understanding of the other in which even identity is shared. In this goal of identification, Philips presents a paradigm shift in representation that is fundamentally outside of a conventional mimetic relationship. This is not imitation but a profound achievement of ontological union: "I am not thine, but Thee." With this limpid statement, Philips makes explicit the harmony between herself and Lucasia, which she has already expressed in the intertwining vowels of long *i* and long *e* (*thine* and *thee*) that permeate this passage. Her use of Petrarchan hyperbole in a female-to-female poem signals her appropriation of idealized love and may also signal a homoerotic content to the relationship. Carol Barash has focused on the political nature of Philips's "Society of Friends," as a "model of political loyalty" as well as a threat "both to heterosexual marriage and to the very myth of political stability it initially figures"; but Philips's Society of Friends is also a *poetic* community in which she redefines poetic and political authority through the bonds of female friends.[13]

Rejecting standard poetic authority, Philips renounces the self as a discrete entity. In "Friendship's Mystery, To my dearest Lucasia," each friend becomes the other as they share emotions:

> We are our selves but by rebound,
>   And all our Titles shuffled so,
>   Both Princes and both Subjects too.
>   (23–25)

In what is a daring appropriation of male roles, Philips proposes community and identity through a shuffling that dissolves hierarchy. Such a notion of female friendship carries over to a nonhierarchical notion of representation based on the immanence of subject and object or their interchangeability. She crafts a communal approach to representation that imitates the other through an identification *with* the other rather than an identification *of* the other.

This nonhierarchical representation appears in *"To the Excellent Mrs. Anne Owen, upon her receiving the name of Lucasia, and Adoption into our Society*, Decemb. 28. 1651."[14] The poet and the Society of Friends serve as a mirror that localizes Lucasia's brightness in an image of contraction and diffusion:

> But as though through a Burning-glass
>   The Sun more vigorous doth pass,
>   Yet still with general freedom shines;
>   For that contracts, but not confines:
> So though by this her beams are fixed here,
> Yet she diffuses glory every where.
>   (7–12)

This society, Philips explains, is its own medium of representation. In using the analogy of sunlight passing through a "Burning-glass," she suggests that this society can represent a powerful, elevated nature, but also that her representation does not constrict that which it represents. The burning glass is an intriguing alternative to the image of the mirror, which necessarily has its own boundaries that limit representation. Philips's glass allows for permeation, or "passing through," that paradoxically intensifies and invigorates through the act of diffusion. Lucasia can be represented as a member of the society while maintaining her nature and freedom. Philips explores further the poetic and social representation of Lucasia within this society:

> Her Mind is so entirely bright,
> The splendour would but wound our sight,
> And must to some disguise submit,
> Or we could never worship it.
> And we by this relation are allow'd
> Lustre enough to be *Lucasia's* Cloud.
>
> (13–18)

Using the conventional notion of accommodating representations of the divine to mortal limits, Philips develops a notion of both society and poetic community in relation to its members and objects of representation. "By this relation" of the contracting glass, both Lucasia and the others are transformed: those who would represent her are figured as lustrous clouds, imbued with her radiance. Philips effectively authorizes her poetic work through a society of friends that, she explains, is itself a system of representation founded on reciprocal illumination.[15] This mimetic relationship, based on like-mindedness as well as shared gender, provides a fascinating revision of mimesis that rejects difference and domination.

Philips's approach to authority and representation would be revised by Finch. But, however much the Matchless Orinda was cited as a model for the woman poet, as the Restoration wears on (Philips's poems were published in 1664 and, posthumously, in 1667), there is a stronger sense of the burden of being a woman poet—a problem that Philips avoided through the construction of her Society of Friends as well as through her relative seclusion in Wales. Although she visited London and had associates at court, her position of Welsh retirement reinforced her appearance as a modest woman poet shunning publication. "Despite her spasms of modesty and reticence over the allegedly pirated publication of her poems in 1664," James Anderson Winn reminds us, "Katherine Philips was actually an aggressive promoter of herself."[16] Women poets would use her as their champion and muse in a poetic field vexed with gender politics as early as Philips's death.[17]

In the pseudonymous Philo-Philippa's "To the Excellent Orinda" (1667), Philips as muse provides Philo-Philippa with powerful inspiration: "Let the male Poets their male *Phoebus* chuse, / Thee I invoke, *Orinda*, for my Muse" (1–2).[18] Philips serves Philo-Philippa in an almost militant segregation of the sexes: Philo-Philippa makes clear that her gender and that of the muse and other figures, such as Daphne and Nature, give women poets a greater right to the laurel wreath. According to these "identity politics," although Phoebus

> could but force a Branch, *Daphne* her Tree
> Most freely offers to her Sex and thee,
> And says to Verse, so unconstrain'd as yours,
> Her Laurel freely comes, your fame secures:
> And men no longer shall with ravish'd Bays
> Crown their forc'd Poems by as forc'd a praise.
> (3–8)

The startling conflation of poetic reputation (winning the laurel) and sexual aggression shows how vividly the muse's female gender was seen as a way of figuring masculine poetic authority through sexual conquest: in referring to the forced branch, the poet suggests that rape leads to poetic fame. Nature's traditional identity as feminine justifies Philo-Philippa's claim that women, not men, should reign over poetry:

> Nature doth find that she hath err'd too long,
> And now resolves to recompence that wrong:
> *Phoebus* to *Cynthia* must his beams resigne,
> The rule of Day, and Wit's now Feminine.
> (21–24)

Poetry as an index of power between the sexes is underscored in this use of conventionally gendered images, where feminine Nature finally subsumes all other powers. Philo-Philippa expresses a woman poet's assertion of her authority in the face of narratives of sexual conquest.

II

By the time Anne Killigrew (1660–85) ambitiously circulated her poems at court as a lady in waiting to Mary of Modena, Philips's positive reception as a woman poet by both men and women was an enviable and distant ideal. More than one critic has observed a shift in the status and reception of women's poetry in the seventeenth century: a shift from Philips's reception as a talented and virtuous woman poet to Killigrew's reception as a poetic pretender violating cultural norms of proper female behavior.[19] Contrasting her reception to Philips's, Killigrew points to a generational shift in which women poets look back to Philips's era as a "female 'golden age' of literature [that] lies in the mid-century past."[20]

In her role as lady in waiting, Killigrew found herself in a privileged environment of high culture, to which she herself could contribute, and one that obviously centered on the Queen.[21] With the Queen serving as her female muse, gender predominates in Killigrew's articulation of her authority. But it is an authority that ultimately cannot counter sexual politics beyond the protective circle of the Queen's domain. In the very first poem in the collection of her work, "Alexandreis" (1686), published only months after her death from smallpox at age twenty-five, Killigrew aimed high. She attempted the highest of poetic kinds in this unfinished epic. Although the poem begins by echoing the *Aeneid* to substantiate its own epic claims—"I sing the Man that never Equal knew, / Whose Mighty Arms all *Asia* did subdue" (1-2)—the poet is staggered by doubts that the muse, "Coy Goddess" (33), might reject an invocation written by a woman.[22] Killigrew insists that it ought to be acceptable for a "Female Pen" (22) to write Alexander's epic, but she has another plan if the muse is not forthcoming: Alexander's own merits will inspire her and "make my Verse Divine" (38).

In fact, rather than relying on Alexander's merits, the poet replaces ambitious themes with detailed visual description that eclipses heroic action and masculine virtue. This shift in sources of authority arises from her suspicion that the muse may not help a woman poet and from her doubts about Alexander's merits as a hero. Killigrew's use of visual imagery dislodges epic values: vivid images of the dawn, the landscape, and military armor take precedence over the exploits of Alexander, who emerges indirectly through stories remembered by Queen Thalestris.[23] Through Killigrew's painterly eyes, we see the beautiful details of military regalia dissociated from violent action: a "Troop in Silver Arms" brighter than the sun's rays, with "Dire Scarlet Plumes [that] adorn'd their haughty Crests," and "crescent Shields" that shaded "their shining Brests" (41, 43, 44). Vision replaces epic action. Only after she describes the scene does the poet reveal the identity of the soldiers to be Amazons, led by Queen Thalestris. Emphasizing visual description allows Killigrew to include women warriors in an epic frame before naming them.

Departing from Alexander and his heroism, the poem is divided against itself and appears as a broken fragment. As an epic, it certainly fails. Her editor (presumably her father) considered it a failure, appending an apologetic note to it. The poem, he wrote, "was the first Essay of this young Lady in Poetry, but finding the Task she had undertaken hard, she laid it by till Practice and more time should make her equal to so great a Work."[24] But as a revision of epic standards and invocations the poem fulfills another purpose: the ambitious placement of a female speaker and an alternative principle of representation in an epic frame. It is not so much Killigrew's authority but epic norms that are negated in the poem. Killigrew's poem announces the problems for women to write epics, problems that turn on her conception of the muse. A female character's vision has disturbed the praise of Alexander as heroic ideal, resulting in an aesthetics of stasis and fragmentation at odds with epic goals.

While the female character replaces the male, and vision replaces action, there is another opposition that explains this fragmented poem: the poet's preference for heroic feminine virtue over masculine martial exploits.[25] In the poem that immediately follows "Alexandreis" in the collection, "To the Queen," Killigrew delineates a new kind of authority in which women and feminine virtue prevail. In this poem, the Queen, not the muse, inspires Killigrew's verse. The poet explains why she abandoned "Alexandreis": the spiritual and moral authority of the queen is a greater theme than Alexander's exploits. "I saw," she explains, "that Pitch was not sublime, / Compar'd with this which now I climb" (17–18). Developing the idea of spiritual heroism ("A Throne i'th'inward Parts" [37]), Killigrew refigures herself and the queen. In her extreme isolation and privileged relationship with the queen, the poet does not focus on imitating the world "without" but instead constructs her poetic self, demonstrating its worth through her relationship with the queen. In their shared feminine virtue, the poet and the Queen can oppose the baleful outer world of her audience. Feminine virtue allows Killigrew to establish a moral authority that legitimates her position as a woman poet entering the public arena. "Poetical character," to use William Collins's term, *is* feminine virtue.

Expecting that virtue will make and preserve her poetic integrity, Killigrew finds that she is denied this very quality because she is a woman. This dissonance between her self-fashioning and how society will fashion her is the focus of her poem on her reception as a poet: "Upon the saying that my Verses were made by another" (1688). The poetic authority figured in her relation to the queen-muse is overwhelmed by what Killigrew figures as a sexual attack on her poetic identity: her best work is attributed to others, she explains, since few can believe a woman could write so well. Yet she is condemned for having written at all, an act promiscuous enough to put into question her chastity. In this classic double-bind for the woman writer, Killigrew uses myth to explain the attack on her poetry and to claim it as her own.

She begins with an invocation that recalls her former invocations of the muse, remembering the poetic self that she would have developed:

> Next Heaven my Vows to thee (O Sacred *Muse!*)
> I offer'd up, nor didst thou them refuse.
>
> O Queen of Verse, said I, if thou'lt inspire,
> And warm my Soul with thy Poetique Fire,
> No Love of Gold shall share with thee my Heart,
> Or yet Ambition in my Brest have Part. . . .
>
> (1–6)

In defining the muse as sacred and royal, Killigrew compactly establishes her poetic authority as spiritual and political. The poet's direct invocation of the muse is at once insistent and humble—suspended in parentheses at the end of the first line. In a position of humility, Killigrew defines her poetic function as a surrender of herself. Enlisting a convention of devotional poetry, she figures the poet's *spiritual* commitment as *sexual* surrender:

> An Undivided Sacrifice I'le lay
> Upon thine Altar, Soul and Body pay;
> Thou shalt my Pleasure, my Employment be,
> My All I'le make a Holocaust to thee.
>
> (9–12)

By constructing the muse as a sacred queen and herself as a willing sacrifice, Killigrew defines her poetic ideal as the surrender to transcendent power.[26]

In these opening lines, Killigrew establishes a coherent poetic authority carrying political and sexual valences. But it is of no consequence to the public's reception of her work (a small public who would have seen her poems in manuscript circulation). Killigrew intertwines the sexual metaphors that described her sublimated relation to the queen with her readers' sexual misrepresentations of her.[27] She renders this assault on her poetic reputation and her poetic self through the most prominent myth that sexualizes poetic authority: Apollo's attempted rape of Daphne. As Ovid tells it, Apollo's desire for Daphne even penetrates her transformation into the laurel tree, as he becomes the first artist to sublimate sexual frustration into artistic triumph. In her arboreal form, Daphne is transformed from the woman Apollo cannot have into a symbol of artistic achievement: "at, quoniam coniunx mea non potes esse, / arbor eris certe" (Since thou canst not be my bride, thou shalt at least be my tree) (*Metamorphoses* 1.557–58).[28] In his new, aesthetic, relation with Daphne, he exerts even greater power over her physically, suggestively swearing, "mea! semper habebunt / te coma, te citharae, te nostrae, laure, pharetrae" (My hair, my lyre, my quiver shall always be entwined with thee) (1.558–59). Killigrew identifies with Daphne, who in rejecting Apollo is condemned to woody silence.

The Apollo-Daphne myth allows Killigrew to explore (1) her society's dismissal of her work precisely because she is a woman, a dismissal that condemns the woman writer as sexually promiscuous and (2) a fundamental problem of the woman writer's relation to Nature, the object of imitation according to her era's poetics. In the Apollo-Daphne paradigm, women cannot represent Nature because woman is Nature—and in her transformation into Nature she becomes the very occasion for the male god of poetry to achieve his poetic reputation. When Killigrew's speaker recounts her earlier view of Nature, in particular, her vision of the laurel tree, she had assumed the Apollonian right to see Nature as an occasion for her art:[29]

> By thee deceiv'd, methought, each Verdant Tree,
> *Apollos* transform'd *Daphne* seem'd to be;
> And ev'ry fresher Branch, and ev'ry Bow
> Appear'd as Garlands to empale my Brow.
>
> (21–24)

In the convoluted word order that reflects her struggle to represent Nature, she finds that her poetic vision leads not to aesthetic triumph but to deranged perception. Nature will neither be transformed by her nor be her crown; instead, she herself becomes an object of nature rather than its artificer. Identifying with the laurel, she complains, "My Laurels thus an Others Brow adorn'd" (39). In applying the Apollo-Daphne myth to her own perception of her stymied poetic self, Killigrew defines mimesis as a kind of madness for the woman poet—in the eyes of society. She also suggests the violence of traditional mimesis, figured as a substitution for rape.[30]

Killigrew continues to use sexual metaphors to describe her tragic relation to her audience. In this, she still figures herself as a sexual object, but she no longer freely sacrifices herself as she did to the queen. Poetic Fame, personification of the public world, first supplants her private communion with the muse and introduces Killigrew's greatest poetic obstacle: her objectification through rumor, particularly, the rumor that someone else wrote her poetry. The fame of her poems, the poet discovers, places her in a sexual context unlike the rarified one she willingly submitted to with the muse. With this exposure to the public, her rarified and willing sexual contact with the muse now becomes like rape, which she emphasizes by the words *rapture* and *ravish*. In the seventeenth century, both could denote rape. She reformulates the ruin of Daphne in other images from nature: "Like *Esops* Painted Jay I seem'd to all," she complains, "Adorn'd in

Plumes, I not my own could call" (35–36). As the accused bird, Killigrew describes herself physically probed: "Rifl'd like her, each one my Feathers tore" (37).[31] She is both Nature and a false imitation of it; instead of painting, is herself painted.

Robbed of her poetic property, which she figures as the theft of her self, Killigrew's solution is to abandon representing the present in favor of representing the future.[32] Again appropriating classical myth, Killigrew affirms her existence as a poet through the story of Cassandra.[33] The poet explains her own paradox of being denied the power of speech while granted the liberty to speak of this denial:

> Th' Envious Age, only to Me alone,
> Will not allow, what I do write, my Own,
> But let 'em Rage, and 'gainst a Maide Conspire,
> So Deathless Numbers from my Tuneful Lyre
> Do ever flow; so *Phebus* I by thee
> Divinely Inspired and possest may be;
> I willingly accept *Cassandras* Fate,
> To speak the Truth, although believ'd too late.
>
> (57–64)

Even the enjambed lines weight the truth of her artistry toward the future, deferring meaning to the next line—"So Deathless Numbers from my Tuneful Lyre / Do ever flow; so *Phebus* I by thee / Divinely Inspired and possest may be." Like Daphne who rejected the sexual advances of Apollo, Cassandra incurred his revenge. Although he had given her the ability to prophesy—a vatic role long ascribed to great poets—he condemned her to an audience that would not listen. Whereas Cassandra rejected Apollo, Killigrew accepts Apollo's gift of inspiration and physical possession, with its sexual overtones. Despite this submission, she still endures Cassandra's punishment. That Apollo is the god of poetry and commands the muses is fundamental to Killigrew's analogy. Appropriately, he appears as the final source of her restriction and eclipses the place of the muse with which the poem began. She defers her claims to poetic authority, the power to imitate Nature, asserting, rather, her claims to prophetic authority.

Killigrew would have found that Dryden's ode to her memory confirmed her complaints in "Upon the Saying." The very images and myths that Killigrew used to describe the theft of her authority are the images Dryden later appropriates to praise her. Both poets use the same images and myths to end up with different versions of Killigrew's history. Dryden's elegy, like Killigrew's "Upon the Saying," emphasizes the muse and sacrifice, but unlike Killigrew, he does not sacrifice himself to a muse but sacrifices her status as a poet to ensure his and society's purification. There is, undoubtedly, a violence to be discovered in his definition of Killigrew as the human sacrifice that he prophesies will purify the poetic and political filth of Restoration England and renew its poetry. Dryden's praise eerily reproduces Killigrew's announced fears in her poem that she will not be acknowledged as a poet. The moral authority Dryden attributes to Killigrew to make her a sacrifice for other poets is the same moral authority Killigrew had once hoped would *entitle* her to poetic authority.[34]

She seems to have prefigured her fate in Dryden's poem in her descriptions of sinister relationships derived from mythology. Dryden's use of the Daphne myth is much more submerged than Killigrew's, but it still indicates his fusion of Killigrew with Nature, precluding her artistic distance and control: "Art she had none, yet wanted none: / For Nature did that want supply" (71–72). Instead of encasing Killigrew within the laurel's bark, Dryden's version of the Daphne myth surrounds her with Christian palms, her virtue framed by the leaves that celebrate Christ's entry into Jerusalem (1–5). Such spiritual privilege, rather than establishing Killigrew as equal or superior to poets, confines her to a domain frequently assigned to women in this era: that of moral exemplar. Disgusted with "This lubric and adulterate age" and seeking to "excuse our second fall," Dryden figures Killigrew as a chaste stream:

> Let this thy *Vestal*, Heav'n, attone for all!
> Her *Arethusian* Stream remains unsoil'd,
> Unmixt with Forreign Filth, and undefil'd,
> Her Wit was more than Man, her Innocence a Child!
> (67–70)

Arethusa was another nymph who, like Daphne, fled the cupidity of a god (Alpheus). Although she was changed into a stream to elude him, it was in this form that Alpheus raped her by reverting to his fluvial state and tunneling through the earth to find her. This sinister aspect of the tale was what Killigrew conveyed in her poem, where she uses a variation on the myth of Arethusa to show the loss of her poetic identity. What ought to have been *her* "Sacred Wreaths" (42) were given to another credited with writing her poems. Her own wreath, Killigrew explains, was

> quite lost, (like a small stream that ran
> Into a Vast and Boundless Ocean)
> Was swallow'd up, with what it joyn'd and drown'd,
> And that Abiss yet no Accession found.
>
> (43–46)

Boldly violating the end of the line (ran / Into), she imitates her violation by others. As in earlier images, she figures herself destroyed by her connection with Nature. In both Killigrew's and Dryden's poems, she is removed from the poet's conventional relation to Nature that requires the writer's difference and distance from the object of representation.

For Dryden, these myths allow him to move from an unsavory past into a purified future. For Killigrew, myths seem to create her historical circumstances with a menacing determinism that closes in on her. Dryden converts this historical woman into an element that allows for his own sublime transport. Killigrew's poem, painfully self-conscious, identifies the historical reception of her poetry with violent, transhistorical sexual narratives that deny her access to poetry. Although aware of her difficulties in constructing her own poetic authority, she makes relatively minor changes to the rhetorical function of the muse and thus her poetic ambition is marked by tragic frustration.[35] Even with the Queen as her muse, Killigrew's relation to a larger audience is untenable. Killigrew identifies patriarchal prohibitions against the woman poet rather than develop an approach to the muse and poetry that would reconstitute the work and reception of the poet.

III

Unlike Killigrew's rebellious content framed in a conservative rhetoric, many of Anne Finch's poems present a conservative veneer to veil her radical rhetorical and mimetic experiments. Finch uses the muse as a site for some of her most complex gestures of elevating and circumscribing her authority as a poet, a role that she often reminds her readers is carried out by a woman. She seems well aware of Philips's earlier solutions to poetic authority and representation. Using many of this poet's strategies, Finch takes on related problems for both the woman poet and for poetry in general as she tackles the power relations of representation and questions the extent to which language can represent an object at all. In her "poetics of replacement," Finch accepts the failure of language to represent, replacing conventional representation with moments in which the subject attempts to stand in the position of the object or stand for (in favor of) the position of the object.

In a poetics that may be considered antimimetic, Finch opposes poetry's conventional claim to representational competency. Through a variety of approaches to the eighteenth–century writer's tropological heritage, Finch's poetry redefines the boundaries between the poet and the nonrepresentable object, providing a model in which poet and object of representation achieve an identification that may be emotional or rhetorical.[36] Her poetry does this in part by revising the poet's invocation of the muse.[37] Whereas Dryden and Pope extend their mimetic privilege by establishing the poet's mimetic domination over an avowedly empirical world troped as feminine, Finch counters this masculinization of the poet and feminization of the object of representation by establishing an identification of the poet with these objects.

In the "Preface," which she did not include in her volume published in 1713, she suggests how her poetic aims are curtailed by what today we would call gender politics. The "Preface" explicitly describes her early clash with classical standards of poetic authority: "some of the first lines I ever writt," she tells, "were part of an invocation of Apollo."[38] In his "wise and limited" advice he tells her

> I grant thee no pretence to Bays,
> Nor in bold print do thou appear;
> Nor shalt thou reatch Orinda's prayse,
> Tho' all thy aim, be fixt on Her.[39]

Judging her ability, Apollo categorizes Finch as a woman poet and thus consigns her to what her contemporaries considered a sphere of lesser talent. Even in Apollo's suggestion that Finch find another object of inspiration in Katherine Philips, the "Matchless Orinda," he denies her access to Orinda's poetic power. In her description of Apollo's rejection of her, Finch yokes together her alienation from classical poetic standards and her status as a woman poet.[40] The similarity between Apollo's answer to Finch's ambition and his answer to Killigrew's in "Upon the Saying" is striking. But Finch smoothes over the pathos of this rejection by couching it in an urbane essay that wittily conveys her acceptance of restriction, unlike Killigrew's defiant prophecy that seeks escape from present restriction through an appeal to the future.

When Jonathan Swift praised Finch's talent in "Apollo Outwitted. To the Honourable Mrs Finch (since Countess of Winchilsea, under the name of Ardelia)" (written probably in 1709), he frames her poetic modesty in terms of an encounter with the womanizing Apollo.[41] Swift recounts Apollo's visit to Finch while she was still a lady in waiting to Mary of Modena. The sun god approaches, shielded by his crown of laurel leaves to shade his eyes from the bright beams of Finch's. As is his wont, Apollo intends to seduce the young woman and promises he will give her anything for her maidenhead. Outsmarting the god of poetry, Ardelia asks that the muses always attend her. With the muses at her side to protect her chastity, Swift's Ardelia stymies the would-be seducer.

In having Apollo condemn Finch to pridefulness and indifference to her poetic reputation, Swift makes comic what Finch had elsewhere described in more serious terms. The conclusion of Finch's "The Introduction," another work she did not include in her published volume of 1713, describes an environment where the woman writer must squelch her ambition and retreat to the shade:

> And if some one, wou'd Soar above the rest,
> With warmer fancy, and ambition press't,
> So strong, th' opposing faction still appears,
> The hopes to thrive, can ne're outweigh the fears,
> Be caution'd then my Muse, and still retir'd;
> Nor be dispis'd, aiming to be admir'd;
> Conscious of wants, still with contracted wing,
> To some few freinds, and to thy sorrows sing;

> For groves of Lawrell, thou wert never meant;
> Be dark enough thy shades, and be thou there content.
>
> (55–64)[42]

Here "my Muse" is not a source of inspiration but her poetical character that requires social subordination and mimetic redirection, figured as "shades." Clearly Finch describes the woman poet's authorial modesty in an unsympathetic environment. But Finch also revises subject-object relations. Her self is designated not in the first person but in the third, aligning the speaker with the object of representation precisely while describing herself as a subject-author. In doing this, she preserves the ultimate inviolability of this "other self"—or object—in a dark obscurity that allows it to survive. Swift's hyperbolic praise and playfulness with poetic conventions contribute to his poem's comic mood. But from the perspective of the woman poet, his narrative is a grim reminder of the tenacious sexual narratives that inform women's writing and would seem to make female poetic authority unimaginable.

Although generally excluding classical sources of inspiration that exclude the woman poet, Finch sometimes identifies with rather than invokes them, thereby effecting a rhetorical substitution between the caller and the called upon. In "From the Muses, at Parnassus," she engages the muses as authors: according to the poem's title, the muses make the verses rather than inspire the poet to write these words congratulating Lady Maidston, mother of Charles Finch (Finch's husband's nephew), on her son's eighteenth birthday.[43] The physical source of this message from the muses is Parnassus, that hill in Eastwell, which replaces its classical predecessor.

With the muses themselves addressing Lady Maidston, the poem calls attention to its direct access to poetic privilege. Conceding that this access is indeed unusual (lines 1–4), the poem asserts that the muses even prefer Lady Maidston's hill to the more restrictive Greek one, "Since from your own Parnassus, they receive / Pleasure's, which theirs in Phocis, never gave" (lines 5–6).[44] The poem never states the nature or source of these pleasures, but, by enlisting Christian typology, Finch underscores their worth: the muses "own, whilst here they reach the height of blisse, / Their forked hill, was but a type of this" (lines 7–8). Throughout the poem, the muses' references to themselves in the third person blurs the distinction between their words and those of an implied author who may at times be describing them. Here the implied author's verses imitate the very merits of the muses' songs they describe in this account of the entrance of the muses:

> See where they come, their brows with lawrel bound,
> And hear the neighbouring woods, repeat the sound,
> Of silver harps, and voyces that proclame
> To all the expecting world, his growing fame....
>
> (9–12)

Verses of muses and of poet mingle through sound devices and imitative form. A pun on the word *line* underscores the double application of these praises, which describe the worth of Lord Winchilsea and the worth of the poem itself: "Hark! How they sing the Line from whence he springs" (15). Finch's muses are not the unheard sources that inform great poetry by men; they are themselves poets, and their songs sound like Finch's—or vice versa. The depth of the poet's identification with these feminine figures appears in this imitative form. Instead of representing the mother of Lord Winchilsea, or Lord Winchilsea himself, this poem presents and represents the muses' song through enacting and describing it. Finch solves the problem of her poetic privilege by presenting a rhetorical tour de force that binds the inhabitants of Kent with the classical origin of poetic utterance. The transference of authority from muses to poet lies in exposing their similarities. In this shift in enunciative positions, Finch collapses the roles of speaker and object, unconcerned with establishing conventional mimetic authority. By the end of the poem, representation has given way to presentation and imitation to identification.

Poems such as "From the Muses" permit Finch to engage and deflate traditional sources of poetic power through a playfulness with classical myth indulged in by many early modern poets. But in her transformation of humans into muses, Finch thoroughly destabilizes the role of the poet. In "To Mr. F. Now Earl of W.," her husband serves as a muse when he desires "Ardelia to write some Verses upon whatever Subject she thought fit, against his Return in the Evening." Despite such spousal encouragement, Finch still asks the muses for help, who refuse, given her unusual theme: a husband. Urania, however, urges Finch to "dictate from the Heart" (78), recalling Sidney's muse in *Astrophel to Stella* who ordered him to "looke in [his] heart and write" (1.14). Unlike Sidney's loquacious heart, Finch's finds "that ev'ry tender Thought, / Which from abroad she'd vainly sought, / Did there in Silence rest. . . ." (82–84). Without the muses and without a speaking heart, Finch reaches an impasse of silence, one that cannot offend her readers by her presumption to articulate. "*Hymen*'s Endearments and its Ties, / . . . shou'd mysterious be," she decides (92–93). Her husband, then, must imagine her thoughts, which will remain secret. Rhetorically undoing her role as a poet, Finch seems to anticipate a Romantic aesthetic goal of expressing the inexpressible as she bows to the authority of her husband's ability to imagine what she would say.

Finch uses contemporary relationships rather than classical mythology to replace representational goals in the poem to her husband called "A Letter to the Same Person." There the poet eventually instructs her husband to finish—in a medium other than words—that which she cannot write. Although Love, she explains, "do's ev'ry tender Line endite" (2), without the inspiration of classical Love and Apollo, she complains, it is difficult to tell him how

>   impatient of your Stay
> Soft Hopes contend with Fears of sad Delay;
> Love in a thousand fond Endearments there,
> And lively Images of You appear.
>
> (21–24)[45]

Love and Apollo fail her, but not because she lacks poetic skill; rather, it is the general failure faced by every poet since "Thoughts of a Poetick Mind / Will never be to Syllables confin'd" (25–26). Faced with language's limitations—"whilst to fix what is conceiv'd, we try, / The purer Parts evaporate and dye" (27–28) —Finch asks Lord Winchilsea to compose the lines of her own thoughts. "You," she tells him, "must perform what they want force to do, / And think what your Ardelia thinks of you" (29–30).

In this surrender of poetic authority, Finch and Lord Winchilsea trade places as representer and represented: she asks him to be the author of the object of her own thoughts—which are about him. Although Lord Winchilsea may seem a modern replacement to the muse, his function is quite different, for, unlike the muse, who gives the poet the best words, Lord Winchilsea keeps the poet's meaning locked in his own mind; there are no words to give. Her husband, it seems, knows her thoughts that escape the order of representation. Grasping authorial intention, he is an ideal reader, but more importantly an ideal writer who creates in potentia though in a different tonal range from the melancholy of Gray's mute Miltons in the *Elegy*. Finch's love poem possesses an un-Romantic contentment with that which escapes language.

Does a poem such as "A Letter to the Same Person" merely add one more treatment of linguistic failure to English literary history? Is it a Restoration version of Donne's lovers in "A Valediction: Forbidding Mourning," who share a "love, so much refin'd, / That our selves know not what it is" (17–18)?[46] Although Donne's poem announces that "T'were prophanation of our joyes / To tell the layetie our love" (lines 7–8), these joys *are* communicated to the happy few through metaphor, including the conceit of "stiffe twin compasses" (line 26). Despite the rejection of "Dull sublunary lovers love" (13) that cannot endure separation, Donne provides the reader with a concrete image of absence that converts the "breach" into an "expansion" (23): "gold to ayery thinnesse beate" (24). In Finch's poem, however, there is no attempt to use figurative language to describe the indescribable, to fill literal language's representational gaps. Rather, linguistic limits leave the condition and knowledge of personal relationships inviolable to representational control.

The poem uses an ideal of marriage to replace the subject-object relation that undergirds mimesis. This replacement provides a model that assumes the willingness of one self to share the place of the other, annihilating poetic selfhood through this view of companionate marriage. Although its use of the socially authorized relationship of husband and wife seems to respect the decorous humility expected from a woman author, this restructuring of poetic authority challenges *any* poet's capacity to represent the objective world. The poet requires her reader to accept language's limits—leaving the unwritable, the rest of the poem, in her husband's thoughts.

In "An Epistle. From Ardelia To Mrs. Randolph in answer to her Poem upon Her Verses," Mrs. Randolph functions as Finch's muse when the poet explains that their friendship makes Finch a poet. Rhyming *heart* with *Art*, Finch underscores the importance of friendship:

> Might I the paralell yett more improve,
> And gain as high a Station in your Love,
> Then shou'd my Pen (directed by my heart)
> Make gratefull Nature, speak the words of Art. . . .
>
> (35–38)

Friendship here is the origin of Finch's notion of representation, creating equivalence between poetic subject and object of representation. As did Philips before, Finch takes to an extreme the convention of using friendship to found authority and art. This is a lesson Pope learned from Finch and Philips.[47] In "An Epistle. From Ardelia to Mrs. Randolph" and in "Friendship between Ephelia and Ardelia," Finch constructs poetic authority on the social and sentimental foundations of friendship, but she also exposes these foundations as an ontological ideal.

From her alternating roles as object of Randolph's poem to her and as speaker in her poem to Randolph—"Nor, lett itt to your Verse, objected be, / That itt has stoop'd so low, to find out me" (19–20)—Finch inverts the hierarchy of poetic kinds. Her modesty about serving as an object of Randolph's poetry—or, perhaps, her resistance to being represented—leads her to argue that "a mean subject greater skill requires / Then one, which of itts self, high thoughts inspires" (21–22). Thus she can accept Randolph's verses to her by praising Randolph's ability to write on such mean subjects as those of Finch and her poetry. To justify her argument, Finch cites Virgil's claim "That if to lowly Plaines, he did repair, / His Song, shou'd make 'em worth a Consull's care" (25–26). In a variation on her attention to the limits of language, Finch argues that not only is the high, those "purer thoughts," resistant to words, but so too is the low, in this case, the lowly theme of herself in Randolph's poetry. Ostensibly deprecating her work in this passage, Finch actually elevates her own poetic achievements, whose objects she often admits are mean.[48] She inverts the poetic hierarchy by referring to the very author whose career established this order: the conservative theme of friendship between women leads her to reverse the course of Virgil's poetic progress from pastoral to epic, placing friendship at the top of a new poetic hierarchy. As did many women writers, Finch contributed to the eventual ascendancy of the lyric that ultimately overshadowed the hierarchy of poetic kinds.

A poem that typifies Finch's mimesis of friendship is "Friendship between Ephelia and Ardelia," where Ephelia asks her friend Ardelia, Finch's poetic persona, to explain "What *Friendship* is" (1).[49] Finch uses the occasion to show the limits of language.[50] Since the concept and experience of friendship cannot be defined beyond "'Tis to love, as I love You" (2), Ardelia tries to explain friendship by offering a list of great sacrifices that friends perform for each other:

> 'Tis to share all Joy and Grief;
> 'Tis to lend all due Relief
> From the Tongue, the Heart, the Hand;
> 'Tis to mortgage House and Land;
> For a Friend be sold a Slave;
> 'Tis to die upon a Grave,
> If a Friend therein do lie.
>
> (7–13)

The abstraction "friendship" is not defined per se but exemplified by a series of imitative actions in which one person takes another's place or lends some replacement, some "due relief" (8): mimetic representation is replaced by mimetic action. The short lines of trochaic tetrameter do not suggest light-heartedness but rather underscore the intensity of this spartan sacrifice. The pressure of the trochaic foot records the difficulty of ideal friendship. Despite Ephelia's repeated demands for a better definition, Ardelia at last concludes that "Words indeed no more can shew: / *But 'tis to love, as I love you*" (19–20).

Friendship resists representation in language except insofar as language points to its own incapacity to represent friendship.[51] Why, though, should this problem of language arise in a poem about friendship?[52] Or, what in the poet's relation to a friend serves to exemplify the poet's relation to language? Friendship as standing in for another—giving "the Tongue, the Heart, the Hand," or life itself—provides a paradigm for the poet's work. In this and in other poems by Finch, "representing" is the willingness to suffer the place of another—human or not. In such poems she provides an influential model of values that privilege sensibility and lyricism. The poetic function lies less in a verbal authority to imitate the other and more in an emotional authority to acknowledge the other's resistance to the order of language. Finch relinquishes the power to imitate directly through language (conventional representation) while using language to point toward an imitation in experience (identification).

Even pointing to the nonrepresentable requires some zero degree of representability, of course, but Ardelia's difficulty with words is more troubling to the notion of representation than, for example, Astrophel's difficulty with words in Sidney's sonnet 35. In trying to render his praise of Stella, Astrophel asks:

> What may words say, or what may words not say,
> Where truth it selfe must speake like flatterie?
> ....
> Wit learnes in thee perfection to expresse,
>   Not thou by praise, but praise in thee is raisde;
>   It is a praise to praise, when thou art praisde.
>   (1–2; 12–14)[53]

Murray Krieger has described this poem as typifying the effort of poets of the English Petrarchan sonnet "to force into the network of language the elusive object that words—his words of love—have not been able to capture."[54] But whereas Finch's poem underlines the insufficiency of words by concluding with the answer given at the beginning of the poem, "'Tis to love, as I love You," Sidney's poem has continued to test the powers of words through a series of paradoxes, including, "It is a praise to praise, when thou art praisde." Finch insists on the very limits of which she speaks through repetition rather than defying those limits through the language of paradox.

Rejecting the powers to objectify what she represents, Finch defies the predominantly empirical claims of many of her contemporaries.[55] In defining the limits of poetic performance, hers is an "Augustan" acceptance of limits but of limits not accepted by most of her contemporaries.[56] Finch's efforts to revise the power relations of representation are derived from her position as a woman as well as from her position of political marginalization, which has been analyzed so thoughtfully by Carol Barash and Barbara McGovern.[57] In looking at Finch's avowed modesty and images of retreat, Barash has concluded that Finch "transformed political defeat into emotional retreat figuring both the landscape and this turn from public to private worlds itself as authoritatively female," and that Finch in turn "invented the poetic psyche."[58] When examined from the perspective of Finch's revisions of representation, however, Barash's oppositions of political versus emotional and public versus private tend to dissolve or resolve themselves. Recognizing the ordering of relationships that is fundamental to representation, Finch developed an alternative not only to "Augustan poetics" but to political exclusion—an exclusion that, as a woman, she might have felt even if the Stuarts had remained in power. In other words, Finch's poetics of replacement need not have the tragic tonality that we tend to associate with what Barash describes as the "poetic psyche": "a figure at once of desire and absence, spiritual fulfillment and the tragic distance that separates it from life and even the most powerful dreams of the material world."[59] Rather, Finch's poetics may be seen as solving both personal and political exclusion through a mimesis that includes the other. Her poetry performs a relation to the other that "makes it possible for individuals to step out of themselves."[60]

IV

Philips, Killigrew, and Finch hailed from privileged circumstances that contributed to their boldness in revising the mythological source of poetic power. The range of women poets' uses of the muse is wide in the Restoration and eighteenth century as this figure allowed them to convey a gender-specific subjectivity as well as other material conditions. Elizabeth Singer Rowe (1674–1737) would transform the muse-poet relationship to exploit her identity as a woman poet and to transcend the material realm (as Killigrew ruefully attempted in comparing herself with Cassandra). According to Germaine Greer, Rowe remade her image after what was at best an awkward relationship with John Dunton, editor and publisher of *The Athenian Mercury* in the last decade of the seventeenth century. Dunton's "chief stock in trade" was "excited panting by females or pseudo-females."[61] Significantly, Rowe did not acknowledge her contributions to Dunton's publication presumably rejecting "some of the torridness of her breathy enthusiams."[62] Kathryn R. King argues that Rowe's use of print and manuscript publishing shows her to be strategically choosing her means of accessing readers.⁶³ In the second phase of her career, Rowe's devotional poetry replaced secular with spiritual passion as she constructed a relation to God as a male muse that freed her from contaminating associations with mortal men and the public literary marketplace. In her focus on the religious sublime, Rowe like other women writers could claim her access to the divine content based on a tradition of female prophets.⁶⁴ Using a sexual dynamic of spiritual communion between a female worshipper and a male God—a convention established by female mystics—Rowe capitalizes on her gender. She can thus establish her poetic authority and dispense with the problem of a mortal reception of her poetry by claiming the audience of God Himself. While male poets of devotional verse, such as Isaac Watts, might figure an ecstatic sexual relationship with God, Rowe's gender allowed her to resuscitate this ecstatic tonality that was becoming obsolete for men.

Her sexually charged invocations are more than a means of establishing her authority; they become the whole of the poem. In "The Vision," Rowe describes her reformed role as a religious rather than secular poet when she encounters a masculine muse. This muse, however, *addresses* the poet, rather than in typical muse-like fashion being *addressed*. Robbed of inspiration to write secular poetry, the poet falls asleep and has a dream-vision.⁶⁵ "The Vision" inaugurates Rowe's infusion of ardent eroticism into religious praise that is based on regendering the conventions of poetic authority. The intensity of Rowe's devotion appears in a series of soliloquies. Labeling them soliloquies, she highlights her earthly isolation, obviates the need for a human readership, and suggests her oneness with God, the source of her addresses. In Soliloquy 7, although she protests that "the pomp of language" (1) fails to describe her love of God, she cannot restrain her poetic devotions (20–21).⁶⁶ Sexual metaphors describing Rowe's spiritual love expand in soliloquy 8, as she echoes the *Song of Songs*:

> Fountain of love, in thy delightful streams
> Let me for ever bathe my ravish'd soul,
> Inebriated in the vast abyss,
> The plenitude of joy; where all these wide,
> These infinite desires shall die away
> In endless plenty, and complete fruition.

(1–6)

By expanding sexual imagery into a spiritualized landscape where God is the fountain of love, she creates a material image through which her body may contact the source of divinity and locate the authority of her poetic devotion.[67]

Rowe recasts representation as the pure expression of overflowing love, a "spontaneous overflow of powerful feeling," not "recollected in tranquility" but uncontainable and, avowedly, unedited, with all the authority of a divinely inspired utterance. Ironically, this appeal to a natural spiritual expression made through claiming contact with the divine was less audacious to her contemporaries than had she claimed the secular authority of perspicuity and judgment.[68] As long as her material could be framed within religious devotion, made authentic by vivid metaphors of sexual intensity, Rowe could write even in the most ambitious genres among mortals, including the Christian epic, as she did in *The History of Joseph* (1736).

For many women writers, the muse's gender provided terms of solidarity between the mythical figure and the woman poet.[69] The muse as alter ego appears in the poetry of Mary Leapor (1722–46). Daughter of a gardener and herself a "some time cook-maid in a gentleman's family in the neighborhood," Leapor used the muse to represent her own laboring-class perspective as in "The Proposal" (1748), where the muse is a gossipy upper servant so familiar that poet and muse walk "cheek by jole" (6).[70] In the light-hearted "The Sacrifice. An Epistle to Celia" (1748), Leapor satirizes the rites of homage to Apollo and the muses by turning them into domestic chores: the first rite of purgation is handled with a "soft Utensil call'd a Broom" (20). A utopia of women poets, "The Muses Embassy" (1751), shows the muses' contact with the human Parthenessia, who serves as a kind of wet nurse to the future great woman poet, Polyhymnia, "Beauteous Darling of the Nine" (68).

Women poets' most complex manipulations of the muse yield new notions of the business of the poet that tend to dislodge models of domination between subject and object. In these confrontations women poets question the source of poetic power and privilege by addressing the cultural symbols through which they themselves have been figured. The results include complex and varying definitions of poetic subjectivity: Philips's and Finch's different versions of identity through sameness, an identification *with* rather than *of* the other; Killigrew's attempt at an ambitious and authoritative subjectivity that is destroyed but returns to speak from the grave; Rowe's poetic subjectivity wholly emptied to serve as the vessel of ecstatic communion with the divine; and Leapor's fully material subjectivity in which poetic authority is defined and enlarged through her position in the laboring class. With each of these subjectivities emerges a revision of the poet's traditional mimetic role of imitating Nature. In the next chapter, I examine the notion of Nature through men and women poets' representations of the landscape, where the feminization of the land replaces the function of the muse.

3
Gender and Order in the Prospect

THE PROSPECT POEM EPITOMIZES THE GENDERED STRUCTURE OF ART, where the poet imitates feminine Nature. Typically in the prospect, the male poet orders the scene of feminine Nature from his position on a hill. Much is at stake in this genre: ordering the politics of the land, claiming poetic territory from Parnassus to the literary marketplace, and formulating the relation between the subject and Nature, the object of Art.[1] With a panoramic view, the poet constructs a *paysage moralisé*: a view of Nature through a descriptive survey of rural scenes and a distant view of the city that spur the speaker to reflect on moral, philosophical, and historical concerns. Scholars have long observed the moral and political objectives in these poetic landscapes.[2] More recently, critics have examined the ways in which class distinctions operate in the speaker's elevated view over the land and its laborers.[3] Carole Fabricant and Jacqueline Labbe have demonstrated poets' persistent figuring of the landscape as feminine.[4] In her study of Romantic landscapes, Labbe argues that the prospect view is "distinctly gendered," indeed, "one of the defining characteristics of masculinity."[5] In this chapter I focus on how the gendering of the poet's relation to Nature in the prospect fundamentally defines how writers represent not only the land but also complex subjectivities. In the pages that follow, I consider how the gendered structure of representation is the means by which men and women construct the observing self and the Nature observed. The prospect demonstrates the subject's ordering of the landscape and in turn how this Nature orders the subject.

The poet's identification with Nature as feminine entity articulates a complex and elusive subjectivity. This elusive self reflects what is ultimately the intractability of Nature—what is coded as its femininity. Thus Nature is both that which Art *imitates* and a formal and ontological condition the poet often seeks to *emulate*. While the prospect's panoramic view allows the poet "to appear clear without plainness, inspired without fantasy, pious, visionary, but strong on fact," the femininity of the landscape continually escapes empirical observation.[6] As discussed in the introduction, by figuring Nature as feminine, poets exceed the bounds of empirical representation. In this tradition, Nature and the feminine are so elastic, varied, and, ultimately, figurative that they are everywhere and nowhere. Both Nature and the feminine have the privilege of not existing.[7] Thus in a mimesis that reproduces the romance plot, Nature and the feminine assure the male poet of an eternal chase, fueling the desire that prompts most structures of representation.

In the prospect poet's pursuit of the feminine, the poet transforms the object, emulating Nature's transforming powers. This dynamic notion of Nature—a *natura naturans*—predates that mode of representation usually identified with Romanticism. In the prospect, the male writer typically retains a romance paradigm for inspiration but internalizes the muse's powers as his own or disperses the muse's characteristics onto land and abstractions gendered female.[8] Although appropriating the figure's femininity and privileged vision for themselves, poets such as Denham, Pope, and Thomson figure this vision as masculine, objective, and disinterested.[9] These objective claims about observing the landscape are always eroded by the poet's reliance on figures of the feminine, figures that expand and complicate the boundaries of subject, object, and the possibilities of representation. That is, descriptions of landscape give the appearance of an empirically based mimesis to a mimesis based on myth, figuration, and idealization. Lawrence Lipking has described "part of the century's shift towards sensory perception that would culminate in the psychological," with the landscape becoming a "locus of ideas and feelings."[10] But even early versions of the prospect show psychology, feeling, and myth very much alive in feminine Nature, the ordering principle of the landscape.

In general, we may say that figuring Nature as feminine solves certain problems in representing Nature and subjectivity for male writers who use sexual narratives to expand the restrictions of an empirical approach. Thus I begin the chapter with the range of possibilities that feminine Nature offered men poets: for John Denham the feminine instantiates the poet's political and visual powers; for Joseph Addison, the gendered structure of the prospect underpins the powers and pleasures of the imagination, which reach their apex in connecting the earthly to the divine. But the poet's authority over the land, and in turn the poet's authority over self, is precarious, as Tim Fulford has argued: "the representation of landscape was never simply a disguised ideology presenting gentlemanly aesthetic judgement as naturally, and by implication socially and politically, valid. It was also a discourse in which that judgement could be redefined, challenged and even undermined."[11] Rachel Crawford argues that by the last decades of the eighteenth century, "the prospect had become correspondingly fraught with conflicting meanings," as easily associated with tyranny as with liberty.[12]

For women writers the feminization of Nature inherited from the poetic tradition would seem to block their participation as poets in this gendered system of representation. Jean Adams shows precisely how restrictive is feminine Nature to the woman poet, where Nature reflects, ironically, not natural but cultural restrictions on women's conduct, including their writing. And yet Lady Mary Wortley Montagu turns this restrictive Nature and conduct into an exploration of moral virtue that privileges the landscape of the heart—an early version of what will come to be called Sensibility. Ultimately, in teasing apart the differences in men's and women's representations of subject and object in the landscape, I turn to ways in which men and women poets construct an androgynous subjectivity, exemplified by Aphra Behn and Alexander Pope. In this androgynous model, which was also used by Milton and Dryden (chapter 1) lie the most complex explorations of subjectivity and Nature as the poet seeks to be like the Nature s/he represents.

I

For Sir John Denham (1615–69), establishing both Charles I's and the poet's right to the land is essential in his poem often

3 / GENDER AND ORDER IN THE PROSPECT

identified as the first prospect poem, *Cooper's Hill* (1642; rev. 1655). Denham's was a response to the political tensions that would result in the beheading of Charles I, ushering in Cromwell's rule. This ur-prospect is a political and poetic manifesto that orders the landscape and designates it, rather than the muse, as the source of poetry. In Denham's prospect, gender serves as the fulcrum to order politics, where the power of poet and king depends on their incorporation of the feminine: the muses, the personification of feminine Fancy, and Nature Herself. Beginning with the problem and the solution of poetic inspiration, Denham proposes,

> Sure there are Poets which did never dream
> Upon *Parnassus*, nor did tast the stream
> Of *Helicon*, we therefore may suppose
> Those made not Poets, but the Poets those....
>
> (1–4)[13]

Using the visual "evidence" of the terrain rather than the muse's reputation, Denham creates an authority of place not restricted by reality but expanded by poetic and political fiat.[14] Denham emphasizes the similarities among kings, muses, and poets through their shared positions of authority high on a hill: he conflates the muse with the poet when he refers to Waller as "a Muse whose flight / Has bravely reach't and soar'd above thy height" (19–20).

Denham's gambit for power depends on integrating feminine Fancy when the poet explores vision itself:

> if (advantag'd in my flight,
> By taking wing from thy auspicious height)
> Through untrac't ways, and aery paths I fly,
> More boundless in my Fancy than my eie:
> My eye, which swift as thought contracts the space
> That lies between, and first salutes the place
> Crown'd with that sacred pile, so vast, so high,
> That whether 'tis a part of Earth, or sky,
> Uncertain seems, and may be thought a proud
> Aspiring mountain, or descending cloud....
>
> (9–18)

The poet moves through "untrac't ways" seen through the naked eye *and* the eye of Fancy. Conflating empirical observation with the vision of feminine Fancy, Denham exposes the ambiguity of the land and the monarchical power it represents: the "sacred pile . . . may be thought a proud / Aspiring mountain, or descending cloud . . . ." (15, 17–18).[15]

In *Cooper's Hill* the levels of naked and fanciful vision blend in the Thames, which itself embodies the King's power. Denham presents a plausibly realistic view of an English face mingled with the landscape when an English youth looks into the river's shining surface. On the river's surface Denham creates an English Narcissus of topographical poetry who avoids the dangerous self-infatuation of the classical youth. The Thames is

> so transparent, pure, and clear,
> That had the self-enamour'd youth gaz'd here,
> So fatally deceiv'd he had not been,
> While he the bottom, not his face had seen.
>
> (213–16)

Leaning over the Thames, the English Narcissus' features assume great proportions: "his proud head the aery Mountain hides / Among the Clouds; his shoulders, and his sides / A shady mantle cloaths" (217–19). Whereas the classical Narcissus has no power because he sees himself, the English face gains power by seeing himself in relation to the English landscape, a prospect informed by fancy and empirical vision.

Image of mimetic desire and symbol of royal might, the river Thames runs through the prospect from Cooper's Hill. Denham reminds us again and again that the river is Charles I and that the river is what the poet wants to be. The crescendo of water imagery shows the poet's rhetorical command and the King's political command over the landscape.[16] The poet exclaims, in two of the most famous couplets in Augustan poetics:

> O could I flow like thee, and make thy stream
> My great example, as it is my theme!
> Though deep, yet clear, though gentle, yet not dull,
> Strong without rage, without ore-flowing full.
>
> (189–92)

Both in its objectives for language and for poetic power, this passage was to be a model for Restoration and eighteenth-century writers (a model so frequently invoked that it was soon parodied). On the one hand, the poet is modeled on Nature itself, the Thames River; on the other hand, this Nature figures the monarch, albeit an embattled one on the verge of being overthrown. Such naturalized politics would serve other poets in their later claims for political stability and for truth. As characterized by Denham, the river embodies an avowedly just, moderate power—"Strong without rage, without ore-flowing full" (192)—that defines ideal poetic language and its subject matter: "Though deep, yet clear, though gentle, yet not dull" (191). Denham's definition of poetic representation relies on the assumption that the King's/poet's power is as natural and irrepressible as that of the Thames. The poem attempts to establish poetic control independent of circumstances just as it attempts to assert the king's control on the verge of civil war. Although Denham explicitly masculinizes the river, superimposed by images of the male monarch, youth, and yearning poet, masculine power exists within the order of feminine Nature, who unites the "huge extreams" that give "Wonder" and "delight" (211, 212).

The river Thames is the *natural* ideal of the poetic subject. The one conventionally masculine element in Nature, the river images the Nature that the poet would both represent poetically and emulate ontologically.[17] From his earlier stance of replacing the muses, the poet now aspires to emulate the river, a monarchical version of the genius of the landscape. As this kinetic subject that cuts through and even threatens to destroy the land, the poet aspires to *be* transforming Nature. And yet, as will be seen in later versions of the prospect, this bid for poetic authority always requires submission—"O could I flow like thee." Denham's model of poetic representation already shows the poet's desire for immanence with nature that characterizes the poetry of Pope and Thomson.

Although Judith Butler has described the male subject as "constituted through the force of exclusion and abjection," my readings show that the seventeenth- and eighteenth-century male poetic subject represents himself not through excluding but through including the feminine.[18] One of the most important features of Restoration and eighteenth-century poetry lies in male poets' attempts to emulate the feminine. In the familiar opening of Pope's *An Essay on Man,* Pope and Bolingbroke range through feminized Nature, where they "beat this ample field" and "Try what the open, what the covert yield" (1.9, 1.10). But Pope ultimately defines himself and Bolingbroke as incorporating the feminine they penetrate. Addison describes this imaginative roving through the landscape in one of his essays on the Imagination:

> Our Imagination loves to be filled with an Object, or to graspe at any thing that is too big for its Capacity. We are flung into a pleasing Astonishment at such unbounded Views, and feel a delightful Stillness and Amazement in the Soul at the Apprehension of them. The Mind of Man naturally hates every thing that looks like a Restraint upon it, and is apt to fancy it self under a sort of Confinement, when the Sight is pent up in a narrow Compass, and shortned on every side by the Neighbourhood of Walls or Mountains. On the contrary, a spacious Horison is an Image of Liberty, where the Eye has Room to range abroad, to expatiate at large on the Immensity of its Views, and to lose it self amidst the Variety of Objects that offer themselves to its Observation. Such wide and undetermined Prospects are as pleasing to the Fancy, as the Speculations of Eternity or Infinitude are to the Understanding.[19]

Addison assumes a communal subject with unrestricted views, a liberty-loving subject reveling in unlimited space.[20] His statement on the imagination in fact evokes aspects of the sublime—a topic I discuss in chapter 5. But my concern here is with the assumed liberty of the spectator of the landscape, which results in the Imagination *losing* itself in this feminine space.

Addison's liberty-loving subject scans the heavens and earth, that "spacious Horison." In his 1712 "Ode," the eye moves through an infinite expanse with the prospect ordering the divine:[21]

> The Spacious Firmament on high,
> With all the blue Etherial Sky,
> And spangled Heav'ns, a Shining Frame,
> Their great Original proclaim:
> Th' unwearied Sun, from day to day,
> Does his Creator's Pow'r display,
> And publishes to every Land
> The Work of an Almighty Hand.
>
> (1–8)

Key to the representation of this male-authored order is the poem's feminine figures. Addison uses them to translate the infinite divine into a representable deistic landscape. The feminine figures that populate this poem connect vast expanses of space, unify different ontological orders, and simplify complex power relations. The feminine explains divine poetic power:

> Soon as the Evening Shades prevail,
> The Moon takes up the wondrous Tale,
> And nightly to the listning Earth
> Repeats the Story of her Birth:
> Whilst all the Stars that round her burn,
> And all the Planets, in their turn,
> Confirm the Tidings as they rowl,
> And spread the Truth from Pole to Pole.
>
> (9–16)

Whereas the feminine served Denham's imagination of the political, in the "Ode" and in his essays on the imagination, the feminine serves Addison's imagination of creation itself. The very communication of the divine—transferred from the Creator to the publishing sun and finally to the repeating moon—uses gendered paradigms to figure, rather than explain, the shift from divine power to human understanding. The conventionally masculine sun serves as the original transmitter that generally publishes the divine. But the familiar, more human, expression of this divinity that accommodates itself to human understanding appears in the conventionally feminine moon. Addison uses the moon's association with the feminine to create a connection to the earthly realm (mother earth). The feminine moon is both "wondrous" and familiar, with the stereotype of female gossips repeating the tale of the divine to the earthbound. In this and in many other more explicitly topographical poems, the creating word, whether God's Word or the poet's, will be usefully figured through this access to the feminine, and, as Addison explicitly shows, through the convenience of metaphors of birth, which the female best supplies. In this paradigm of the canon's gendered structure of representation, the feminine accommodates the divine to human understanding. Addison's discourse of self-evidence gives the momentary appearance of the visual, empirical evidence often assumed to predominate in prospect poetry and to underpin deism. But in transmitting the divine to the human realm, the poet emulates the feminine earth that repeats the tale.

II

The feminine figure in Addison's poem resembles the position of women vis-à-vis the land. As Susan Staves explains it, "in the property regimes of patriarchy, descent and inheritance are reckoned in the male line; women function as procreators and as transmitters of inheritance from male to male."[22] For women poets the prospect presented obvious dilemmas in its gendered structure of representation, its tone that is "strong without rage," and its mastery of a vast landscape. Women's approaches to prospect poetry rarely expatiate freely over a distant survey of Nature but instead present complicated visions of constraint.[23] The order of things in their prospects is often based on an identification with objectified feminine Nature. Women poets' uses of the landscape show (1) a drastic reduction of space, (2) abrupt shifts in tone that according to more traditional aesthetic standards might be considered aesthetic incompetence, and (3) reversals in, or fluidity between, the subject and object of representation.

Anne Finch responded to the difficulty of the prospect poem in her unpublished "Preface." There, when she imagines writing about the land in the tradition of a topographical poet like Denham, who "Might bid the Landskip, in strong numbers stand, / Fix all itts charms, with a Poetick skill," her inspiration flags. She cannot write a poem such as Denham's, she claims, because "he by being a real Poet, cou'd make that place (as he sais) a Parnassus to him; whilst I, that behold a real Parnassus here, in that lovely Hill, which in this Park bears that name, find in my self, so little of the Poet, that I am still restrain'd from attempting a description of itt in verse, tho' the agreeablenesse of the subject, has often prompted me most strongly to itt."[24] Although Finch complains that she cannot conquer the landscapes of her own world—having too little of the poet in her—in that same preface and in many of her poems, she articulates a poetic relation to the landscape through a model of participation rather than control:

And now, whenever I contemplate all the several beautys of this Park, allow'd to be (if not the Universal yett) of our British World infinitely the finest,

> A pleasing wonder throo' my fancy moves,
> Smooth as her lawnes, and lofty as her Groves.
> Boundlesse my Genius seems, when my free sight,
> Finds only distant skys to stop her flight.

Her rendering of the landscape of Eastwell Park resembles traditional descriptions of a male poet's movement through the muse's groves but with an important variation. Rather than penetrating the secret places of the goddesses, Finch describes her artistic spirit absorbing her surroundings.

As we have seen, Addison's prospects allow both imaginative expansion (as in his essays on the Imagination) and a link between the human and the divine (as in the "Ode"). Such a vast and unifying prospect contrasts sharply with the narrow view in Jean Adams's (1710–65) "To the Muse" (published 1734).[25] Adams's working-class background—a sometime maid and governess whose life ended in indigence—may inform her limited prospect that contrasts so sharply with Addison's.[26] We must also bear in mind that in this era women of all classes had limited access to property. (In essay No. 411 in *The Spectator*, Addison took care to limit even women's figurative access to the land while he extended it to the "Man of a Polite Imagination": "the Prospect of Fields and Meadows . . . gives him, indeed, a kind of Property in every thing he sees."[27]) Adams's "To the Muse" renders the problem of the prospect for the woman poet with deceptive simplicity. The landscape restricts instead of amplifies the scene through an implacable code of gender decorum. The poem, quoted here in its entirety, presents the muse with a restrictive prospect:[28]

> Come hither to the Hedge, and see
> The Walks that are assign'd to thee:
> All the Bounds of Virtue shine,
> All the plain of Wisdom's thine,
> All the Flowers of harmless Wit
> Thou mayest pull, if thou think'st fit,
> In the fair Field of History.
> All the Plants of Piety
> Thou mayest freely thence transplant:
> But have a Care of whining Cant.

For Adams, representing the prospect entails an oppressive encounter with regulations of feminine propriety. In her poem, both speaker and muse are subjected to a symbolic landscape bounded by social norms for women: the speaker gains no power, as Denham did, in assuming the muse's powers.[29] Adams's is a secular and social view—any inclusion of the divine would enlarge the scene. The muse is not invoked as an elevated source of poetic power but, rather, is inducted as a young woman into a prescriptive landscape, a man-made garden, small, limited, literally hedged in. The brevity of the poem confines and alienates the addressee. As an epistle it has the effect of inscribing the reader/addressee into its narrow walls, bringing both muse and reader to the confining hedge. The muse walks, not flies, with this domestication of poetic energy. Gender decorum has made both the poet and muse incapable of controlling the landscape as the prospect poet would do.

Adams has contracted the *paysage moralisé* of the prospect poem into a landscape of distilled abstractions, where a series of views overlap and restrict each other creating a narrower and narrower code of behavior that contracts the speaker within the "Bounds of Virtue," the "plain of Wisdom," and the "fair Field of History." The poetic subject seems alienated from an artistic relation to the object of nature but at the same time is defined by this claustrophobic landscape. Such a contracted state of being concludes with a warning against the misuse of language. As allegory the poem represents women's limited access to literary territory, poetic ambition, and language itself. This poetic alienation from the landscape imitates women's legal-economic alienation from the land—that "women were supposed unfit 'to meddle with the land.'"[30] With few rights to the land, Adams's speaker could never take on its political stakes as Denham does in *Cooper's Hill*. For Adams, the sexual politics of women's relation to Nature preempt considering the politics of nation.

Lady Mary Wortley Montagu's (1689–1762) "Epistle to Bathurst" (written probably in 1725; published 1748) shows a more passionate response to the gender politics of the prospect in a complicated narrative of sexual betrayal.[31] Her revision of the prospect poem identifies the landscape as a site of sexual politics that inform writing and being. While Adams's speaker and landscape contract as they are rendered, Montagu's speaker and landscape aspire to annihilation, fulfilling the objectification of woman and nature at the hands of the male landscaper. Bathurst controls and is charmed by the landscape at his fingertips: "Plans, Schemes, and Models, all Palladio's Art / For six long Months has gain'd upon your Heart" (3–4).[32] His intrigues in the country are succeeded by those at Court (where he is "Full of new projects for—allmost a Week" [34]), which are then succeeded by schemes of romance. In these schemes, Montagu emphasizes Bathurst's view of women as landscapes: he sees an audience of beautiful women at the opera as a "gay Parterre" (42) and admires Cloe's "bloom" (43), in the conventional diction of the pastoral. Montagu exposes the roving eye of Bathurst as restless and exploitative, not purposive and exalted as defined by Denham and Addison.

To attack this landscaping roué Montagu figures him as an unarable and indefinable landscape—as sterile and mutable as the grains of desert sand:

> Thus on the Sands of Affric's burning plains
> However deeply made no long Impress remains,
> The lightest Leaf can leave its figure there,
> The strongest Form is scatter'd by the Air. . . .
>
> (61–64)

By landscaping the landscaper into grains of sand Montagu reduces the womanizer to the lowest particle in a system of tropes that control women as well as that larger object of representation, Nature. Montagu goes one step further than objectifying Bathurst: in his insubstantiality he even fails to function as an object. In countering Bathurst's system of conquest over Nature and woman, the poet asserts not so much the female subject as the existence of the *object*, which she explores in the remainder of the poem.

If the poem had ended with Bathurst's dispersal, we might consider it a fairly successful satire, with the customary urbanity of tone and controlled rage recast to represent the experience of sexual betrayal. But these verses take a sharp turn that alters the tone and mode of the poem when the poet contrasts her steadfastness with Bathurst's fickleness. Still relying on the appearance of the landscape to manifest personal values, the poet depicts her powerful moral authority earned by enduring emotional trauma (what Emily Dickinson would describe as the "formal feeling" after "great pain"). With the speaker's shift from satirical attack to a melancholy self-consciousness, she inhabits the position of conscious invisibility and immobility:

> Unseen, unheard, the Throng around me move,
> Not wishing Praise, insensible of Love,
> No Whispers soften, nor no Beautys Fire,
> Careless I see the Dance, and coldly hear the Lyre.
> (68–71)

Montagu develops her speaker's object-like status when she figures her integrity as an element in a landscape. Like Bathurst she does not receive an impression, but this is because of her adamantine substance as opposed to Bathurst's insubstantiality:

> So numerous Herds are driven o're the Rock,
> No print is left of all the passing Flock,
> So sings the Wind around the solid stone,
> So vainly beats the Waves with fruitless moan,
> Tedious the Toil, and great the Workman's care
> Who dare attempt to fix Impressions there.
> (72–77)

In this new landscape of emotion that has replaced the observable prospect at the beginning of the poem, the speaker is the object. Montagu offers the invisible secrets of the heart as an alternative to empirical views. A rock that cannot be eroded by herds, wind, or waves, the speaker is figured as a deep self through her resistant objectification. As a sublime landscape that defies the topographer's control, the speaker is reduced to immobility and what will ultimately be a much deeper submission when she transforms herself from a rocky cliff into an art object, a funerary stone.[33] This stone is incised not by the speaker who confidently began the poem; rather, "some Swain more skillfull than the rest" writes "his Name on this cold Marble Breast" (78, 79).

When the satirist hands her pen to an unspecified male pastoral poet, the metamorphosis of Montagu's speaker—from satirist to sentient stone—dissolves her initial trope, her tone, and her voice. Here Montagu yields poetic authority to assert moral authority. In a variation on the figure of Daphne, this transference of voice depends on her final identification with feminized tropes rather than her actual role of poet. Montagu's revision of the prospect poem collapses the poet-subject with the object of representation. The desire that fuels representation becomes in Montagu's conclusion the death of the female subject pleading to be written—only differently—by a devoted male pastoral poet. Oppressed romantically rather than by codes of conduct, Montagu's poet seeks to be represented. In Montagu's system of landscape values to be writable is to be a virtuous self, in contrast to the unimpressable, wind-blown Bathurst. Although this writable subject may appear to be in a condition of defeat, this is not the death of the female subject but the articulation of conscious emotion in the object without agency.[34] In this final image of her breast incised, Montagu invokes the ancient notion of "writing as cutting": "the basic image is the receptive heart as a blank writing surface, a 'table' or tablet for recording impressions in the form of words."[35] Thus, Montagu transforms the feminine Nature exploited by Bathurst at the beginning of the poem into a landscape of the heart. This heart—inviolable in its virtue—demonstrates the deep self of the speaker who can only be "written" by the rare swain. Writing has become virtuous feeling and being.

Adams's and Montagu's versions of the prospect show the restrictions women poets often find in the landscape and the consequences of such restrictions on representation and subjectivity. We could argue that both poems expose the class positions of their authors. Adams's extremely restricted view reflects the poor woman's alienation from property; whereas Montagu's emphasis on sexual politics suggests an alienation from property corresponding to the attenuated power of a female aristocrat: in her relations to men the female aristocrat may have a modicum of control over the landscape. Such class differences appear throughout prospect poetry. With comical flair, Mary Leapor specifically connects her status as a servant to her lack of access to the prospect in her poem "Crumble-Hall" (1751): just after reaching the rooftop of the old mansion where she serves, the speaker and muse are dragged down to the "nether World" of the kitchen.[36] Mary Collier's (1690?–c. 1762) poem "The Woman's Labour" (published 1739) summarizes the bitter lot of women working in the fields by describing the absence of spatial and temporal prospects: "For all our Pains, no Prospect can we see / Attend us, but *Old Age* and *Poverty*" (200–1).[37]

In its attention to spatial constraints, Jonathan Swift's poetry resembles certain features of women's use of the landscape. In her study *Swift's Landscape*, Carole Fabricant argues that he identifies more "with the objects of perception" than with the perceivers—a feature seen in many landscape poems by women.[38] Swift "portrays himself as a figure *in*, rather than overlooking, the landscape, often as someone on alien turf."[39] His "Drapier's Hill" (published 1729) mocks the prospect poem as he emphasizes the financial burden of "improving" the land he will christen Drapier's Hill. Swift provides no wide-ranging view of the prospect that might be. For him the hill would function temporally rather than spatially: when the Irish have forgotten what the "Drapier" did for them, this hill will remind them. Yet the very purpose of Swift's hill places the poet and the land he *might* control in a domain of politics (however neglected and powerless Swift claims to be). In mock vanity, the poet claims his model hill will vie with Cooper's, but this mockery asks the reader to weigh the liberty of the Irish with Denham's concern for national, monarchical stability in *Cooper's Hill*. Not surprisingly, Swift's poem "The Dean's Reasons for Not Building at Drapier's Hill" (written probably 1730) is a much longer and ultimately more serious poem than his "Drapier's Hill," asking, "How could I form so wild a vision, / To seek, in deserts, fields Elysian?" (15–16). The social, political, and even psychological restrictions of Swift's prospects, thus, are of a different *kind* from those described by women poets discussed here. But Swift shares with them a sense of exclusion from controlling the land.

III

Prospects in this era are always mixed forms (e.g., Addison's deistic ode, Adams's prospect of conduct, and Montagu's satirical and elegiac landscape), but the pastoral is central to these landscapes. Because of its explicit artifice, the pastoral may be admitted in quaint contrast to the prospect poem's empirical claims without appearing to destroy them. In its artificial context the pastoral permits the inclusion of female characters and sexual narratives. The political implications of pastoral elements in the prospect pastoral are manifold: as one of the lowest kinds on the poetic hierarchy, the pastoral was considered a relatively acceptable kind for women poets and thus could provide a modest veil for ambitious experimentation.[40] Emphasizing the pastoral in the prospect, poets could focus especially on Nature as feminine and domestic. More intimate than many other poetic kinds, the pastoral often foregrounds relations between the sexes. Pastoral prospects often focus on sexual politics rather than the explicitly governmental politics epitomized in Denham's *Cooper's Hill*. Most importantly, because the pastoral is a more intimate depiction of the landscape where individual characters take precedence over prospects, women poets find it a more flexible mode than the prospect for exploring relations between subject and object. Most of Aphra Behn's poetry is overtly pastoral rather than topographical, presenting bold female subjects well aware of sexual politics in the landscape.[41]

In "On a Juniper-Tree, cut down to make Busks" (1680) much of the poem's significance is lost if it is not seen as revising assumptions of the prospect from the perspective of pastoral. The poet replaces the conventional meditations on the meaning of landscape—its relevance to humans—by personifying a tree, allowing the landscape to speak. From this position the poet is herself the landscape with irrefutably "natural" authority. As a speaking tree, Behn's juniper is a revision of the position of the silent Daphne. But, instead of Daphne's violated female figure (see Killigrew's version of Daphne discussed in chapter 2), Behn turns woman's association with Nature from a paralyzing condition to a powerful and provocative one.[42] Behn's juniper tree can basically "tell it like it is" because it is the voice of Nature unbound by social constraints. But it is also the voice of Nature that knows itself to be constructed by society—not natural at all. By using a trope to identify with Nature, literally speaking through the landscape, Behn immerses her speaker in the landscape to reveal the artifice of sexual politics and sexual reputation. If the prospect allowed writers a distant and avowedly objective view of English society, Behn's use of the landscape as itself the vantage point, specifically the speaking tree, asserts the poet's physical proximity to and wise familiarity with the ramifications of sexual and gender politics.[43]

In a poem that demonstrates several contradictions, chiefly, the speech of the mute, the movement of the immobile, and the consciousness of the nonhuman, the tree begins by praising its own chaste sensual delights:[44]

> Whilst happy I Triumphant stood,
> The Pride and Glory of the Wood;
> My Aromatick Boughs and Fruit,
> Did with all other Trees dispute.
> Had right by Nature to excel,
> In pleasing both the tast and smell:
> But to the touch I must confess,
> Bore an Ungrateful Sullenness.
>
> (1–8)

The tree here is in a position of triumphant elevation normally reserved for the prospect poet, its authority both natural and artificial in its command of pastoral expression. Here is the voice of "Nature": a coy rhetoric that exposes and suppresses sexual content. Representing the landscape from the inside out, Behn wittily exposes the assumption that Nature is feminine and that Nature is natural. Through her personification of the tree, which is the poem's speaker, Behn makes "Nature" the subject of art and the object of imitation. Most important to Behn's artful revision of the landscape is her subtle marking of the tree as both feminine and masculine. As an element of Nature the tree is conventionally understood as feminine, and Behn underscores its stereotypical femininity in the tree's initial coyness. At the same time, Behn's tree stands prominently, boasting its supremacy in the landscape (1–6). Throughout the poem the tree combines symbols of femininity, such as the tree's maternal protectiveness (28), with its masculine elements, such as its phallic trunk and root, on which Cloris leans her head (26). The tree's ambiguous gender identity runs parallel with its ambiguous sexual preferences (33–40). Its androgyny allows Behn to unite nature with art, poetic subject with object of representation.[45]

The poet plays with decorous rhetoric in order to express and suppress sexual content. When a male and female lover regularly visit the tree and copulate under its branches, the tree participates, despite its earlier dislike of touch:

> My Grateful Shade I kindly lent,
> And every aiding Bough I bent.
> So low, as sometimes had the blisse,
> To rob the Shepherd of a kiss. . . .
>
> (33–36)

The tree claims to enjoy this sexual behavior that it conceals under its sheltering "Canopy" (28). Behn exploits the personification of the tree to expose the cultural metaphors that connect female sexuality with commodification, the economic value of women's chastity.[46] The tree announces that

> My Wealth, like bashful Virgins, I
> Yielded with some Reluctancy;
> For which my vallue should be more,
> Not giving easily my store.
>
> (9–12)

When the lovers must stop meeting under the juniper tree, the speaker grieves at her loss: "No more a joyful looker on, / Whilst Loves soft Battel's lost and won" (93–94).

Behn literalizes the figurative connection between feminine chastity and commerce when the tree is cut down and made into a woman's corset.[47] In this "happier state" the tree finds not the innocence of a pastoral Golden age but the condition of artful dress in the form of a corset that defines, protects, and provides access to women's sexual parts. Behn mocks the confounding of sexual, religious, and rhetorical powers in her use of the word *translate*:

> She cut me down, and did translate,
> My being to a happier state.
> No Martyr for Religion di'd
> With half that Unconsidering Pride;
> My top was on that Altar laid,
> Where Love his softest Offerings paid:
> And was as fragrant Incense burn'd,
> My body into Busks was turn'd:
> Where I still guard the Sacred Store,
> And of Loves Temple keep the Door.
>
> (99–108)

The poem's shift in tone lies not in the speaker's change in voice, which remains light-hearted, but in the transformation of the object speaking. Pastoral pleasures condoned by the personified tree can maintain a veneer of modesty. But when these pleasures are condoned by the speaker's new position as a woman's undergarment, the superficially modest tone turns bawdy.[48]

The poet's figuration of the tree may be read as an allegory of Behn's own poetics. Nature is converted into art by combining Nature's femininity with the tradition of feminine sexuality as artful, but the tree's androgyny complicates this. Emphasizing the busk's role as covering and uncovering, Behn values neither empirical argument nor sublime suggestion but an erotic wit that exposes the habits of gendered rhetoric. What makes it different from traditional canonical displays of wit in this period is the degree to which it considers the artistic and social implications of feminine figures. Behn's approach to the boundaries of speaker and object denatures Nature and "de-genders" gender by making it masculine and feminine. While the speaker's position is from the beginning overtly fictional, by the end of the poem, when the last shreds of pastoral ideals have vanished, the speaker's powers are so intertwined in artifice that art can no longer be said to imitate Nature. Language is indeed the "dress of thought" in this poem, but what it clothes remains elusive. Behn's radical restriction of "Nature" playfully asserts the agency of the object represented.[49]

In this highly contracted landscape that ultimately encircles the woman's body, Behn creates a subjectified object that colludes with Cloris in controlling access to the woman's sexuality. The landscape initially presided over by the tree is now the yonic site of Cloris's body, thus collapsing outer and inner.[50] Unlike Adams's contracted landscape, Behn's shows the liberty of this collapsed space for Cloris, and arguably, for the woman writer. The poem began with a bower-like setting and ends with a brilliant variation on the woman as a walled garden: the *hortus conclusus*. But rather than emphasizing "real" female chastity, Behn's female body enclosed by busks represents control over female sexual reputation.[51] Behn's androgynous speaker-object at the beginning of the poem introduces the poem's focus on Cloris's sexual reputation and the necessity of disguise.[52] That Cloris's reputation is shielded first by the tree and then by busks suggests that for Behn the elusiveness of sexual identity is part of a larger system in which subject and object metamorphose as needed.

To defy representation is to protect the fulfillment of desire. Behn uses this playful strategy in "To the fair Clarinda, who made Love to me, imagin'd more than Woman" (1688):[53]

> Fair lovely Maid, or if that Title be
> Too weak, too Feminine for Nobler thee,
> Permit a Name that more Approaches Truth:
> And let me call thee, Lovely Charming Youth.
> This last will justifie my soft complaint,
> While that may serve to lessen my constraint;
> And without Blushes I the Youth persue,
> When so much beauteous Woman is in view.
> Against thy Charms we struggle but in vain
> With thy deluding Form thou giv'st us pain,
> While the bright Nymph betrays us to the Swain.
> (1–11)

Clarinda may be represented as man, woman, or both. Her capacity to be either sex—and hence to elude a single mode of representation—protects, like the busks of the juniper tree, the speaker's reputation:

> In pity to our Sex sure thou wer't sent,
> That we might Love, and yet be Innocent:
> For sure no Crime with thee we can commit;
> Or if we shou'd—thy Form excuses it.
> For who, that gathers fairest Flowers believes
> A Snake lies hid beneath the Fragrant Leaves.
> (12–17)

In representing Clarinda's alternating identity, Behn underscores representation as an illusory imitation of identity, an illusion that preserves the fulfillment of female desire.

Returning to "A Juniper Tree," then, although Behn integrates the speaker-subject with the object of representation, the subject, if we may call it that, remains elusive, founded as it is on Behn's exploration of the object. There is no "deep self" but rather an intractable one that emerges through performance and disguise. Thus, "A Juniper Tree" contrasts poems of a later generation, such as those by Collins and Gray, where the poet's gambit is based on the *desire* to integrate subject and object rather than to achieve it. Collins's and Gray's, and, before them, Thomson's, poetics are based on the dynamic of sexual difference and an enunciation based on yearning. Behn's poetics is based on identification rather than difference and on an enunciative and sexual satisfaction conveyed through wit. This wit lies in taking literally the gendering of landscape and revising it to include agency and androgyny. In Behn's poem the speaker does not aspire to enter feminized Nature because the speaker is feminine—and masculine—Nature as well as art.

IV

Gendered landscapes permeate the Restoration and eighteenth-century canon, supporting Dryden's representations of history and Pope's representation of politics and Man.[54] Pope's poetry shows the most comprehensive use of feminine landscapes and abstractions to order ideas and arguments. He uses the feminization of Nature to push an ostensibly empirical representation into the realms of myth and imagination—the quintessence of "Augustan" poetry's reliance on the feminine. Central to the complexity of Pope's approach to representation is his incorporation of Nature's femininity into the character of his male poet-subject—a strategy that coincides with Pope's relation to his garden at Twickenham. "Gardening," argues Helen Deutsch, "was the highest form of self-fashioning for Pope."[55] His poetic mastery of the landscape is established through the authority of gender and depends on the suppression of his status as a Catholic, unable to possess the land literally.[56]

Subtly reordering gender decorum, Pope appropriates feminine characteristics in an avowedly manly way. More than any other canonical "Augustan" poet, Pope uses the malleability of femininity's symbolic power to elevate man-to-man discourse. In chapter 1 we saw that Pope's male conversationalists imitated the muse's omniscience by assuming an elevated and presumably disinterested view of society from a hilltop, whence the feminine landscape beneath them served as an object to be described and controlled through familiar romance paradigms. As an *idée reçue* defined by reigning cultural stereotypes, feminine Nature figuratively connects Pope's exposition of man's relation to God and to other men. The feminine's metaphoric capacities serve Pope's characterization of himself in "Epistle to Arbuthnot" as one who "stooped to Truth." But the Truth that Pope seeks is continually compromised or transformed by his reliance on the metaphoricity of the feminine. For Pope, the muse as feminine entity authorizes his access to the truth that, for him, is the object of poetry and the foundation of its moral power. Pope's use of the symbolic power of the feminine allows him to exceed the material and historical limits of representation ultimately through figuring his own androgyny.

By making political order intelligible through feminine figures, Pope affirms the poet's indispensability to that order, as Denham did in *Cooper's Hill*. But far more than in *Cooper's Hill*, Pope's poet-subject incorporates the feminine in variations on Behn's poet-speaker in "A Juniper Tree." But whereas in Behn the subject and object of representation vacillate, now feminine, now masculine, in Pope, the masculine subject incorporates the feminine object that is Nature. This verbal incorporation found its horticultural equivalent in Pope's garden at Twickenham: at the center of his garden was the "obelisk in memory of his mother, inscribed, 'Ah Editha! Matrum Optima. Mulierum Amantissima. Vale.' (Ah Edith! Best of Mothers. Most Beloved of Women. Farewell)."[57] In Pope's political prospect *Windsor Forest* (1713), feminine figures in the landscape play a central role in organizing the poem's artistic and political concerns. His emphasis on pastoral elements in this Eden of the Stuarts, specifically, of Queen Anne, establishes a network of feminine characters and characteristics. International political tensions and the domestic political tension over succession from a childless queen are displaced onto a simpler narrative of seduction that shows feminine powers checked by masculine voices. The numerous feminine elements in the poem, including the landscape, the queen, Lodona, and various abstractions, veil or alter specific governmental operations, including the Treaty of Utrecht, the extent of monarchical powers with its related problem of monarchical succession, and England's mercantile economy.[58]

These feminine entities are contextualized and interpreted by male speakers, convincing insofar as it is assumed that masculine entities naturally control feminine ones. Pope calls forth the spirituality and seductiveness of the feminine in a description of Windsor Forest that echoes Milton's rendering of feminine Paradise. Volatile political power resembles the play of light and shadow through the trees, a "coy Nymph" whom "her Lover's warm Address / Nor quite indulges, nor can quite repress" (19–20). The poem begins by establishing sexual authority within the landscape, subordinating the muses in the landscape to Granville: "What Muse for *Granville* can refuse to sing?" (6).[59] The authority placed in Granville is expressed through sexual images in which the Sylvan Maids cannot refuse him entrance. Thus Pope initiates the poem's masculine authority while the feminine persists as a volatile power that can simplify or obscure. The poem will repeatedly circumscribe women, nymphs, feminized land, and, ultimately, even the poet himself by masculine authority.

Pope repeatedly intertwines political and poetic power, introducing the landscape that belongs to Queen Anne in artificial pastoral diction:

> See *Pan* with Flocks, with Fruits *Pomona* crown'd,
> Here blushing *Flora* paints th'enamel'd Ground,
> Here *Ceres'* Gifts in waving Prospect stand,
> And nodding tempt the joyful Reaper's Hand,
> Rich Industry sits smiling on the Plains,
> And Peace and Plenty tell, a Stuart reigns.
>
> (37–42)

To contain the political within the poetic, Pope describes the Queen's success in a tableau ordered by Flora and Pan, god of pastoral poetry. The pastoral here serves to heighten poetic myth-making as central to the Stuarts' success, and, possibly, succession, as it provides a setting for sexual narratives that transform political complexities.[60] Although often seen as stabilizing political tensions, the pastoral includes narratives of desire, in this case of female agency, that allow for pockets of instability tolerated precisely because of pastoral's overt artificiality.

The poet's circumscription of the feminine, central to his demonstration of poetic might and political finesse, appears in the poem's lengthy "digression," a digression that might seem to compromise the unity of the poem. In fact, the digressive story of

Lodona epitomizes Pope's gendered system of representation. Lodona, who is almost seduced by Pan, elaborates the poem's fundamental gesture of subsuming the poetical and the political within the category of the feminine, which is in turn controlled by male figures. In recounting the story of the Loddon stream, Pope transports the reader into a mythological frame where metamorphosis and sexuality dominate. The story of Lodona is the story of the hunt, appropriate given that Windsor Forest is the royal hunting ground.[61] As a hunter herself Queen Anne leads us to the history of the nymph Lodona: despite the fact that the queen was married, both she and Lodona are presented as devotees of the principles of Diana—virginity and the chase. Lodona's rejection of sexual contact disrupts the order of Pan; similarly, Queen Anne's childlessness disrupts the succession and so endangers the governmental order.[62]

Lodona's transgression of traditional sexual roles is represented through her crossing of geographical limits and the threat of sexual punishment (rape) that follows: "It chanc'd, as eager of the Chace the Maid / Beyond the Forest's verdant Limits stray'd, / *Pan* saw and lov'd" (181–83).[63] Rich in meaning for the place of desire in poetry, Pope's story echoes Ovid's version of Apollo's close pursuit of Daphne in this description of the hunted Lodona: "And now his shorter Breath with sultry Air / Pants on her Neck, and fans her parting Hair" (195–96). Daphne-like, Lodona asks for help from greater powers and is metamorphosed into a "silver Stream," a tributary of the Thames. In the ancient myths both Apollo and Pan parlay their *failure* to conquer the women they desire into symbols of artistic achievement. For Apollo, Daphne's laurel leaves will crown victorious poets to signify his command of the realm of poetry, and for Pan Syrinx's reeds are joined to make a pipe for his legendary songs. Emblem of Pope's own recurring poetic strategy and its political implications, the Pan-Lodona myth represents political and poetic territory brought within a recognizable sexual narrative where masculine power dominates through art.[64] The royal forest remains the Queen's, and the Queen/Lodona retains her chastity, precisely because the poet/Pan renders her artistically, rather than conquering her body. Through this figuration Pope demonstrates the poet's indispensability to the ruler in formulating the order of politics, gender, and representation, all of which overlap.[65]

With the containment of Lodona, Pope emphasizes her role as an instrument of poetic and political achievement. That a feminine stream is used as instrument of this artistic production establishes Pope's methods to be one with Apollo's. Like Denham's English youth who gazes at the reflecting Thames, Pope's youth sees not himself but the English landscape in Lodona:

> Oft in her Glass the musing Shepherd spies
> The headlong Mountains and the downward Skies,
> The watry Landskip of the pendant Woods,
> And absent Trees that tremble in the Floods;
> In the clear azure Gleam the Flocks are seen,
> And floating Forests paint the Waves with Green.
> (211–16)

As an altering mirror, the feminized stream defines the shepherd's musings and transforms the actual into art through its refracting difference.[66] Imaging artistic perception through myth is typical of Pope's authority in this and many other poems: he animates the landscape through feminized personifications that unite poetic and political powers, thereby demonstrating the political efficacy of poetic voice.[67]

Unlike Denham, Pope does not strive to flow like the Thames in this poem. Rather, he lets the river speak. Scanning the prospect from "High in the midst, upon his Urn reclin'd" (349), the Thames

> turn'd his azure Eyes
> Where *Windsor*-Domes and pompous Turrets rise,
> Then bow'd and spoke; the Winds forget to roar,
> And the hush'd Waves glide softly to the Shore.
> (351–54)

Like Lodona's narrative, the Thames's long speech appears to be a rhetorical interruption if not a thematic one. But the Thames stands in as the manly and sublime alterego of the avowedly pastoral poet, only to be boldly interrupted by the poet—"Here cease thy Flight" (423)—who would assert his modesty. As the poem concludes, Pope subordinates himself once again to Granville, figuring himself as muse and denizen of this feminine domain (425–26). He accentuates his subordination through pastoral imagery that translates matters of state (Peace and mercantile prosperity) into the actions of a dilettante:

> My humble Muse, in unambitious Strains,
> Paints the green Forests and the flow'ry Plains,
> Where Peace descending bids her Olives spring,
> And scatters Blessings from her Dove-like Wing.
> (427–30)

In this scene of enveloping feminine Peace, Pope peaceably submits to the order he has created. Returning to his poetic self as muse, Pope takes us back to the pastoral scenes that had opened *Windsor Forest*. But this innocent landscape has now lost its simplicity, despite the humble claims of Pope. The green forest and its peace represent the fundamental power of the British monarch. The pastoral world that Pope has remade is the imaginary of the political. He has transformed the sexual paradigm of the male poet's call on the female muse into the male poet's possession of contemporary power figured as feminine land and abstractions. The poet as muse makes this royal demesne his own poetically and returns it, transformed, to the Queen.

In his subsequent poems, Pope uses feminine and masculine categories far more subtly, developing in his poetic personae and his male guides a more comprehensive incorporation of the feminine. He maintains the model of masculine authority over feminine powers by developing one of the most important themes in his oeuvre—friendship—which he expresses through an increasingly conversational tone in his poetry.[68] Together, male poet and male friend stoop to moral truths by incorporating them as feminine features. In *An Essay on Man* Pope tackles one of his most complex mimetic objectives when he attempts to represent the truths of human nature.[69] The hidden art of his conversation with Bolingbroke masks the philosophical difficulty of the topic. Their feminization of landscapes and abstractions mask the aporias of their argument.[70] The metaphoric assumption that underpins *An Essay on Man* is that whatever is feminine or female is conquerable by men or God.[71] It is through this conquest that Man can be defined. The suppleness of the feminine allows it to occupy apparently contradictory positions, offering at times an image of materiality, especially, maternal nature, and at other times feminine vulnerability, in contrast to which Man can mark his own limits and abilities. Pope and Bolingbroke determine "Man in the Abstract" by relying on figurations of feminine Nature, from the feminine landscape to its personified inhabitants such as Virtue and Peace.[72] And yet in what appears to be an epistemological ordering of the prospect, both Pope and Bolingbroke must order themselves ontologically to imitate feminine Nature.

Pope's explanation of God's dominion over man depends on this metaphoric shortcut: that God's power can be figured in feminine Nature, which presents an unfathomable maternal power as well as a controllable female body.[73] As a mother figure, Nature has a mysterious power not shared by men, but as a woman she is conquerable by physical contact. This sexual contact in fact "naturalizes" the poem's first lines, where Pope must win the reader's interest in and sympathy for his argument. "Let us," he invites Bolingbroke,

> Expatiate free o'er all this scene of Man;
> A mighty maze! but not without a plan;
> A Wild, where weeds and flow'rs promiscuous shoot,
> Or Garden, tempting with forbidden fruit.
>
> (1.3, 5–8)[74]

The quest for "Man in the abstract" is visual, tactile, and discursive. The attention to seeing Nature, Pope's "almost obsessive concern with 'seeing,' as both fact and metaphor," has been described by Patricia Meyer Spacks as Pope's way of imaging "man's struggle to understand and accept his place in the universe, a struggle embodied as a drama of seeing."[75] Pope and Bolingbroke's philosophical objectives are realized through a figurative penetration of a feminine landscape whose submission is assumed:

> Together let us beat this ample field,
> Try what the open, what the covert yield;
> The latent tracts, the giddy heights explore
> Of all who blindly creep, or sightless soar;
> Eye Nature's walks, shoot Folly as it flies,
> And catch the Manners living as they rise. . . .
>
> (1.9–14)

Men of good sense pursue Nature to find her Truth, but it is only accessible as another feminine figure.

In his inquiry into the Nature of Man, the poet-subject only initially desires to control the feminine landscape in a narrative of sexual conquest. The poet's fundamental relation with Nature is one of deep emulation that at first requires his and Bolingbroke's joint penetration of Nature. Whereas in *Windsor Forest* Pope pursues a relationship of gallantry with the Queen, in *An Essay on Man* he pursues a relationship of intimacy with Bolingbroke through their shared emulation of Nature. This version of Nature—which is also Man's Nature, according to Pope—is a profound and inscrutable interstice that connects man to Man and man to God.

Pope interposes feminine Nature in crucial passages that confront a doubting interlocutor. When presented with the question of whether the universe is man-centered or God-centered ("Is the great chain, that draws all to agree, / And drawn supports, upheld by God, or thee?" [1.33–34]), Pope relies on feminine nature as irrefutable truth, with a rhetorical question whose imagery impresses more than its answer: "Ask of thy mother earth, why oaks are made / Taller or stronger than the weeds they shade?" (1.39–40). Nature as authoritative mother not only silences the interlocutor's doubts about his relation to God but also his doubts about his relation to earthly authorities. The scale of economic inequity is swept away by Nature's maternal gesture: "Know, Nature's children all divide her care; / The fur that warms a monarch, warm'd a bear" (3.43–44).

With feminine nature, Pope has recourse to a dialectic in which these men who seek Man must oscillate between a confidence in Reason and an abject humility about their own limited powers. Through this dialectic Pope demonstrates a knowledge that can only be grasped as an interstice: that is where the feminine resides, linking together the Great Chain of Being. The road to happiness, a feminine middle way, dwells between extremes:

> Take Nature's path, and mad Opinion's leave,
> All states can reach it, and all heads conceive;
> Obvious her goods, in no extreme they dwell,
> There needs but thinking right, and meaning well....
> (4.29–32)

In his prologue, "The Design," Pope announces this method of "steering betwixt the extremes of doctrines seemingly opposite." The vague advice of the poet to think right and mean well acquires its substance through the paradoxical combination of mystery and matter that constitutes the feminine. It is also through the feminine that Pope develops his approach to representation founded in sympathy. In *An Essay on Man*, often mistaken by Romantics and post-Romantics as a bastion of dry imitation, Pope fashions a poetics and ethics of affect that, like the feminine he figures, exists between extremes.[76]

Feminine Nature plays public, personal, and poetic roles that represent Pope's relation to Bolingbroke. Their intimacy and its importance to political and poetic realms is powerful insofar as they imitate and contact feminine Nature.[77] Bolingbroke's authority in the final lines emerges from Pope's subtle characterization of him as a man who understands nature and is even like "her."[78] His strength lies in his intimacy with Nature (he is "in various nature wise" [4.377]) and in his control of his own nature (he can "fall with dignity, with temper rise" [4.378]). That both Pope and Bolingbroke shared a profound interest in gardening as a form of self-expression adds material weight to these ideals.[79] Bolingbroke is Pope's "Genius," a term which underwent much variation at this time but would have most commonly pointed to a masculine deity presiding over a particular landscape, a *genius loci*. Its shifting use in the eighteenth century is often cited as marking the changes from "Augustan" to "Romantic."[80]

In his praise of Bolingbroke, Pope himself adopts the malleability and submissiveness of the feminine Nature he and his friend penetrated at the beginning of the poem. This submissiveness parallels what Brean Hammond has described as Pope's "quasi-feminine passivity" that he assumed in his friendship with Bolingbroke.[81] Shaped by Bolingbroke's "converse" (4.379), Pope sees self-love as the foundation of social love. Self-love expands:

> Self-love thus push'd to social, to divine,
> Gives thee to make thy neighbour's blessing thine.
> Is this too little for the boundless heart?
> Extend it, let thy enemies have part:
> Grasp the whole worlds of Reason, Life, and Sense,
> In one close system of Benevolence:
> Happier as kinder, in whate'er degree,
> And height of Bliss but height of Charity.
>
> (4.353–60)

The transforming power of self-love resembles the power of genius exercised by Bolingbroke on Pope who, guided by him, "turn'd the tuneful art / From sounds to things, from fancy to the heart" (4.391–92). While asserting the importance of self-knowledge, Pope explains that this search is the imitation of Nature's light, when the poet

> For Wit's false mirror held up Nature's light;
> Shew'd erring Pride, Whatever Is, Is Right;
> That Reason, Passion, answer one great aim;
> That true Self-Love and Social are the same;
> That Virtue only makes our Bliss below;
> And all our Knowledge is, Ourselves to Know.
> (4.393–98)

In this enigmatic copula, "whatever is, is right," lies the interstice that defies empirical representation and resorts to a notion of being based on figuration. In other words, Pope's copula of existence (is || is) shows *being* as figuration. This self-knowledge suggests a poetry that reveals, rather than imitates, the self.

Characterizing himself as the landscape manipulated at the beginning of the poem, Pope defines his friendship with Bolingbroke as one that imitates man's relation to Nature. As in many of his passages establishing his intimacy with a patron or friend, Pope assumes the stereotype of feminine passivity, incorporating a heterosexual model to establish homosocial power relations. Yet because of his control of tone in *An Essay on Man* and the homosocial prerogative of controlling the feminine landscape that he shares with Bolingbroke, ultimately Pope subsumes Nature rather than lose himself in this feminine figure. Retaining and emphasizing his own consciousness through judgment and argument, Pope maintains his stereotypically masculine position as speaker while he incorporates the feminine into his *being*, openly declaring his acquisition of feminine qualities. Thus Pope encloses within himself the mystery of the feminine that resides, for him, in the middle way of the poet. In this notion of representation, the interstice both defies representation and embodies it in the figure of Nature.

Pope and Behn use androgynous ideals to explore the figures of Nature. But Behn, writing decades before Pope, converts feminine Nature into an androgynous Nature in order to confound the oppositions between male and female, Nature and Art, and the subject and object of representation. In such a system, female desire escapes social censure through a mode of representation that conceals (ultimately, refuses to represent) as well as selectively reveals. Pope, however, locates the power of androgyny not in Nature itself, which he insists is feminine, but in the poet's ontological imitation of Nature, which depends on a manly incorporation of the feminine. This androgynous combination yields a mode of representation where figures liberate empirical vision, expanding Pope's territory of representation. Behn's earlier use of androgyny approximates an elusive subjectivity, while Pope's use of androgyny establishes the (male) subject precisely through its incorporation of the feminine. Pope's development of poetic subjectivity, thus, contributes to the larger emergence of the subject in Western representation. For Behn androgyny is part of the elusiveness of the self; for Pope it is the core of creating a complex identity.

These prospects of Nature by Pope, Behn, Montagu, Adams, Addison, and Denham show us Nature as a projection of the poet's position as subject, object, or a convergence of the two. While the poet's gender identity certainly shapes the poet's relation to Nature, we have seen vast differences within each gender. In focusing on the ordering of the poet and Nature, the intertwining of subject and feminine object, we have moved farther and farther away from our modern notion of external nature. Is there such a nature to be found in Restoration and eighteenth-century poetry? The next chapter examines the voices and faces poets give to Nature to articulate its specificity, and, ultimately, its separateness from the human.

4
The Voice of Nature and the Poet's Labor

THE VERSIONS OF THE PROSPECT SEEN IN CHAPTER 3 SHOW US THAT the poetic "self" and its poetic functions are never autonomous but always supported or bound by a relation to the feminine. That the subject emerges, or is suppressed, in relation to gender is a familiar claim, as is the subject's reliance on the object to articulate itself. In the prospect poem Nature leads us to the poet's subjectivity in a variety of convergences between the two. This chapter considers the significance of personifying Nature to assert the poet's labor as a condition of being.[1] Nature is, of course, the fundamental personification of eighteenth-century poetry and poetics.[2] Through this projection of the human onto abstract forces and entities, poets demonstrate poesis, or making.[3] But personifications may themselves have the power to make—to generate Nature and other personifications.[4] In his series of essays on the imagination, Addison describes these generative qualities:

> Thus we see how many ways Poetry addresses it self to the Imagination, as it has not only the whole Circle of Nature for its Province, but makes new Worlds of its own, shews us Persons who are not to be found in Being, and represents even the Faculties of the Soul, with her several Virtues and Vices, in a sensible Shape and Character. (*Spectator*, no. 419, 1712)[5]

To analyze the role of personification in constructing subjectivity and representation in the eighteenth century, we must imagine the trope in the same energetic spirit of an eighteenth-century reader who was "trained to see pictures in poetry . . . even when the poet gave him only the slightest visual hint."[6]

With the great majority of personifications feminine, scholars have attributed their gender to the original Latin nouns such as Nature, Science, and Imagination, but others have also observed the tenacity with which poets have maintained the gendering of these nouns in a language that ceased to gender others.[7] But given that poets and readers did see these nouns as persons, it is not surprising these "persons" maintained their gender. Thus with numerous feminine personifications the poet tapped into abstract categories with the same benefits that the feminine provided in the form of the muse or in the feminine landscape. Personification is as much about a relationship to gender as it is a relationship to person.

As poets increasingly elaborate on Nature as person, this "object" may speak. Thus the voice of Nature challenges the poet's, generating radical inquiries into language. In their focus on the voice and consciousness of Nature, poets redefine their own work. In granting Nature agency and voice, the poet's labor shifts from writing to yielding—a quality already seen as early as Denham's *Cooper's Hill*. This use of personification destabilizes the model of Nature as property to be surveyed and owned, at least imaginatively. Rather, in exploring the *voice* of Nature, the poet may assert Nature and the self as intangible.[8] "Working" the land involves another kind of labor, a labor of *being* rather than *doing*, where self and nature elude representation and resist commodification.

I

In the landscape poetry of Anne Finch we discover what is arguably the most profound representation of immanence with Nature to be seen in this era. Central to Finch's representation of Nature is her recurring figuration of her poetic self as a bird—figure of the natural poet. Such immanence with Nature leads her to blend with the skies rather than anatomize the grove. Indeed, she depicts her perception of Nature as the feminine personification of "free sight." Flying through the landscape like a bird, "free sight" is a liberating poetic perception that *is* the Nature it perceives, like a bird only stopped by "distant skys."

4 / THE VOICE OF NATURE AND THE POET'S LABOR 113

Finch delicately identifies with the bird to render perceptions as both subject and object of Nature.[9] She takes pains, however, to distinguish the differences between the poet and Nature (viz. "The Bird and the Arras" and "To the Nightingale").[10] Indeed, the bird typifies Finch's complex approach to personification. Never taking the figure for granted, Finch engages it as a temporal possibility for temporary immanence. Approaching Nature as not only animate but also conscious, Finch's poetry shares much in common with approaches to Nature in Cambridge Platonism and vitalism. Carolyn Merchant's summary of vitalism equally serves to define Nature in Finch's poetry: "As a philosophy of nature, vitalism in its monistic form was inherently antiexploitative. Its emphasis on the life of all things as gradations of soul, its lack of a separate distinction between matter and spirit, its principle of an immanent activity permeating nature, and its reverence for the nurturing power of the earth endowed it with an ethic of the inherent worth of everything alive."[11]

Finch's intimate relation with Nature begins with an emphasis on Nature's abjected spaces rather than with the powerfully elusive order found in poets such as Denham and Pope. In the position of woman poet, Finch finds an alternative community in Nature, a strategy we have seen in the work of other women poets. As discussed in chapter 2, in "The Introduction," a poem she never sent to the press, Finch anticipated the harsh public reception of a woman poet. Finch seeks a *modus vivendi* in the shades of Nature, where her Muse as bird finds political and poetic protection: "For groves of Lawrell, thou wert never meant; / Be dark enough thy shades, and be thou there content" (63-64).[12] That this shelter echoes the classical *locus amoenus* for the pastoral poet indicates it is not only a domain of social exclusion but also a domain of poetic creativity.

The paradox of Finch's poetry is that what is worth writing about is the unwritable that exists in the relation between the writer and the written. Personification signifies the temporary bridge that links the writer and the written, but it points ultimately to the inexpressible. We see a version of this relation in the single fifty-line sentence that constitutes "A Nocturnal Reverie" (1713). The poem's use of present tense, accretion of images, and all-inclusive syntax attempts to record the speaker's proximity to and identification with the creatures "in such a *Night*." And

Finch's use of imitative form allows poet and reader to be one with Nature through structures of sound and time. She engages all of the senses so that instead of the visual prospect, founded on a division between speaker-subject and object of representation, there is an immediate sensory engagement that evokes temporality and movement. The visual images that are included are kinetic: the reflection in the river shows a moving, sentient Nature. In the freshened grass that "bears it self upright" (11) and the "swelling Haycocks" that "thicken up the Vale" (28), Nature is consciousness. We participate in Nature's kinesis through imitative sound when "unmolested Kine rechew the Cud" (34).

Much of the poem's power lies in its images that swiftly fluctuate between the nonhuman natural world and human consciousness, a fluctuation conveyed in the poem's sense of temporal fluctuation. The reader enters Nature temporally through the poem's torrent of *whens* that support an elusive time present. Finch's personifications inhere in the landscape because it is depicted more temporally than spatially, as much a timescape as a landscape. While this animated nature derives from a conventional seventeenth-century view that made no clear distinction between "the order of nature and the life of man," Finch subtly animates Nature's "self" awareness as it "bears it self upright" and "watch[es]" its hour.[13] Personifications in "A Nocturnal Reverie" are emerging persons that collapse as soon as created, replaced by other inchoate personifications. Aware of the potential of personification to deface Nature, Finch uses personification delicately.[14]

The delicacy of this vital Nature challenges poetic language. In this nocturnal reverie,

> When a sedate Content the Spirit feels,
> And no fierce Light disturb, whilst it reveals;
> But silent Musings urge the Mind to seek
> Something, too high for Syllables to speak;
> Till the free Soul to a compos'dness charm'd,
> Finding the Elements of Rage disarm'd,
> O'er all below a solemn Quiet grown,
> Joys in th' inferiour World, and thinks it like her Own. . . .
> (39–46)

Finch rarifies the poetic self as a "Spirit" that joins the landscape and shares Nature's relation to a Light that gently reveals rather than disturbs. In this alternative use of the senses, the poet does not survey Nature but moves *with* it in the moonlight. This parallels Finch's linguistic approach to Nature: "silent Musings urge the Mind to seek / Something, too high for Syllables to speak." The poet-spirit-mind muses *silently* and confronts the insufficiencies of language. Perhaps this at-one-ness with Nature undoes the engine of language based on absence: the absence that language may seek to fill, the desire that may drive representation, is gratified during the temporal duration of the poem. Finch calls this yearning for words to accommodate spirit nothing less than *Rage*.[15] But freedom of Soul can transform this Rage: the poet hears the silence of Nature and in this silence finds joyful connection. Rather than simply personifying this "inferiour World," the speaker "joys" in it "and thinks it like her Own" but does not *make* it her own. Thus Finch provides a model of the poet in relation to Nature that, while acknowledging the imaginative act of resemblance, is based on immanence and participation.

The poem confronts the limits of language when the mind makes its sublime forays, but rather than develop this potentially agonizing aspect of the ineffable—"Something, too high for Syllables to speak"—Finch renders this encounter with the ineffable as a condition of freedom. It is the "free Soul" that can find composure through the intimate identification with personified Nature, but the speaker returns to a domain of limits and human defects in her fable-like coda:

> In such a *Night* let Me abroad remain,
> Till Morning breaks, and All's confus'd again;
> Our Cares, our Toils, our Clamours are renew'd,
> Or Pleasures, seldom reach'd, again pursu'd.
>
> (47–50)

The conclusion unravels the formerly intertwined speaker and objects. Assuming the position of the fable-writer explaining the moral, Finch sharpens the difference between speaker and object. Finch's temporal re-creation of perceiving the landscape rejects the authority of vision and property associated with the prospect poem—until the break of day.[16] Notably, she does not associate the limits of language with a woman poet's inadequacy; rather, she satisfactorily replaces linguistic limits with nonlinguistic immanence.

Finch's most radical representation of Nature appears in "To the Right Honourable Frances Countess of Hartford who engaged Mr Eusden to write upon a wood enjoining him to mention no tree but the Aspin and no flower but the King-cup."[17] In this playful, sometimes fantastic, poem, Finch elaborates the connection between the voice of Nature and that of the natural poet. She inquires into the poet's words, Nature's words, and the pen that writes both. The gender politics of the poem underscore Nature as a feminine realm where women, not men, have authority: Finch reorders the "masculine" claims to the landscape by using Hertford's class to override Eusden's privilege of gender.[18] "Hartford 'tis wrong," she begins her wry chiding of her friend and fellow aristocrat, "if Poets may complain / To bid them write yet dictate to the Brain" (1–2). Reversing the gendered access to the landscape, Hertford has denied the male poet access to the landscape, who, writes Finch, "labour'd under Pharoah's hard decrees / To raise a Wood tho' you denied him trees" (5–6). Eusden has been given the abjected parts of the landscape—the very parts that Finch routinely embraces. Thus, for Finch, Hertford's restrictions on Eusden provide the occasion for Finch to depict the landscape he might have composed. Significantly, rather than replace the abject Aspin and King-cup with a commanding survey of the landscape's overrated treasures, Finch attends to what can be perceived intimately and is often overlooked, as in "A Nocturnal Reverie."

To the "Rattle" of the "grave Dame" Nature that Hertford allowed Eusden (9–12), Finch contrasts a relation to the landscape that highlights both the plenitude of feminine Nature and its agency:

> But Flora's gifts shou'd amply there be seen
> And every beauteous die emblaze the green
> Cowslips and Dazies over all shou'd run
> And the broad oxe-eye stare against the sun.
>
> (31–34)

She personifies Nature in Flora, the "Cowslips and Dazies" that run, and most boldly in the individual flower that stares back at the sun. By highlighting personification as the conjunction of subject and object, the "object" of Finch's hypothetical landscape, the "broad oxe-eye," emerges as an inscrutable subject that looks back. She suggests the depth and shades of Nature on a perceptual level by including the "Brakes and clustred Hazell under grown" (45) that lie beneath the "embowering arches" (43)—analogous to the "deep self" of a human subject. This poetic freedom *within* but not *over* the landscape acknowledges Nature's complex agency.

When the poet perceives Nature as subject—or more precisely as subject and object—language breaks down. This collapse emerges from the writer's ontological rather than epistemological relation to Nature. Thus, Finch's representation of Nature's agency and complexity works reciprocally to convey the agency and complexity of language itself. The medium of representation is less scrutable and more vital:

> A miscellany every grove affords
> Where trees confused disdain the form of words....
> (101–2)

Although the image shifts from Nature as person to the Book of Nature, this "language" of Nature resists words. Whereas poets such as Denham and Pope yearn for a natural language fitted to Nature, Finch sees Nature as having its own language. "Every grove" provides a miscellany, offering the writer matter for poetry, but these groves are already poems. As we saw in Behn's "Juniper Tree" the division between Art and Nature collapses, altering, in turn, poetry's function as the Imitation of Nature. Finch has altered the relation between Nature and language: rather than the natural as an ideal for language and, therefore, the figure for language, Finch's "miscellany"—a wordless language—serves to figure Nature.

Finch describes a reciprocal relation between Nature and Art that requires that the poet be natural and that the tools of Art be living nature: the poet of Nature must, like the trees, be "produc't by a rich soil and heat" (103). This compost, union of soil and sun, is the humble model of poetic creativity for the natural poet who is fit to "treat" Nature (104) without constraining it. Although we may compare this with Pope's later figuration of himself and Bolingbroke as Nature, Finch emphasizes the union of poet and Nature on the humblest ground.

Developing the paradox of artless art, she describes the "Ghost of Eusden's injured pen" (127), murdered by the Countess's cruel restrictions, as a "feather stareing and the ghastly quil / Pale in its self yet seeming paler still" (129–30). Addressing the Countess, Finch plays with the elusiveness of the pen:

> Fleet in your way its liberty regain'd
> Haunting the trees from whence it was restrain'd
> To these of generous growth tho' dead aspire
> But from the hated aspin swift retire
> And quivering in the agony of flight
> Shrink to a picktooth e'er it left your sight
> Or on the air such characters impress
> As motes we call whose meaning none can guess
> Which yet may be the ghosts for ought we know
> Of syllables which sunk too soon below
> Who wanting cordial praise in time applied
> When merit claim'd it discontented died.
> (131–42)

The personified pen demonstrates a tour de force of the poet's imaginative making, but it also undoes any transparent relation between Nature and Art. The medium and means themselves acquire agency. In acknowledging this condition of Nature that the poet must share, Finch's poem takes a fantastic turn, representing the poet's pen as embodying both Nature (the feather) and Art. With humor she explores Nature's resistance to objectification in tandem with the natural poet's "cyphers" that become unreadable without a sympathetic audience:

> Were this conjecture true some verse of mine
> Dwindled to motes may hovering now repine
> 'Gainst Criticks who from Pedantry refuse
> The soothing sweetness of the natural muse
> Whilst free she sings as birds from warbling throats
> As large her compass and as wild her notes.
> (153–58)

The model of sympathetic identification between poet and Nature is also the model relationship between poet and reader.

Integrating the "natural" poet with nature through an understanding of language's limits, Finch negates the prospect poem as a genre of power and order: she insists on a remnant that language cannot capture, which is, ironically, a part of language.

Breaking the Countess's bonds on Eusden, Finch renders the liberty of poet *and* object. Poet and Nature cannot be commodified because they reside in consciousness that defies finite language. Given the frequent identification between woman poet and Nature, it is not surprising that Finch's rendering of the landscape's animation and complexity is followed by her self-characterization as a poet who shares this Nature and may be rejected on that very count. What began as Eusden's artistic restrictions (confined to the aspin and king-cup) ends by reordering the relation between artist and Nature as one of freedom though ontological resemblance. Her complexity of representation shows how gender shapes the structure of representation, but it is perhaps inevitable that, given Finch's position as an aristocrat, she represents her relation to Nature at the imaginative level rather than at the material level of the laborer.[19]

II

Liberating the self and Nature by removing both from the order of possessions, Finch gave her successors a model of person and Nature. We see her influence on the work of John Dyer (1699–1757) and James Thomson (1700–1748). In Dyer's "Grongar Hill" (published 1726), so often cited as a typical prospect poem, the poet ultimately seeks a personal contentment removed from the appetitive vision associated with the wide-ranging prospect.[20] At times reclining in the shade and at others moving through the landscape, as Finch does in "A Nocturnal Reverie," Dyer initially describes the widening prospect. The poet luxuriates in the landscape's feminine features that "give each a double charm, / As pearls upon an *AEthiop*'s arm" (112–13).[21] He echoes Finch's animation of Nature in a landscape that "swelling to embrace the light, / Spreads around beneath the sight" (47–48). While such vastness stimulates the poet's appetite for still greater vistas, he reaches a turning point:

> O may I with my self agree,
> And never covet what I see:
> Content me with an humble shade,
> My passions tam'd, my wishes laid;
> For while our wishes wildly roll,

> We banish quiet from the soul:
> 'Tis thus the busy beat the air;
> And misers gather wealth and care.
>
> (129–36)

Turning away from the movement of the eye, Dyer attends to an emotional movement that develops the virtuous, nonmaterialistic self. In self-agreement, the poet hears and feels rather than sees Nature, now birds on the wing who fill the sky with their music (137–45).[22] Dyer's exuberant expansion is noticeably untempered by Finch's awareness of "tyrant Man."

Whereas Finch approaches Nature as nature—still personified but identified as a variety of particularized entities—Thomson personifies Nature as a large, unifying entity. But the voice of Nature in both Finch and in Thomson ultimately defies poetic language. As his senior and as the friend and great aunt of Thomson's patron the countess of Hertford, Finch may well have influenced his poetry.[23] In standard narratives of literary history, James Thomson's representation of landscape in *The Seasons* (1726–46) has been seen as a turning point in eighteenth-century poetics, one that will develop into a more subjectivized landscape that "culminates" in Wordsworth's poetry. But when we trace the function of the feminine in men's and women's poetry, Thomson's achievement appears less radical, especially in relation to Finch's. Like Finch, Thomson represents Nature as "vitally experiential," focusing on the "relationship between perception and external reality."[24]

As in Pope, Thomson inscribes a poetic voice that at times articulates control over the feminine and at other times strives to emulate it. Like Pope's, Thomson's male characters can take on feminine virtues and thereby establish the justness of their relation to Nature and property, and they can also penetrate and work upon things figured feminine. In *Spring*, he invokes Lyttleton in a paradigm that Pope would later use to praise Bolingbroke in *An Essay on Man*.[25] Lyttleton's own complexity and variety parallel his ability to wander through Nature, wooing the muse: his "passions thus / And meditations vary, as at large, / Courting the muse, through Hagley Park you stray" (906–8). Lyttleton can "pensive listen to the various voice / Of rural peace" because of his likeness to Nature (917–18).[26] Rather than providing a more detailed representation of Nature, Thomson's so-called empiricism is as figurative a representation as Pope's, but Thomson emphasizes perceptual details and perception itself more than Pope.[27] That is, Thomson's focus on the perception of Nature turns to the subject's perceptions as they connect with the object. Thomson's personifications of Nature articulate a hybrid subjectivity that replaces the speaker's.

In *The Seasons* his detailed perceptions of feminine Nature prove Thomson's poetic authority.[28] Whether he uses details of Newtonian optics or contemporary politics, the tacit assumption of his meditations is that masculine perception orders feminine Nature, and it often does so in highly erotic images. In his invocation to Spring, Thomson highlights eroticized feminine Nature:

> Come, gentle Spring, ethereal mildness, come;
> And from the bosom of yon dropping cloud,
> While music wakes around, veiled in a shower
> Of shadowing roses, on our plains descend.
>
> (1–4)

Emphasizing the *person* of Spring, Thomson seems to have denatured Nature.[29] He makes a bid for class privilege when he conflates the landscape he represents with the countess of Hertford, whom he bids "listen to my song, / Which thy own season paints —when Nature all / Is blooming and benevolent, like thee" (8–10). If Spring is a woman, the countess is also Spring. Aligning the poet's power with the countess's privilege, Thomson can survey the arduous labor of plowing as a sensuous delight. When winter turns to spring,

> Forth fly the tepid airs; and unconfined,
> Unbinding earth, the moving softness strays.
> Joyous the impatient husbandman perceives
> Relenting Nature, and his lusty steers
> Drives from their stalls to where the well-used plough
> Lies in the furrow loosened from the frost.
>
> (*Spring* 32–37)

Nature yields to the penetrating plow as easily as the mistress of an idyll loosens her stays.

Such eroticism extends to what might seem the empirical realms of vision and science: Apollo-like the "penetrative Sun" exercises "His force deep-darting to the dark retreat / Of vegetation" (*Spring* 79–81). Newtonian analysis not only exposes Nature's parts but also seems to penetrate Nature through its figurative rather than analytic procedure. Newton as the ultimate surveyor of Nature "mounts" the landscape through scientific acumen as Thomson blends eighteenth-century scientific vocabulary (e.g., *refracted, dissolving*) with the attributes of feminine beauty (*fair, red, violet*) contained by masculine power:[30]

>   refracted from yon eastern cloud,
> Bestriding earth, the grand ethereal bow
> Shoots up immense; and every hue unfolds,
> In fair proportion running from the red
> To where the violet fades into the sky.
> Here, awful Newton, the dissolving clouds
> Form, fronting on the sun, thy showery prism. . . .
>
> (*Spring* 203–9)

Newton's ejaculatory prism makes the study of optics look as pleasurable as plowing had earlier.

In contrast to these models of penetration and ejaculation, Thomson also includes his poetic persona within Nature to objectify himself. In *Autumn*, the poet's function is to establish his own immanence with the landscape he figures. In the opening of *Autumn* he seems to make himself one of his own personifications:

>   Crowned with the sickle and the wheaten sheaf
> While Autumn nodding o'er the yellow plain
> Comes jovial on, the Doric reed once more
> Well-pleased I tune.
>
> (1–4)

In passages such as this, poet and Nature begin to converge, and yet the poet still maintains enough separation to depict Nature. Personifying himself as Autumn, he harmonizes his body with the season, and the season simultaneously nods approval. Unlike the personification of Spring, which must be invited, Autumn need not be called: it coexists with the poet's will and capacity. Harmonizing his surroundings and in harmony with them ("well-pleased"), the poet tunes the reed, an instrument plucked directly from nature, while Autumn acts as master of ceremonies to celebrate the harvest. The poet's body blends with Autumn's in a relation of harmony authorized by the approving nod of the season and in an immanence where the poet is Nature, Nature the poet.

From this condition of immanence, the poet figures himself fertilized by his personifications of Winter, Spring, and Summer:

> Whate'er the Wintry frost
> Nitrous prepared, the various-blossomed Spring
> Put in white promise forth, and Summer-suns
> Concocted strong, rush boundless now to view,
> Full, perfect all, and swell my glorious theme.
> (*Autumn* 4–8)

His "glorious theme" incorporates all of the seasons in full perfection, but instead of *making* the landscape, the poet *is* a receptive landscape nourished by chemical processes. Fertility swells the theme of the poem through the chemistry of personification: its capacity to engender so that it may contain and be contained.

Able to contain nature and create "new worlds," Thomson's personifications parallel his definition of Nature itself: he defines Nature as his contemporaries did to include the earth and the universe (the universe of the cosmos and the universe of human character, wherein all persons have common characteristics) as well as a general ordering and creating principle. In his description of Nature as a system of progression, inclusive like the great chain of being, Thomson locates its summit in the mind: "The varied scene of quick-compounded thought, / And where the mixing passions endless shift" (*Autumn* 1363–64). In containing the mind, personified Nature in *The Seasons* is less something that means than it is something that figures—thus repeating the function of the feminine discussed in previous chapters.

Attributing creative power to personifications constitutes one of Thomson's complicated achievements: the redundancy of recreating through language the creating Nature to which the poet has already given the power of language. In letting Nature speak for "herself," creating "her" own Nature poetry, he complicates poetic authority and agency: he imagines Nature's voice supplanting the poet's. Addressing the God of the Seasons, Thomson proclaims:

4 / THE VOICE OF NATURE AND THE POET'S LABOR

> And yet, was every faltering tongue of man,
> Almighty Father! silent in thy praise,
> Thy works themselves would raise a general voice;
> Even in the depth of solitary woods,
> By human foot untrod, proclaim thy power....
> (*Summer* 185–89)

Compared with the authenticity of Nature's voice, the poet's is superfluous and inadequate, a problem that Thomson will define in another section of *The Seasons* as the failure of language and imagination. When Nature calls on the Muse to represent her, the poet measures his capacities against Nature's:

> Behold yon breathing prospect bids the Muse
> Throw all her beauty forth. But who can paint
> Like Nature? Can imagination boast,
> Amid its gay creation, hues like hers?
> Or can it mix them with that matchless skill,
> And lose them in each other, as appears
> In every bud that blows?
> (*Spring* 467–73)

The voice of Nature seems to be free from the limits of language that constrain the poet, in part because Thomson has *defined* Nature as voice and vision. And yet Nature demands a repetition of her voice in the poet's.[31]

In a series of personifications, where Nature bids and paints, and the poet wonders if imagination can boast, the ideal language is figured as something visual and palpable. But because personified Nature can be seen and felt, it eclipses the faint power of words:

> If fancy then
> Unequal fails beneath the pleasing task,
> Ah, what shall language do? ah, where find words
> Tinged with so many colours and whose power,
> To life approaching, may perfume my lays
> With that fine oil, those aromatic gales
> That inexhaustive flow continual round?
> (*Spring* 473–79)

In the search for words *of* Nature and *for* Nature, even language is personified ("what shall language do?"). Nature figures language itself: the ideal words would have the properties of flowers or spices, generating a flow of "aromatic gales." Just as Thomson blends poet and Nature in his introduction to *Autumn,* in this excerpt from *Spring,* he would have the poet's language share the properties of the Nature it describes—a reproduction instead of a representation.

If language should be like Nature, and yet always fails, what remains of the poet's function? Thomson tries to solve this dilemma by objectifying the body of the poet and making it the poet's labor to listen rather than speak.[32] At the close of *Autumn,* the last season Thomson wrote, the poet supplements his inadequate language with his body:

> But, if to that unequal—if the blood
> In sluggish streams about my heart forbid
> That best ambition—under closing shades
> Inglorious lay me by the lowly brook,
> And whisper to my dreams. From thee begin,
> Dwell all on thee, with thee conclude my song;
> And let me never, never stray from thee!
> (*Autumn* 1367–73)

Describing poetic failure by figuring the poet's body contained by and containing the landscape, the "sluggish streams," Thomson's body tropes the poetry that will not flow, his own blood forbidding poetic expression.[33] Instead of containing the landscape in an inadequate representation, the poet asks that his body be contained by the landscape, where the poet's surrender finally signifies Nature's supremacy over poetic language and, ironically, the authenticity of poem and poet. Language will be replaced by the restoration of the poet's body in Nature. Interred alongside the brook, the poet will listen to Nature's language, which is a whisper—a closed circle of communication, preserving its purity, unheard by the reader.[34] As he is permeated by Nature rather than penetrating "her," the poet's sexual imagery recedes.

In this attempt at immanence with feminine Nature, the poet appears in a position of Orphic submission. Revising the river god's authority to survey the landscape (cf. the Thames in Denham's *Cooper's Hill* and in Pope's *Windsor Forest*), Thomson figures himself submitting to Nature by enlarging his body to contain the variety and fluidity of the river. Thus he answers

Denham's address to the Thames, "O could I flow like thee."[35] Thomson elaborates the poet's connection with the literal springs of poetry by figuring his ability to internalize it. When the poet asks for the nightingale's inspiration, the images of poetry as river and poet as river express his authority: "pour / The mazy-running soul of melody / Into my varied verse!" he commands (*Spring* 576–78). His landscape may seem to resemble those of women poets, who often represent their identification with conventionally feminine Nature. But it is important to observe that Thomson's mimesis is based on a dynamic of difference, where the gesture of surrender is based on a sexual dialectic, one that recalls Orpheus's destruction by the Maenads. In his surrender to Nature Thomson enlarges and disseminates poetic subjectivity, as the still singing decapitated head of Orpheus travels down the river of poetry making its way through flowing Nature.[36] In his imagined death, his corpse floating on the river, Thomson transforms poetic labor from the plowman-like penetration of the land to the poet's disappearance within it.

III

Finch's poetic experiments in the late seventeenth and early eighteenth-century reorient our understanding of the shifts associated with midcentury poets such as Collins and Gray.[37] In close comparison of Collins's "Ode to Evening" with Finch's "Eusden" and "A Nocturnal Reverie," we can identify important areas of overlap and divergence. Collins's "Ode to Evening" replaces the external structure of prohibition seen in Finch's "Eusden" with a more internalized prohibition. Whereas Finch's Countess forbids Eusden parts of the landscape, which Finch meets with a tone of playful awareness, Collins imposes on *himself* a restricted relation to Nature that shapes his poem's meditative, reverential tone. Finch's light familiarity with the animated nature she perceives—and that perceives her—contrasts with the distance between the poet and Nature/Evening in Collins's poem. Both Finch and Collins emphasize the theme of representation, but Collins figures the relation to Nature as part of an ironic and erotic structure, where in order to represent Evening, the poet must emulate her chastity and reserve. In this reserve, Collins attempts a representation that would not intrude on or penetrate Nature but rather would respect the space between them. Although Finch's nature is animated and ultimately resistant to language, her "natural poet" is already at one with this Nature; by contrast, Collins's poet must yearn and court.

As we have already seen in other landscape poems, the "Ode to Evening" (1746) rejects the empirical vision typical of prospect poetry in favor of the imaginative potential of approaching darkness.[38] Collins chooses the waning of light in Evening to explore Nature's and his own spatial and temporal liminality. Focusing on Nature as temporal phenomena, Collins combines the principle of transition to the principle of vision as a way to order Nature. To represent Evening as temporal threshold, he elaborates on "her" as feminine personification, joining biblical with feminine associations of Nature:[39]

> If ought of Oaten Stop, or Pastoral Song,
> May hope, chaste *Eve*, to sooth thy modest Ear,
>   Like thy own solemn Springs,
>   Thy Springs, and dying Gales,
> O *Nymph* reserv'd, while now the bright-hair'd Sun
> Sits in yon western Tent, whose cloudy Skirts,
>   With Brede ethereal wove,
>   O'erhang his wavy Bed....
>
>   (1–8)

By complicating the syntax of his lines, the poet participates in evening's accrescence as he recreates a perceiving consciousness that interrupts itself in seeking words that would suit Evening. For twelve more lines this first sentence interweaves its clauses like the light and dark that compose Evening, which finally emerges with the disappearance of the Apollo figure (significantly, god of the sun and of poetry) into the horizon.

The only way for the poet to represent Evening without intruding on her is for the poet to be Evening-like—and so he asks her to teach him to breathe (15–16) (cf. Finch's speaker in "A Nocturnal Reverie" and the natural poet in "Eusden"). Paul Sherwin describes the existential bond between poet and personification in the "Ode to Evening" as one in which "persona and personified are attuned to the same rhythm: all the epithets applied to Evening are implicitly transferable to the poet."[40] But the value of this similarity depends on a distance that remains between the speaker and the personification: "to collapse the distance separating them is to violate the mystery of goddess and poet alike."[41] Unlike poets such as Denham, Pope, and Thomson who associate fertility with the feminine, Collins focuses on feminine chastity, which resists the poet's powers and requires that he establish an ontological rather than epistemological or penetrative relation to these feminine attributes.[42] In this eroticized chastity, Evening resists the poet physically but is accessible to him through his poetic ability to figure, and resemble, her. In the conclusion, where the poet confirms Evening's power through her permanence, Collins finally augments Evening as a woman's body rather than as dispersed effects on the landscape:

> While *Spring* shall pour his Show'rs, as oft he wont,
> And bathe thy breathing Tresses, meekest *Eve*!
>   While *Summer* loves to sport,
>   Beneath thy ling'ring Light:
> While sallow *Autumn* fills thy Lap with Leaves,
> Or *Winter* yelling thro' the troublous Air,
>   Affrights thy shrinking Train,
>   And rudely rends thy Robes. . . .
>   (41–48)

Collins has moved from a meditation on her chastity to this depiction of Evening as the object of caresses and finally sexual violence.

Such intimacy with feminine Evening begets its own worshipping speaker-audience in the last four lines, a chorus of admiring personifications:

> So long sure-found beneath the Sylvan Shed,
> Shall *Fancy, Friendship, Science*, rose-lip'd *Health*,
>   Thy gentlest Influence own,
>   And hymn thy fav'rite Name!
>   (49–52)

The speaker becomes a personification in the company of these feminine personifications that represent different modes of intimacy with Evening. In becoming like Evening, Collins enlists imagination (Fancy), sympathy (Friendship), perception (Science), and the sensuous body (rose-lip'd Health). In the final line, all "hymn" Evening's name, whereby Collins confirms the spiritual valence of this scene. The poet who sought shelter from harsh nature in lines 33–40 ("when chill blustring Winds, or driving Rain, / Forbid my willing Feet" [33–34]) here acquires residence in Evening's *locus amoenus* by conflating his perception and position as speaker with these personified modes of attention. Collins's poetic "action" is to attend by surrendering his own identity, including his gender.

The poet's relation to the object in "Ode to Evening" is relatively simple compared with this relation in "Ode on the Poetical Character" (1746) where he mythologizes the centrality and complexity of the feminine's relation to poetic voice. The eroticism of feminine chastity already seen in "Ode to Evening" is fundamental to his explanation of what constitutes poetical character. In "Ode on the Poetical Character," Collins establishes the character of the poet as one that can only relate to Nature by chastely *resisting* her. The innocent *locus amoenus* in "Evening," which the poet may enter syntactically and rhetorically and through the acquisition of feminine personifications, is in "Ode on the Poetical Character" a more challenging landscape that holds the spiritual intensity of a *hortus conclusus*.[43] Chaste Fancy is central to poetic character, analogous to the cest's symbolic value in Collins's reference to Florimel's girdle: "One, only One, unrival'd fair, / Might hope the magic Girdle wear" (5–6). Collins equates the poet's privilege with feminine chastity in his account of the "Cest of amplest Pow'r" (19) while he describes God's love of the feminine. "Long by the lov'd *Enthusiast* woo'd," God,

> Himself in some Diviner Mood,
> Retiring, sate with her alone,
> And plac'd her on his Saphire Throne,
> The whiles, the vaulted Shrine around,
> Seraphic Wires were heard to sound,
> Now sublimest Triumph swelling,
> Now on Love and Mercy dwelling;
> And she, from out the veiling Cloud,
> Breath'd her magic Notes aloud....
>
> (29–38)

Fancy gives birth to a poet-Apollo-sun figure that Collins himself apostrophizes as "Thou rich-hair'd Youth of Morn" (39), a primordial figure of the poet.[44] As the invoked, the "Youth of Morn" holds a rhetorical position as object, but he holds a thematic position as poet-speaker. This duality of object-speaker roles is reflected in the youth's origin in feminine Fancy and the masculine God.

If we understand the poet's achievement as a condition of *being* poetic rather than writing a poem, the poetic character may be understood as emulating the object's essence rather than representing the object.[45] This paradox helps explain the poet's achievement in the concluding section, which defines the poetic character by an achievement other than speech:

> High on some Cliff, to Heav'n up-pil'd,
> Of rude Access, of Prospect wild,
> Where, tangled round the jealous Steep,
> Strange Shades o'erbrow the Valleys deep,
> And holy *Genii* guard the Rock,
> Its Gloomes embrown, its Springs unlock,
> While on its rich ambitious Head,
> An *Eden*, like his own, lies spread. . . .
> (55–62)

Collins explains his relation to Milton's landscape, which, like the initial narrative of the cest, bears its own chaste symbolism. The object resists representation but exists within the consciousness of the poet: both the landscape's and the poet's purity is maintained by this inaccessibility. Running away from Waller's pastorals and toward Milton's sublime paradise, the poetic character confronts the loss of landscape:

> In vain—Such Bliss to One alone,
> Of all the Sons of Soul was known,
> And Heav'n, and *Fancy*, kindred Pow'rs,
> Have now o'erturn'd th' inspiring Bow'rs,
> Or curtain'd close such Scene from ev'ry future View.
> (72–76)

Failure to represent the opaque object *testifies* to the character of the poet. Milton provides the exception to—not the epitome of—poetic character as the "one and only one" whose work establishes what is inaccessible, the paradisal landscape. Like Milton's chaste *hortus conclusus*, Collins's poet preserves himself in his erotic chastity. According to poetic models as diverse as those of Waller and Milton, the lineaments of poetic character are those in which neither the speaker nor the object can be realized. Unlike Finch, who perceives animated nature and allows room for its voice, Collins collapses Nature with Art—specifically, Milton's —whereby the landscape disappears. (Cf. Pope's description of Virgil in *An Essay on Criticism* [1711]: "*Nature* and *Homer* were, he found, the *same*" [135]). Collins brings us to the point where subject and object eclipse each other: the poetical character neither listens for Nature's voice nor presumes to speak of or for Nature. Thus he walks the tightrope of representing the impossibility of representation.[46]

IV

In the *Elegy Written in a Country Church-Yard* (1751), Gray is concerned with, among other things, hearing and rendering the voice of personified Nature. But he defines this voice in relation to class and labor. Henry Weinfield has argued that, unlike Gray's use of personification in his early odes, "in the *Elegy* his field of representation embraces the sociopolitical realm," with personification functioning "in relation to particular *types* and *classes* of individuals."[47] Personification, argues Weinfield, "may be considered Gray's master trope in the *Elegy* . . . connected to his investigation of the problem of value."[48] Through a complex integration of subject and object and masculine and feminine, Gray constructs a voice of Nature in the *Elegy* that attempts to shield Nature, poem, and poet from commodification.[49]

The *Elegy* replaces visual images of the prospect poem with aural and tactile images, which effectively "leaves the world to darkness and to me" (4).[50] This "me" is at once the speaker and object of the first stanza, an identity that Gray will expand temporally while attempting to maintain its inscrutability. By attributing characteristics of feminized objects to "me," the poet develops the speaker's objectification, completed in the concluding epitaph. The plowman, who in Thomson's *Seasons* penetrated feminine nature, becomes in Gray's poem a vehicle by which the poet subsumes feminine characteristics. Such an expansion of the faculties of the self involves the objectification of the speaker, still more than Thomson's self-objectification in *The Seasons*, that so complicates an analysis of voice in the *Elegy*. Most discussions of voice in the poem center on the problem of identifying "thee" in line 93: "For thee, who mindful of th' unhonour'd Dead / Dost in these lines their artless tale relate."[51] But "what is especially ironical about the formalist attempt to resolve the pronomial ambiguities," argues Weinfield, "is that the blurring of the pronouns coincides with a blurring of class distinctions that is in the service of this vision."[52] The poet asserts that the afterlife of the laborer is worthy of poetry and that the poet himself is capable of rendering it by establishing his shared position of isolation from the external world (hence, the lack of a prospect) and, in turn, his intimacy with a variety of kinds of exclusion. As the poet and laborers acquire feminine characteristics, they assume the voice of Nature rather than assume the role of her spectator.

Gray thus combines characteristics of the feminine and the laboring class, a union epitomized in his revision of the muse from a figure of grandeur—the Muse of "Luxury and Pride" (71), who is the object of the "great"—to the muse as a figure of the unexpressed and the inexpressible in the lives of laborers:

> Their name, their years, spelt by th' unletter'd muse,
> The place of fame and elegy supply:
> And many a holy text around she strews,
> That teach the rustic moralist to die.
>
> (81–84)

Whereas in his "Ode on the Spring" Gray demonstrates his place in the landscape and his familiarity with its details by placing himself and the muse in the midst of the landscape—"Beside some water's rushy brink / With me the Muse shall sit, and think / (At ease reclin'd in rustic state)" (15–17)—in the *Elegy*, the muse resembles the role of excluded laborer-poet. By replacing visual images with aural and tactile ones, visual and material representations of the feminine give way to aural representations. Thus Gray alters the referent of the feminine from material accomplishments of the great to a domain of intangible values that can be assimilated by the poet.

The plowman's exclusion from material power underscores alternative values that the poet acquires. Again, the darkening landscape provides descriptive space for the poet's focus on himself as perceiver of the landscape and his attention to what is not seen: the dead laborers, "Each in his narrow cell for ever laid"

(15). Gray elaborates the plowman's relation to the feminine through a series of vignettes that convey the inner worth of the laborer. The farmers are imagined in a former scene of feminized domesticity: "For them no more the blazing hearth shall burn, / Or busy housewife ply her evening care" (21–22). The poet imagines the potential of these "rude Forefathers" (16) by combining feminine images of acute sensibility ("Perhaps in this neglected spot is laid / Some heart once pregnant with celestial fire") with masculine power ("Hands, that the rod of empire might have sway'd, / Or wak'd to extasy the living lyre" [45–48]).

Darkness allows for the integration of the feminine by the male characters. For example, Gray defines the laborers' potential by modifying the tropes of gem and flower, customary in traditional blazons of feminine beauty:[53]

> Full many a gem of purest ray serene,
> The dark unfathom'd caves of ocean bear:
> Full many a flower is born to blush unseen,
> And waste its sweetness on the desert air.
>
> (53–56)

The feminine is pivotal to valuing the laboring class and rendering it compatible with poet and poetry. Rather than figure women's *physical* beauty, the gem and flower evoke men's subjectivity. Gray accomplishes this transfer by taking the tropes out of an empirically verifiable landscape into one that exists only in imaginative perception. This revaluation of the gem and flower participates in Gray's attempt to free laborer, poet, and poem from commodification. He transforms the gem, argues Suvir Kaul, to give it "value without being commodity, without coming into contact with the social labour that creates value."[54] This passage on the gem and flower figures in John Guillory's well-known analysis of the *Elegy*'s participation in canons and cultural capital: "When we relate this telltale blush to its predecessor in the line 'Full many a flower is born to blush unseen,' the homology of poverty and obscurity produces ... a curious equation between social and *literary* ambition."[55]

Thus in the *Elegy* the voice of Nature is epitomized in unheard human cries beyond the material to bind the living and the dead:

> On some fond breast the parting soul relies,
> Some pious drops the closing eye requires;
> Ev'n from the tomb the voice of Nature cries,
> Ev'n in our Ashes live their wonted Fires.
>
> (89–92)

The voice of Nature is the overarching figure of this poem: its "femininity" accommodates lower and upper social strata while its status as disembodied person asserts poetic *and* material labor as inward and thus incapable of commodification.

The culmination of the speaker's feminization and objectification is the placement of the poet's body in the plowman's earth. Having achieved an acute feminine sensibility, the poet can now objectify his own soul.[56] In his imagined objectification of himself the speaker chooses the position of river god, but instead of Father Thames' survey of empirical achievements, Gray's poet-cum-river-god reads the intricacies of the water, where the "object" is his reflective musings:

> 'There at the foot of yonder nodding beech
> 'That wreathes its old fantastic roots so high,
> 'His listless length at noontide wou'd he stretch,
> 'And pore upon the brook that babbles by.
>
> (101–4)

Omitting the reflections his poet sees, Gray preserves poetic interiority.

In the "Epitaph" Gray defines the poet's place in the afterlife in relation to feminine Nature and feminine personifications:

> *Here rests his head upon the lap of Earth*
> *A Youth to Fortune and to Fame unknown,*
> *Fair Science frown'd not on his humble birth,*
> *And Melancholy mark'd him for her own.*
>
> (117–20)

Embraced by the feminine, the poet defines his spiritual and poetic worth.[57] Objectifying itself via an incorporation of the feminine (or the masculine incorporated by the feminine), the poetic self defines its boundaries within this double feminine embrace. We may compare this articulation of subjectivity to other interpretations of subjectivity in the poem. Gleckner takes exception to "those readings that one way or another regard Gray as 'disappearing' in the poem." But Pat Rogers has argued for the importance of this poem's "'vanishing subject,'" and Bogel sees the *Elegy* as emphasizing the "perception of insubstantiality."[58] In the *Elegy*, argues Kaul, "the object of pathos is in fact the Subject(ivity) of the Poet."[59] Kaul sees the poet's self-entombment as a crisis in language, particularly "the failure of poetic language to bridge the gulf between cultures"—that of the city and that of the country.[60] "The poet's art," argues Kaul, "that would speak for the villagers, discover value in them, cannot speak to them or be valued by them."[61] Guillory argues that the poem's closing focus on literary subjectivity is its "final product": "the poem discovers this melancholy subject as the solution to its intractable problems."[62] Straining against ambition and the poet's public circulation of himself and his words, the poem requires the assertion of a repressed self, the literary correlative of what was a social requirement for many women.

V

In Gray and Thomson, the poet personifies Nature to disembody it along with the poet. Thus figuring the person *as* disembodied, poets dissolve both subject and object and unite them in their nonmateriality. Finch's approach to the voice of Nature is one in which subject, object, and language live in her category of the natural. But when the poet Mary Leapor approaches the voice of Nature as inescapably material, she exposes as fantasy the imaginative convergence of poetic subject with feminine Nature. Leapor's "On Winter" (1748) presents the collision of material and imagined Nature—perhaps an inevitable perspective from a woman who was a poet, servant, and daughter to a gardener-laborer. In "On Winter" Leapor chooses the harshest of English seasons to confront a lack of poetic inspiration in a poem that challenges the figurative integrity of Nature.[63] In Leapor's poem fecund nature and inspiration abandon the speaker in her attempt to combine poetry with the laboring poor. Whereas Adams's "To the Muse" (discussed in chapter 3) expressed the restrictions on the woman poet derived from codes of gender conduct, Leapor's "On Winter" expresses the restrictions on the laboring poet when Nature must be approached materially—restrictions which the poet necessarily overcomes.

"On Winter" begins with the problem of finding matter and means for the poem: "What Pictures now shall wanton Fancy bring? / Or how the Muse to *Artemisia* sing?" (1–2). Realism impinges on the pastoral vocabulary when the poet accounts for her lack of inspiration:

> Now shiv'ring Nature mourns her ravish'd Charms,
> And sinks supine in Winter's frozen Arms.
> No gaudy Banks delight the ravish'd Eye,
> But northern Breezes whistle thro' the Sky.
>
> (3–6)

Leapor's restrained couplets imitate the chill of winter: Nature's conventional abundance is shown to be patently false. Birds cannot sing in the bitter cold: "No joyful Choirs hail the rising Day, / But the froze Crystal wraps the leafless Spray" (7–8); and pastoral characters "their aking Fingers blow" (19). This inverted *locus amoenus* yields images of feminine Nature gone awry:

> Poor daggled *Urs'la* stalks from Cow to Cow,
> Who to her Sighs return a mournful Low;
> While their full Udders her broad Hands assail,
> And her sharp Nose hangs dropping o'er the Pail.
>
> (27–30)

Rather than the easy fertility of Mother Earth, Nature for Leapor's laborer is exhausting. The scene that immediately follows continues to depict the laborer's difficult intimacy with Nature, which leads to domestic penury and marital resentment—neither the poetic effusions of Thomson's winter, whose "Vapours, and clouds, and storms / . . . exalt the soul to solemn thought / And heavenly musing" (3, 4–5) nor Gray's warm domestic circle around the plowman returning home. Rather,

> With Garments trickling like a shallow Spring,
> And his wet Locks all twisted in a String,
> Afflicted *Cymon* waddles through the Mire,
> And rails at *Win'fred* creeping o'er the Fire.
>
> (31–34)

Such is the laboring counterpart of Father Thames; instead of locks wet from the majestic Thames, Cymon's are bedraggled by winter rain. Instead of reclining like the lordly Thames on the sedgy bank, Cymon "waddles through the Mire." Instead of prophesying, Cymon rails at Win'fred, confined to the circle of her domestic chores. This scene prompts the poet to ask the "gentle Muses, . . . is this a Time / To sport with Poesy and laugh in Rhyme" (35–36). The poet's blood, like a river, is chilled by Winter: "the chill'd Blood, that hath forgot to glide, / Steals through its Channels in a Lazy Tide" (37–38). Identifying the absence of inspiration in the absence of fertile Nature, the poem concludes with the question, "how can *Phoebus*, who the Muse refines, / Smooth the dull Numbers when he seldom shines" (39–40).[64] The poet's relation to Nature is ultimately to the masculine Phoebus, who *denies* warmth and light. While this passage may recall Thomson's orphic surrender, Leapor's poem suggests that sunless winter affords no poetry.

Although filtering Nature through the artifice of the pastoral, Leapor adroitly focuses on the laborers's point of view:

> While the faint Travellers around them see,
> Here Seas of Mud and there a leafless Tree:
> No budding Leaves nor Honeysuckles gay,
> No yellow Crow-foots paint the dirty Way.
>
> (21–25)

In this landscape, where the pastoral ideal of harmony between humans and nature is gone, Nature is defeminized, infertile, immobile, and silent—an allegory of laboring women writers' lack of poetic access to Nature, which Leapor has, of course, refuted by changing the quality of Nature.

Providing the blankness of what she calls a "white prospect" (17), Leapor explores the possibilities of Nature absent its conventional feminine fertility while she obliquely represents the subjectivity of the laborer constrained by material Nature. Based on negation, Leapor's landscape is one of the grimmest variations on the restricted landscapes seen in other women poets' prospects. (Readers may recall Leapor's demystification of the association between women and Nature in "An Essay on Woman" [1751]: "Woman—a pleasing, but a short-liv'd Flow'r, / Too soft for Business, and too weak for Pow'r" [1–2]). Her Nature is not at the disposal of a countess who may offer its bounty in part or whole, as we saw in Finch's "Eusden." In "Winter," Leapor's Nature has nothing to give: thus she demystifies Nature as object of Art, Nature as person, and the person as natural.

Whereas many other poets explore relationships with Nature free from either physical dependence or ownership, Leapor pursues the possibility of poetry within constrained material relations to Nature. Instead of other poets who desire to join subject and object or show their conflation, Leapor does not seek to merge with harsh Nature but rather show the effects of Nature's brutal materiality on the subject. Deprived by a landscape of deprivation, subjectivity asserts itself through material details (nose, fingers, hair), not metaphysical yearning. Providing little psychological characterization of her laborers, Leapor brilliantly gives us only fragments of consciousness that correspond to their particular material circumstances. To Urs'la, Cymon, and Win'fred, Leapor provides a counter subject, her poet-speaker Artemesia, suggesting the split subjectivity of the poetic imagination and the laborer's body. The breach between poetic subjectivity and the laborer's relation to Nature lies exposed.[65]

What does the act of personifying Nature achieve? Critics have drawn opposite conclusions about whether personification functions conservatively or radically. To Lawrence Lipking, it can "tame the savage, unhuman world," and to Clifford Siskin it can invoke a community of general belief, order chaos, and make the inequitable appear equitable.[66] Margaret Doody describes personifications as "agents of metamorphosis, the energies which make metamorphosis inevitable."[67] Bogel argues that personifications may "exemplify a taming of the other, a partial withdrawing of metaphysical commitments, but in another sense they represent . . . the conferring of a certain independence and substantiality on qualities, on the contingent."[68] In the exploration of subject-object relations in eighteenth-century poetry, does this trope efface the specificity of Nature in a false projection of human subjectivity, or, in vivifying Nature, does it come closest to representing humans' respect for Nature? To grant personhood to that which is not a person takes us to the crux of representation—how can, or should, the poet represent difference? We may recall Emmanuel Levinas's notion of the "face" in ethical discourse: "To be in relation with the other face to face—is to be unable to kill. This is also the situation of discourse. . . . Can things take on a face? Isn't art an activity that gives things a face?"[69] For most of the poets discussed in this chapter, giving a feminine face to Nature underlies their attempts to define the self, and sometimes Nature too, treasured for its intangibility.

5
The Nightingale's Breast against the Thorn: Sensibility and the Sublime

IN THIS LAST CHAPTER I PLACE THE STUDY OF POETRY AND THE feminine at the intersection of three currents: the religious sublime, the culture of sensibility, and less familiar *eighteenth-century* notions of the sublime. In his comprehensive study of the religious sublime in the eighteenth century, David B. Morris describes its permutations in the course of poetry and criticism. Although poetry of the religious sublime continues from the seventeenth century on, Morris marks its conflation with sensibility as occurring in the second half of the eighteenth century, when "feeling and religion became nearly equivalents."[1] Although poets continued to write in the vein of the religious sublime throughout the eighteenth century, Morris has discussed its transformation in the second half of the century under the influence of the culture of sensibility: "to the sentimentalists, sublimity no longer implied the stern grandeur of Milton or the chaste simplicity of Boileau but whatever in art or nature contributes to strong excitement of the feelings."[2]

Although Morris sees this as a dilution of the sublime, I argue that the conjunction of sentiment, or sensibility, and the sublime in the eighteenth century is a complex aesthetic achievement with ethical challenges for the reader.

The structure of sensibility depends on the poet's acute sensitivity to pain—her/his own or another's—that not only demonstrates the depth and delicacy of the self but also an attention to suffering that can extend to issues of social justice, most pointedly in the antislavery poems that appear in the second half of the eighteenth century. *Sensibility* and *sentimentalism* (the two terms are often used interchangeably) are flexible and debatable terms linked to the domains of consciousness, feeling, and sexuality.[3] G. J. Barker-Benfield defines *sensibility*, or *sentimentalism*, as the "receptivity of the senses," based on the "psychoperceptual scheme explained and systematized by Newton and Locke."[4] Although *sensibility* referred to the nervous system, "the material basis for consciousness," it was considered an exercise of morality and spirituality.[5] Whether seen as a feminization of culture (women's delicate nerves, it was argued, rendered them particularly susceptible to sensibility, but it was men who were considered capable of expressing sensibility through the control of art) or as a masculinization of "feminine" emotions, sensibility relied heavily on gendered systems.[6] The poetry of sensibility embraces the cultural values of the feminine we have seen in the muse, the landscape, and personifications.

The literature of sensibility has a long lineage in the element of pathos, a quality extending back to Euripides, medieval morality plays, and Elizabethan and Jacobean drama.[7] In its appearance in devotional poetry, pathos combines with elevated subject matter to produce the religious sublime. William A. Sessions characterizes the seventeenth-century English religious lyric as focused on pathos and the feminization of the male speaker. These religious lyrics written by men prefigure the focus on female and feminized suffering by men writers in the mid-eighteenth century. Sessions argues that speakers in poems by John Donne and George Herbert, for example, "often sound like the hopeless cries of the abandoned women of classical tradition," not surprising given that early modern men would have would have relied on such a tradition of female voices found in Ovid's heroic epistles and Virgil's depiction of Dido.[8]

In the poems discussed in this chapter, the once separate categories of the sublime and the pathetic are seen to interpenetrate each other by the second half of the eighteenth century, in contrast to their longstanding separation. (In the dedication to Young that precedes Joseph Warton's *An Essay on the Writings and Genius of Pope*, Warton maintains the distinction between the sublime and pathetic, which he describes as the "two chief nerves of all genuine poesy."[9]) In the second half of the eighteenth century, the sublime and the pathetic, or its modernized version of sensibility, unite to form a poetic standard that establishes aesthetic values as inseparable from ethical ones. To suffer and to imagine others' suffering in such poetry engages the highest aesthetic and ethical standards.

I

The religious sublime associated with poets such as Isaac Watts provides the foundation for the conjunction of sensibility and the sublime that we see especially in the second half of the century. Indeed, Restoration and eighteenth-century poets' uses of the muse, landscape, and personification have already shown variations on sensibility and the sublime. The identification with or yearning to emulate these feminized entities requires an acute sensitivity that connects poet to object of representation. This ontological dimension of the act of representation—that the poet must *be* poetic to make poetry—is strikingly similar to the ontological requirements of the writer of literature of sensibility. Being poetic is emulating the feminine.[10]

Following Hugh Blair, I call this intersection of sensibility and the sublime the *sentimental sublime*. With roots in the suffering self of the religious sublime, the sentimental sublime is an important intersection of subjectivity and representation. We find the sentimental sublime in Thomas Gray and William Cowper, for example, but also in Christian Carstairs, Anna Seward, and Ann Yearsley. These versions of the sublime do not provide the conclusion of the sublime trajectory found in the theories of Burke and Kant, where typically the subject transcends that which threatens its survival. Although the effect of the sublime is to render the person experiencing it temporarily powerless, the encounter simultaneously expands and raises the mind, allowing it to repossess itself in a dynamic of transcendence.[11] The self must be stable enough to confront and survive the abyss: there is "nothing sublime," wrote Burke in the *Enquiry*, "which is not some modification of power."[12] In the sentimental sublime, however, the subject often remains under threat. As in other gendered structures of representation, the sentimental sublime usually feminizes the object of representation: feminine virtue in distress, as inherited from romance narratives, is the typical object of sensibility.[13] But this object can also be the poetic subject itself: that is, the speaker may articulate his or her own tender pain.

In the eighteenth century, sensibility and the sublime are overlapping discourses found in the work of critics such as John Baillie and Hugh Blair. By focusing on notions of the sublime derived from Longinus, Burke, and Kant, however, post-Romantic critics have created an aesthetic standard that excludes much of eighteenth-century poetry and virtually all of women's poetry in that era.[14] Versions of the sentimental sublime appear in the theories of John Baillie (1747), Alexander Gerard (1759), James Beattie (1783), and Hugh Blair (1763 and 1783). In Baillie's *An Essay on the Sublime* (1747), the sublime is "every thing which . . . raises the Mind to Fits of *Greatness*, and disposes it to soar above her *Mother Earth*."[15] As Baillie describes it, thus "arises that *Exultation* and *Pride* which the Mind ever feels from the *Consciousness* of its own *Vastness*—That *Object* only can be justly called *Sublime*, which in some degree disposes the Mind to this *Enlargement* of itself, and gives her a lofty *Conception* of her own *Powers*."[16] Baillie and others assert that the sublime can reside in virtue; heroism; the "Contempt of *Death*, *Power*, or of *Honour*"; and in "universal *Benevolence*."[17] But Baillie pointedly excludes domestic affections—the "narrow Object" of "a *Child*, a *Parent*, or a *Mistress*"—from the sublime.[18] In his *Lectures on Rhetoric and Belles Lettres* (1783), Blair describes the "moral, or sentimental Sublime" as

> arising from certain exertions of the human mind; from certain affections, and actions, of our fellow creatures. . . . Wherever, in some critical and high situation, we behold a man uncommonly intrepid, and resting upon himself; superior to passion and to fear; animated by some great principle to the contempt of popular opinion, of selfish interest, of dangers, or of death; there we are struck with a sense of the Sublime. . . . High virtue is the most natural and fertile source of this moral Sublimity.[19]

Mary Locke's "Sonnet" (1794) epitomizes Blair's assertion that "High virtue is the most natural and fertile source of this moral sublimity." But rather than "a man uncommonly intrepid and resting upon himself; superior to passion and to fear," Locke shows us a feminine personification achieving the moral or sentimental sublime. In a landscape of darkness, storms, and murder, feminine Virtue "'mid the dreadful scene, / Fearlessly treads the cliff's extremest verge" (9–10): "conscious she of blameless life, / Nor shuns nor fears the elemental strife" (13–14).[20]

In the sentimental sublime, the self remains in a position of obscurity, vulnerability, or decomposition. Burke considers obscurity one of the chief ingredients of sublime grandeur (many will recall his precision in stating that a clear idea is another name for a little idea): visual obscurity overwhelms the imagination and reason steps in to delimit the obscure and preserve the coherence of the self. As opposed to Burke's view in which the sublime can only be experienced from a position of material safety—the danger is faced imaginatively—in the sentimental sublime the danger is often presented as a material "reality" that is nevertheless insignificant compared to the mental or emotional damage that the subject endures.[21] Whereas in the Burkean or Kantian sublime the self may be threatened by the terrifying obscurity of Nature, such as an abyss or mountain peak enveloped by clouds, in the sentimental sublime the obscure is quite different. Rather than a source external to the suffering self, the source of suffering is emotional, or spiritual, and is often intentionally obscured by the speaker—part of the unfathomable, deep self. In the sentimental sublime, then, the interior self rather than Nature is the obscure.

Ashfield and de Bolla have discussed the conjunction of sensibility and the sublime in relation to Adam Smith's moral-sense theory. Smith's *The Theory of Moral Sentiments* rescues sensibility from effeminacy, defining it as supreme manliness:[22]

> Our sensibility to the feelings of others, so far from being inconsistent with the manhood of self-command, is the very principle upon which that manhood is founded. The very same principle or instinct which, in the misfortune of our neighbour, prompts us to compassionate his sorrow; in our own misfortune, prompts us to restrain the abject and miserable lamentations of our own sorrow.[23]

Smith describes high virtue as "exquisite sensibility": "The man of the most perfect virtue, the man whom we naturally love and revere the most, is he who joins, to the most perfect command of his own original and selfish feelings, the most exquisite sensibility both to the original and sympathetic feelings of others."[24]

Such writers assure us that sensibility can inform the sublime. Gray's poetry provides a range of the sentimental sublime, including his *Elegy* in which the "Youth to Fortune and to Fame unknown" establishes virtuous sensibility by giving to "Mis'ry all he had, a tear" (118, 123). Whereas the *Elegy* makes much use of the exercise of virtuous, high sympathy toward this sympathizing youth and the poor in their graves, Gray's *The Bard* invokes the heroic mode in the sentimental sublime. "The Bard. A Pindaric Ode" (published 1757) ("founded on a Tradition current in Wales, that Edward the First, when he compleated the Conquest of that country, ordered all the Bards, that fell into his hands, to be put to death") articulates what Blair would later describe as "a man uncommonly intrepid and resting upon himself; superior to passion and fear." The poet occupies the politically powerful position of bard, which is precisely why Edward I, according to the tradition, wants all bards dead:

> On a rock, whose haughty brow
> Frowns o'er old Conway's foaming flood,
> Robed in the sable garb of woe,
> With haggard eyes the Poet stood;
> Loose his beard, and hoary hair
> Stream'd, like a meteor, to the troubled air)
> And with a Master's hand, and Prophet's fire,
> Struck the deep sorrows of his lyre.
>
> (15–22)

The rock's haughty brow suggests the poet as landscape, and the bard's "hoary hair / [that] Stream'd like a meteor, to the troubled air" is its own threatening sublime landscape. Rather than represent Nature, the bard *is* Nature, is the country he sings—a masculine landscape of emotional intensity meant to evoke a manly conjunction of sensibility and the sublime. The "deep sorrows" of the lyre personify the instrument of art. As the lyre achieves being, the bard achieves death:

> 'Fond impious Man, think'st thou, yon sanguine cloud,
> 'Rais'd by thy breath, has quench'd the Orb of day?
> 'To-morrow he repairs the golden flood,
> 'And warms the nations with redoubled ray.

'Enough for me: With joy I see
'The different doom our Fates assign.
'Be thine Despair, and scept'red Care,
'To triumph, and to die, are mine.'
He spoke, and headlong from the mountain's height
Deep in the roaring tide he plung'd to endless night.

(135–44)

"To triumph, and to die" may signal the poet's perception of his own political insignificance in mid-eighteenth-century Britain, as John Sitter argues.[25] The bard's contempt of Edward's sentence encapsules the masculine heroic version of the sentimental sublime. Whereas Gray's bard plunges to his death as an act of political defiance, the subject of the sentimental sublime prefers, often seeks, a material threat to an obscurely referenced *psychological* suffering. Gray's bard is the masculine and overtly political version of a figure that recurs in the sentimental sublime: the pained nightingale.

II

In the religious sublime of the seventeenth and eighteenth centuries, the poetic self is the suffering soul, and the obscure may lie in the uncertainty about one's spiritual condition and fate (the dark night of the soul, the crisis of faith). Racked spiritually and emotionally, this suffering soul's achievement is to endure spiritual and emotional turmoil. The poetry of Isaac Watts includes many examples of the suffering soul of the religious sublime. In his "The Hurry of the Spirits, in a Fever and Nervous Disorder" (written 1712; published 1734), the body is a sublime landscape—"My frame of nature is a ruffled Sea" (1)—and "my Disease the Tempest" (2).[26] Articulating a spiritual dialectic between reason and imagination that prefigures Kant's discussion of these categories in the sublime, Watts describes the mind disordered by "confus'd Ideas / Of Non-existents and Impossibles" (15–16):

Fragments of old Dreams,
Borrow'd from Midnight, torn from Fairy Fields
And Fairy Skies, and Regions of the Dead,
Abrupt, ill-sorted.

(17–20)

These images of the disordered/disordering imagination "dance and riot wild in Reason's Court" (25). "I'm in a raging Storm" (26), explains the speaker,

>   while my Soul
> Like some light worthless Chip of floating Cork
> Is tost from Wave to Wave: Now overwhelm'd
> With breaking Floods I drown, and seem to lose
> All Being; Now high-mounted on the Ridge
> Of a tall foaming Surge, I'm all at once
> Caught up into the Storm, and ride the Wind,
> The whistling Wind; unmanageable Steed,
> And feeble Rider!
>
> (27–35)

The poem ends with a series of questions in which the speaker wonders when his agony will end. We find here not only the conventional images of Burke's sublime (storms, floods, and precipices) but, more importantly, the speaker's ongoing state of vulnerability—a reverse of the triumphal subject.

Similarly in Edward Young's poem *The Last Day* (1713), a prelude to his highly influential *The Complaint: or, Night Thoughts on Life, Death, and Immortality* (1746), the self endures spiritual torment:[27]

>   Deep anguish! but too late; the hopeless soul
> Bound to the bottom of the burning pool,
> Though loth, and ever loud blaspheming, owns
> He's justly doom'd to pour eternal groans;
> Enclos'd with horrors, and transfix'd with pain,
> Rolling in vengeance, struggling with his chain:
> To talk to fiery tempests; to implore
> The raging flame to give its burnings o'er;
> To toss, to writhe, to pant beneath his load,
> And bear the weight of an offended God.
>
> (3.208–17)

The terrors of the religious sublime make those later described by Burke look mild. Whereas Watts and Young render the soul threatened by a suffering of uncertain duration, William Cowper, writing at the end of the century, is certain of his everlasting agony, described in "Hatred and Vengeance, My Eternal Portion" (written 1774?; published 1816):[28]

> Hard lot! Encompass'd with a thousand dangers,
> Weary, faint, trembling with a thousand terrors,
> Fall'n, and if vanquish'd, to receive a sentence
>   Worse than Abiram's:
> Him, the vindictive rod of angry justice
> Sent, quick and howling, to the centre headlong;
> I, fed with judgments, in a fleshly tomb, am
>   Buried above ground.
>   (13–20)

More familiar is Cowper's "The Castaway" (written 1799, published 1803), where the poet compares his lot to that of the sailor drowning at sea:

> No voice divine the storm allay'd,
>   No light propitious shone,
> When, snatch'd from all effectual aid,
>   We perish'd, each, alone;
> But I, beneath a rougher sea,
> And whelm'd in deeper gulphs than he.
>   (61–66)

In these poems the speaker seeks union with the divine and suffers because that union cannot yet be achieved—or, as Cowper believes, will never be achieved. Such poems provide models of the most radical vulnerability that carry over to increasingly secular models of the self. These models of humility and fear may conform to an orthodox relation to the divine, but readers are often less approving of such humility and vulnerability in a secular environment. A less traumatic humility grounds the desire for union with the muse, feminine Nature, or a friend in the more secular poems of Dryden and Pope.

    These examples of agonized spiritual longing by Watts, Young, and Cowper seem little indebted to the erotic structure of representation seen most famously in Donne's imagery in "Batter my heart" or Milton's in *Paradise Lost* of the Spirit that impregnates "the vast Abyss" (1.21).[29] Rather, it is in poetry of the religious sublime by Elizabeth Singer Rowe (1674–1737), writing at the same time as Watts, that we see again the explicit use of an erotic structure where sublime longing is sometimes satisfied.[30] Erotic tension fuels devotion in much of Rowe's religious poetry. In soliloquy 7, the soul suffers less from fear of perdition than from aching humility and longing:[31]

> Yet I must aim at subjects infinite,
> For oh! my love sick heart is full of thee.
> In crowds, in solitude, the field, the temple,
> All places hold an equal sanctity;
> While thy lov'd name in humble invocation
> Dwells on my tongue, and ev'ry gentle sigh
> Breathes out my life, my very soul to thee.
>
> (20–26)

Margaret Doody suggests Rowe's desire for union with the divine is a sublime longing that takes language to the "edge of the ineffable."[32] Rowe's version of the religious sublime is striking for the pleasure the soul takes in sublime immensity and the destruction of self, as in the blank verse soliloquy 8:

> How my free soul
> Expatiates in these wide, these boundless joys!
> How am I lost to ev'ry thought but thee,
> Forgetting ev'n myself, forgetting all
> But thee, my glorious, everlasting theme!
>
> (23–27)

Rowe's poetry is a striking example of a religious sublime where the soul is both transported and humble. We may recall Addison's description of the imagination soaring unbounded (*The Spectator*, no. 412), discussed in chapter 3. The restrictions on women poets' imaginative movement in secular prospect poetry contrasts sharply with Rowe's flight through spiritual prospects.

III

Sensibility is often itself a feminine personification, as in Ann Yearsley's "Addressed to Sensibility" (1787).[33] Here the religious sublime and sensibility cross-fertilize each other:[34]

> Oh! Sensibility! Thou busy nurse
> Of *Inj'ries* once receiv'd, why wilt thou feed
> Those serpents in the soul? their stings more fell
> Than those which writh'd round Priam's priestly son;
> I feel them here! They rend my panting breast,
> But I will tear them thence: ah! effort vain!
> Disturb'd they grow rapacious, while their fangs

> Strike at poor Memory; wounded she deplores
> Her ravish'd joys, and murmurs o'er the past.
>
> (1–9)

In acute sensibility the self is invaded by some pain—often unspecified—thus recasting the suffering soul of the religious sublime. Feminized and trivialized as "busy nurse," Sensibility even exceeds the suffering masculine heroism of Priam's son. The sharp stings of the "sensible" heart make the speaker's breast a scene of violence. But in fact it is not the acutely sensitive heart that is the source of pain but rather some episode from the past, unstated in this poem but explicit in another poem in the same edition: "To those who accuse the Author of Ingratitude" (discussed later in this chapter). The self is not destroyed but lives in unremitting agony (like Prometheus, whose liver the eagle continually ravages). Announcing itself as a poem of sensibility, Yearsley's work establishes its intense pain by invoking the terror and heroic suffering of the religious sublime.

In the poetry of sensibility the breast, or heart, is often assailed as in Yearsley's "Sensibility" (we may recall Montagu's heart incised by the swain in her poem "To Bathurst," discussed in chapter 3). Sensibility is conveyed in the wounded breast of the "Nightingale" (1786) by Christian Carstairs (fl. 1763-86), quoted here in its entirety:[35]

> O! could my sweet plaint lull to rest,
> Soften one sigh—as thou dreamst,
> I'd sit the whole night on thy tree,
> And sing, — — sing, — —
>   With the thorn at my breast.

In this cryptic gem, Carstairs never specifies what suffering needs to be quelled—is it her own, another's, the "thou" of line 2? But to assuage this pain the speaker would endure the thorn at her breast—image of physical and emotional pain. Carstairs echoes this torment in her wildly fluctuating meter, regular only in the line that describes the speaker steadfastly enduring the night with the bird. In the last two lines the speaker hypothetically surrenders to the thorn of Nature, the rhythm broken by dashes and closing eerily with the dancing anapests: "with the thorn at my breast." This is no distant, imaginative threat that reason can overcome; rather, the subject surrenders her very body to penetrating Nature. Carstairs distills the sentimental sublime, where suffering is unresolved and where physical pain is sought as an alternative to mental or emotional distress: the speaker hangs on a precipice of suffering. No steep cliff or wide ocean terrifies the speaker; rather, the speaker *seeks* the thorn to pierce her breast. The poem's use of the suspending dash suggests that language may be part of the material relief (through pain) or the obstacle sought—or that language is fundamentally inadequate. Carstairs's poem features two elements—the obscure and the inexpressible—that predominate in the sentimental sublime as they do in the more familiar Burkean and Kantian sublimes.

A much earlier poem that incorporates sensibility and the sublime is Anne Finch's "To the Nightingale" (1713). She adopts the venerable goal of imitating the nightingale's song, but the nightingale that reigns as lyrist of the sublime in the beginning of the poem is by the end a bird whose fable plays out the foibles of ambitious and envious poets and critics. The speaker of the poem initially aims for sublime transport when she tells the nightingale, "Free as thine shall be my Song" since poets "Pleas[e] best when unconfin'd" (5, 8). This freedom, she argues, is, paradoxically, a constrained one, for the bird's painful restriction produces its legendary song:

> Cares do still their Thoughts molest,
> And still th' unhappy Poet's Breast,
> Like thine, when best he sings, is plac'd against a Thorn.
> (11–13)

The condition of restrained freedom is paralleled by the restricted powers of the muse, who is instructed to follow the nightingale's song rather than provide the poet with inspiration (15–17). Contrary to the classical plot in which the poet and the nightingale compete until the nightingale finally dies, the poet seeks harmony with the bird.[36] She urges her poetic self, which she calls "muse," to meet inspired nature:

> Canst thou Syllables refine,
> Melt a Sense that shall retain
> Still some Spirit of the Brain,
> Till with Sounds like these it join.
> (18–21)

Unable to imitate the bird's song, the defeated speaker orders the nightingale to "cease thy Tune" (26).

The original object, the nightingale's sublime music, is now dismissed, but in its conclusion the poem recasts the sublime as a *failure* of sensibility:

> Thus we Poets that have Speech,
> Unlike what thy Forests teach,
> If a fluent Vein be shown
> That's transcendent to our own,
> Criticize, reform, or preach,
> Or censure what we cannot reach.
>
> (30–35)

The "I" that inaugurated the poem becomes both generalized and objectified here in the voice of the critic who condemns "what we cannot reach" (35) and in the voice of the poet critiqued, announcing its own objectification in the phrase "we Poets that have Speech." The poem ultimately condemns the critic's incapacity to understand the poet's and the nightingale's positions (a failure of sensibility that recalls that of the unsympathetic critics in Finch's "Eusden," discussed in chapter 4). The poet carries over the limits of words in the first part of the poem to the limits of her readers. That these confrontations arise in Finch's attention to the nightingale is perfectly fitting: Finch used the figure of the bird often to express her own poetic self's effort to understand the object/other.

In her transformation of the poet's "duel" with the nightingale, where instead of the convention of conquering the nightingale this poet *yields* to the bird, Finch creates an aesthetic and ethical pressure that requires the reader to adjust her or his evaluation of poetic speech. The poem, argues Hinnant, is "concerned in the broadest possible sense with the limits of poetic signification."[37] Through this conflict, Finch reproduces the very conditions of poetic beauty she portrayed earlier in the poem: the nightingale sings best when its breast is "plac'd against a Thorn." This painful pressure serves as a controlling metaphor for the poem's mimetic stress. Finch thus obliquely reaches the most difficult poetic goal through the description of putative failure. The poet's imitation of the nightingale's song must fail for the poet's sympathy with the nightingale's position against the thorn to succeed.

The goal of identification through transcendence is not only impeded by the limits of language but also by human relations where selfish envy, another thorn of representation, squelches sympathy and community.

Characterized as a masculine mode inimical to women's abilities, the sublime was for women a "forbidden discourse of transcendence," in the words of John G. Pipkin.[38] The great irony, however, is that women's contributions to dismantling the hierarchy of poetic kinds had opened a space for the sublime prohibited to them. We would indeed expect that few women would attempt this most ambitious and elite of aesthetic domains and yet by incorporating the discourse of sensibility women *and* men poets found a way to explore the sublime in a humble way, one that owes its quality to a continuity with the religious sublime.

In her "Address to Woman" Anna Seward (1742–1809) warns women to "seek not" a landscape characterized by the sublime: "the craggy height, / The howling main, the desert wild!" (3–4).[39] Rather, women should cultivate "peace," "soft delight," "tender love," and "pity mild" (1–2). Alien to the very nature of "woman," the sublime, according to Seward, is meant for "ruffian Man [who] endures the strife / Of tempests fierce, and furious seas" (9–10). Of course, Seward's interdiction participates in the sublime, not only by citing it, but authoritatively cordoning off the sublime mode as a threatening object dangerous to the woman writer. In fact, Seward wrote several poems in the vein of the sentimental sublime, where she uses images of sublime nature to represent a state of mind, but the sublime threat is obliquely assigned to some desolating relationship with another person. The damage done is a permanent inner strife that cannot be resolved except by drugs, dreams, or numbing indifference. Indeed, paralysis rather than transport characterizes the sublime in Seward's "Sonnet 82" (written circa 1790; published 1799), which begins with the image of a violently split tree:

> From a riv'd tree, that stands beside the grave
>   Of the self-slaughter'd, to the misty moon
>   Calls the complaining owl in night's pale noon;
>   And from a hut, far on the hill to rave
> Is heard the angry Ban-Dog. With loud wave
>   Yon rous'd and turbid river surges down,
>   Swoln with the mountain-rains, and dimly shown

> Appals our sense.—Yet see! from yonder cave,
> Her shelter in the recent, stormy showers,
> With anxious brow, a fond expecting maid
> Steals towards the flood!—Alas!—for now appears
> Her lover's vacant boat!—the broken oars
> Roll down the tide!—What images invade!
> Aghast she stands, the statue of her fears!

In this narrative of loss and desolation, the self is destroyed because a personal relationship has been severed. While the turbid river sublimely "appals" the senses, recalling a Burkean notion of sublime obscurity, more fundamental to the poem is its quality of rived Nature (including the tree, the grave, and the maid). Seward's poem is a broader, narrativized version of Carstair's "Nightingale," with the speaker's breast suspended on a thorn; it is also a secularized version of the suffering soul in Watts and Cowper that conveys the desolation of a woman bereft of her lover. All of these poems resonate with James Usher's pronouncement in *Clio: or a Discourse on Taste* (1769) that "in the sublime we feel ourselves alarmed, our motions are suspended, and we remain for some time until the emotion wears off, wrapped in silence and inquisitive horror."[40]

These same elements may be found in many of Anna Seward's poems that, despite her own strictures against women and the sublime, enlist the sublime from an intriguing range of perspectives. In a series of sonnets (nos. 88–90), "The Prospect a Flooded Vale," we find the ingredients already observed in Carstairs's poem: an obscure origin of the sublime threat, a preference for material pain over mental or emotional anguish, and the self suspended. In the opening lines, the speaker *seeks* Nature's terror: "Up this bleak hill, in wintry night's dread hour, / With mind congenial to the scene, I come!" (1–2). The valley is overwhelmed by a flood, but rather than experiencing it as an imaginative terror, Seward's speaker looks on the "wide waste of waters" (12) and responds in an emotional outpouring that emulates the physical environment: "to tides of misery and disgrace / Love opes the flood-gates of my struggling soul" (13–14). In the middle sonnet in this sequence, we find that the speaker has come to the precipice overlooking the flooded valley to throw herself from the cliff. In this and the final, third, sonnet, Seward offers a curious revision to sublime recovery or self-preservation:

the speaker is unable "sublime to rise," whereby s/he might "Rend the conflicting clouds, inflame the skies / And lash the torrents!" (4–6). In the middle sonnet in this sequence, to the speaker's dismay, something "roots my feet" (13). In this inversion of sublime transcendence, where the speaker desires to die, she *fails* by saving her body, rather than her soul. The conventional values of the sublime have been reversed, with the preservation of the subject seen as an act of failure.

But this trio of sonnets is not Seward's only concern with the sublime. In other poems we also find the self represented in a state of dissolution, often vaguely attributable to love lost. This epitomizes that stage of the sublime in which the self is violated, but whereas Dennis had called it "a pleasing Rape upon the very Soul," Seward emphasizes the pain of a danger that cannot be transcended but has already damaged the self.[41] Interestingly, rather than a dynamic of self-preservation or resolution in which reason conquers the imagination, Seward typically shows that to resolve the pain is to delude oneself. Her "Sonnet 71. To the Poppy" (written circa 1789; published 1799) illustrates all of these elements:

> While Summer roses all their glory yield
>   To crown the votary of love and joy,
>   Misfortune's victim hails, with many a sigh,
>   Thee, scarlet Poppy of the pathless field,
> Gaudy, yet wild and lone; no leaf to shield
>   Thy flaccid vest, that as the gale blows high,
>   Flaps, and alternate folds around thy head.—
>   So stands in the long grass a love-craz'd maid,
> Smiling aghast; while stream to every wind
>   Her garish ribbons, smear'd with dust and rain;
>   But brain-sick visions cheat her tortured mind,
> And bring false peace. Thus, lulling grief and pain,
>   Kind dreams oblivious from thy juice proceed,
>   Thou flimsy, shewy, melancholy Weed.

This, too, is a poem that might be associated with the aesthetics of pathos or the cult of sensibility, but much is lost if we do not consider it in relation to the sublime. We can begin with Seward's selection of elements from Nature: not an abyss, a mountaintop, or an ocean, but a flower whose opiate powers have destroyed the figure, or rather, offered sympathetic relief to a human as vulnerable as the flower itself. In this figure of the poppy Seward has brilliantly chosen a flower, the element of nature conventionally used to figure women's beauty. Her choice of the poppy, not the rose, reflects her concern with the inner state, exquisitely detailed by the external features of the loose wind-blown petals. Recuperation of the self comes through false peace and the delusions of "Kind dreams." The source of the sublime threat is not nature but an undisclosed lover, and the "scene" of turmoil is the inner life. The "love-craz'd maid" "personifies" the disordered, disordering Nature—the poppy. The wind-blown poppy figures the woman's rent existence. And the broken octave, ending at line 7 rather than line 8, shows traditional poetic form ruptured by female desire. Strained throughout by heavy metrical variations, the poem brilliantly closes with perfect iambic pentameter to counter the ruin of woman and flower.

In Seward's versions of the sublime, the acute sensibility of the self begets a sublime encounter that cannot conclude with a whole, healed self. Seward's sentimental sublime presents not external Nature (such as a vast, turbid ocean or an abyss) but another human as the source of the obscure. Although in many cases the angst is related to a love lost or betrayed, what becomes obscure in these poems is the reason to live. Although Seward's engulfing flood is visually obscure, the source of psychological anguish *precedes* the subject's encounter with Nature. This obfuscation of the source of sublime distress may hide a narrative of sexual impropriety or it may serve to mark subjectivity itself as obscure. In this discreet obscurity, the subject does not so much transcend suffering as assert an interiority inviolable to representation.

In "Sonnet 10. To Honora Sneyd" (written 1773; published 1799) Seward posits her own suffering in the future as she imagines herself spurned by Sneyd, her close friend and, speculate some scholars, her lover:

> Honora, should that cruel time arrive
>   When 'gainst my truth thou should'st my errors poize,
>   Scorning remembrance of our vanish'd joys;
>   When for the love-warm looks, in which I live,
> But cold respect must greet me, that shall give
>   No tender glance, no kind regretful sighs;
>   When thou shalt pass me with averted eyes....
>
>   (1–7)

Seward imagines her future wounds in the vocabulary of the sentimental sublime:

> ... I could not bear
> Such dire eclipse of thy soul-cheering rays;
> I could not learn my struggling heart to tear
> From thy loved form, that thro' my memory strays;
> Nor in the pale horizon of despair
> Endure the wintry and darken'd days.
>
> (8–14)

The speaker enters a sublime landscape of the future where the visually obscure renders her own disappearance from Honora's consciousness. The only light that remains, "the pale horizon of despair," bespeaks the emptying out of landscape and psyche.

IV

The core experiences of sensibility and the sublime enlist the cultural stereotypes of femininity: in sensibility the "feminine" capacity for acute delicacy and compassion; in the sublime the "feminine threat" of the unruly or the obscure to the rational ego. Sensibility is characterized as an acute sensitivity of the nerves, finely tuned or vibrating to the suffering of another, or oneself. On a textual level when sensibility's object is oneself, the *source* of suffering is obscured or omitted, suggesting the obscure depths of the psyche. But when sensibility is directed toward another, the obscure may be more problematic. Indeed, the compassion we associate with sensibility has often been critiqued as thriving in its position of luxurious distance from the other. Thus some versions of sensibility may exploit the other as an opportunity to exercise compassion, obscuring the other as subject. Indeed, the frequently scopophilic structure of sensibility—where one looks upon an object/other to exercise one's sensibility—is the ethical problem of pity, an exercise that can enlarge the ego of the person of sensibility rather than create a domain of understanding and, presumably, social or spiritual action.[42]

The tension of sensibility as condescension, especially class condescension, overlaps with the class inflections of the sublime, often marked as an elite aesthetic territory of transport to a higher realm. "Matters of social class or rank," note Ashfield and de Bolla, "are rarely explicitly discussed within the context of the sublime, but they nevertheless underpin much of the tradition. If one's education were very rudimentary how could one be able to appreciate aesthetic forms?"[43] We see a complex approach to the sentimental sublime as it explicitly engages issues of rank in the poetry of Ann Yearsley (1752–1806), known in her day as Lactilla, milkwoman of Bristol. Key to her approach to sensibility and the sublime is her redefinition of obscurity. Yearsley associates obscurity with her rank and in turn with her access to education, as she describes it in "To Mrs. V——N" (1785):[44] "In dark obscurity my life began, / Where Science scorn'd to cheer the dreary way" (3–4). The obscurity linked to her inadequate education hinders sublime transport:

>Bright sentiment, if unimprov'd, must die,
>And great ideas, unassisted, fall;
>On Learning's wing we pierce th'empyreal sky;
>But Nature's untaught efforts are but small.
>
>(5–8)

Yearsley's modesty about her education in this first collection of her poems establishes the authority of virtue over knowledge. (Although she had no formal education, her mother was literate and owned a few books available to her children, including *Paradise Lost* and some works of Young, Pope, and Shakespeare.[45]) Indeed, repeatedly in Yearsley's poems her virtue manifests itself in sublime transport. Her speaker even achieves a cosmic perspective:

>Hope, lovely phantom! is, and shall be mine,
>She hovers round, amidst this waste of woe;
>Points my once cheerless soul to views sublime,
>From Earth's sad scene, and Mis'ry's wreck below.
>
>(69–72)

Yearsley's work signals the intersection of obscurity in sensibility and in the sublime as she articulates her own subject position fraught with social displacement. She did not perceive herself as laboring class.[46] "Far from identifying with the community into which she had been born," argues Waldron, "Yearsley only felt at home with the cultured and educated. Since she also saw much to criticize among the wealthy, her position, both socially and culturally, must be recognized as that of an isolate."[47]

Yearsley uses the trope of obscurity to represent her particular position as a laboring-class writer drawn to sensibility and the sublime, a conjunction seen in her poem "Sensibility," discussed earlier in this chapter. Among her more public sufferings was the oppressive patronage of Hannah More. As a milkwoman with no formal education, Yearsley found herself the object of More's condescending sensibility. In the terms of our discussion, More's condescension toward Yearsley obscured Yearsley's position as a subject. In financial terms, this denial of Yearsley's agency manifested itself in More's unwillingness to grant Yearsley rights over money earned from her first book of poetry. After an ugly break with More, Yearsley composed a highly class-sensitive revision of sensibility and the sublime in her poem "To Those Who Accuse the Author of Ingratitude" (1787).

In "To Those Who Accuse," she emphasizes the dignity of her position by her capacity for sensibility and sublime transport and her sophisticated use of blank verse. Characterizing Yearsley's sensibility as "an endless struggle of suffering thought," Jerome McGann aptly identifies her "'clogg'd' verse [that] perfectly represents her difficult mental environment, including her own (mental) self as it struggles to negotiate its obscurities, which replicate those of its world."[48] Yearsley uses the sublime and sensibility to reimagine her subjectivity outside of class prejudice, representing her own subjectivity as impervious to the gaze of her "superiors." Her purblind accusers suffer from high-flying arrogance:[49]

> You, who thro' optics dim, so falsely view
> This wond'rous maze of things, and rend a part
> From the well-order'd whole, to fit your sense
> Low, groveling, and confin'd; say from what source
> Spring your all-wise opinions? Can you dare
> Pronounce from proof, who ne'er pursu'd event
> To its minutest cause? Yet farther soar,
> In swift gradation, to the verge of space;
> Where, wrapt in worlds, Time's origin exists:
> There breathe your question; there the cause explore,
> Why dark afflictions, borne upon the wing
> Of Love invisible, light on the wretch
> Inured and patient in the pangs of woe?
>
> (1–13)

Yearsley has figured her accusers as attempting a sublime position in the landscape, an elevated position from which they can discern her soul and know the true cause of things. And yet their sense is "low" and "groveling" as they fail at not only the sublime but sensibility. Indulging in a kind of satanic self-transport through the cosmos, Yearsley's accusers can not know her intentions or situation, which is the genuine obscure.

She cleverly uses the trope of elevation to show her accusers' false transcendence, signaling their class superiority, presumption, and littleness of soul. Their elevation makes them the least capable of judging Yearsley. She addresses them as "incapacious souls" who attempt to "confine, within your narrow orbs, / Th'extensive All" (17–19). In their false sublime, one that lacks sensibility, Yearsley eggs them on:

> Fantastic group!
> Spread wide your arms, and turn yon flaming Sun
> From his most fair direction; dash the stars
> With Earth's poor pebbles, and ask the World's great Sire,
> Why, in Creation's system, He dare fix
> More orbs than your weak sense shall e'er discern?
> Then scan the feelings of Lactilla's soul.
>
> (42–48)

Figuring herself as an object and subject of sensibility in the poem's conclusion, Yearsley asserts the sublime obscurity of her "soul" in an interiorized subjectivity that preserves the self while refusing to represent it. Yearsley's version of the sublime is neither the canonical transcendent self nor the self in dissolution, as seen in Seward's poetry. It is, rather, a version that articulates the subject within a class structure and relates this to the hierarchical aesthetics of the canonical sublime. The threat in this poem is neither Nature nor a vaguely referenced psychological trauma; it is society's persistence in seeing her as a milkwoman and not as an artist.

From what Moira Ferguson has described as a "complex vantage point," Yearsley comes to articulate in her poetry the notion of "social love"—a social and metaphysical perspective that resolves many of the tensions between sensibility and the sublime that inform her art in "To Those Who Accuse."[50] Yearsley's "Remonstrance in the Platonic Shade, Flourishing on an Height"

(1796) expands issues of the suffering soul to social and cosmic domains. Matters of rank and hierarchy seem irrelevant to spiritual and intellectual development in a poem that shows her departure from orthodox religion.[51] The speaker describes herself in a spiritual and intellectual space *despite* her chains. The Platonic spirit, the "purest spirit" (1), melts away her despair. Typical of the sentimental sublime, she does not specify the origins of her suffering:[52]

> In this sacred shade,
> Whilst cruel duty fetter'd every sense,
> I saw my morning sun ascend with tears,
> And sink at eve with heaviness; the night
> Came burthen'd with despair; yet unsubdued,
> I frown'd indignant on my chains, and tun'd
> My rural lay to universal love.
>
> (6–12)

The poet expresses a refinement of being that she achieves as she sings in her chains. This "expansive confinement" is brought out by her wonderfully ambivalent syntax. "I saw my morning sun ascend with tears" can refer to the speaker's tears through which she views the sun as well as a more startling image of the personified sun weeping. Similarly, both she and the sun may "sink at eve with heaviness." Yearsley forges the speaker's cosmic connections that depend on her own sensibility with an imaginative power that feels for Nature personified when the night comes "burthen'd with despair." Assisted by "sober contemplation" (42), the speaker asserts her capacity for social love precisely as she suffers. In this love where cosmic perspective transcends worldly contamination of spirit, reason and passion join (two elements at odds in the sublime), and "Love breathes corrected sentiment" (44).

Yearsley soars "to the farthest bound / My sense of words can bear" (65–66), where she reflects on the hazards she has survived:

> have I not climb'd an height
> So frightful, e'en from comfort so remote,
> That had my judgment reel'd, my foot forgot
> Its strenuous print, my inexperienced eye
> The wondrous point in view; or my firm soul,

> Made early stubborn, her exalted pride,
> Though of external poor; the stagnant lake
> Of vice beneath, than Cocytus more foul,
> Had oped its wave to swallow me, and hide
> My frame for ever.
>
> (68–77)

For the speaker, this sublime precipice is the very edge of language—the obscure that language can never articulate. It takes her to a region of moral, physical, and spiritual danger. From this terrifying height, the speaker is not concerned with the survival of self but with the depths of suffering on historical, social, and spiritual levels: she sees "the turf / That covers long descended kingdoms" (105–6), hears "The tyger roar, where tyrants scourg'd mankind" (107), and "learn[s] the hymn / Sweet Philomel sings to the warriors shade" (109–10).

And yet Yearsley blends social love with an elitism that recalls her position in "To Those Who Accuse." Gazing back at the crowd who would make her the object of their gaze, the speaker describes

> yon motley crowd
> Who eye me through a medium all their own.—
> I like them not, their pageantry contemn—
> They know not to communicate delight—
> But square my compass with a mimic skill.
>
> (113–16)

This tension is part of the poet's ongoing attempt to balance a reverence for the self with a reverence for society, as she seeks to balance the sublime with social love—"to revere / Myself, adore in solitude," and "perform / More social duties" (126–28). In the Platonic shade, Yearsley places Love within the sublime landscape. As in other poems of the sentimental sublime, the speaker in "Remonstrance in the Platonic Shade" does not once and for all conquer affliction, but the "Platonic shade" serves as a domain of intellectual and spiritual meaning. Yearsley's experience of the sublime, with its topoi of obscurity and the inexpressible, in the words of Tim Burke, "becomes a precondition for achieving higher, idealized planes of conception in which she might at once preserve her silent interiority."[53] Not surprisingly, Yearsley's version of the sublime resembles that described by critics in the Platonic tradition, such as Shaftesbury, who "stress the oneness of the human and the divine. The numinous for them is not 'wholly other,' but rather the divine in man freed of all limits and therefore released into the infinite and eternal."[54] For Shaftesbury and for Yearsley in this poem, "the sublime is a moment both of a supreme self-realization and of rhapsodic oneness with a divine ordering power in the world at large."[55]

The sentimental sublime makes it widest and deepest claims in antislavery literature: here sensibility attempts to imagine the greatest human suffering while elements of the sublime make issues of equality and freedom part of moral and aesthetic imperatives. In Helen Maria Williams's "On the Bill Which Was Passed in England for Regulating the Slave-Trade; A Short Time before Its Abolition" (1788), the poet distinguishes between the fanciful sublime and the sublime based on real horror: this sublime confronts the sufferings of those treated most inhumanly. In articulating the horror of what slaves endure, Williams begins her poem with the disappearance of the conventional features of a sublime landscape—"the hollow winds of night" heard by Fancy (1)—and instead introduces the sensory deprivations of the slaves chained on the ship as it leaves the African shore:[56]

> The groan of agony severe
> From yon dark vessel, which contains
> The wretch new bound in hopeless chains!
> Whose soul with keener anguish bleeds,
> As Afric's less'ning shore recedes....
> (4–8)

At the poem's close, Williams returns to the distinction between the art of fancy and that of reality—a sublime that attends to social suffering:

> Fancy may dress in deeper shade
> The storm that hangs along the glade;
> Spreads o'er the ruffled stream its wing,
> And chills awhile the flowers of spring;
> But where the wint'ry tempests sweep
> In madness o'er the darken'd deep,—
> Where the wild surge, the raging wave,
> Point to the hopeless wretch a grave;
> And death surrounds the threat'ning shore—
> Can fancy add one horror more?
> (261–70)

In Williams's comparison, the imagination can indeed augment the harshness of Nature in more traditional images of the sublime ("The storm that hangs along the glade"), but the imaginative work required by the sublime horror of slavery depends on developing a social sensibility to justly represent and understand this suffering.

V

Recent critics, among them John G. Pipkin, Laura Runge, and Barbara Claire Freeman, have analyzed the gendered structure of the sublime as defined by Burke and Kant: the male subject confronts and conquers an obscure, threatening "feminine" element. According to Lucinda Cole and Richard G. Swartz, by the end of the century a writer's engagement with the sublime establishes his or her status in the "market of official aesthetic and literary discourse."[57] Barbara Claire Freeman describes the sublime as a misogynistic process in which the female imagination must be sacrificed to male reason.[58] Pipkin has described the "set of rhetorical maneuvers concurrently establishing the sublime as a tropological and phenomenological index of masculinity while representing female experiences and articulations of sublimity as 'unnatural.'"[59] Peter de Bolla argues that "the discourse [on the sublime] produces the subject, and produces it in gender differentiated terms."[60]

And yet in the sentimental sublime, we do not find such a gendered structure of authority. Rather, it seems to dispense with a heterosexual dialectic of conquest and submission. The sentimental sublime yokes what the culture identifies as a "feminine" capacity for acute delicacy and compassion with the experience of the conventionally feminized virtue in distress. That is, feminine virtue-in-distress is embraced as the subject's own nature in the sentimental sublime. These poets thus explore what would be the object of representation in the culture of sensibility, but they do so within a context of sublime transport. Ultimately they may achieve a horizontal rather than vertical transport—not rising to a privileged or rarified realm but moving toward another (kind of) being. This articulation of subject and object corresponds to what de Bolla has described as amorphous notions of the self in midcentury accounts that "resist" the notion of a "uni-

5 / THE NIGHTINGALE'S BREAST AGAINST THE THORN 165

fied subject."[61] "The sublime is an order of representation," he suggests, that disturbs representations of the self.[62] As we have seen, poetic versions that both articulate and dissolve what we would now call a "unified subject" (and its myth) were explored in the seventeenth century by Philips and Behn, among others.[63]

Practiced by women poets in the long eighteenth century and by men poets especially in the second half of the eighteenth century, the sentimental sublime should not be confused with what some critics have called the feminine sublime.[64] For example, in Mellor's notion of the feminine sublime in the Romantic era, women writers represent nature in a manner characterized by their deep identification with the natural world.[65] My study of men and women poets of the eighteenth century, however, problematizes the category of Nature (see chapters 3 and 4) and explores a range of different kinds of identification. Critiquing the feminine sublime as described by Mellor and Freeman, Pipkin rightly observes that these theories are "unable to account for the ambivalent responses to nature's power" seen in many poems by women.[66]

In the sentimental sublime we approach the dissolving of the gendered structure of representation. Because the sublime inevitably participates in what de Bolla calls the "ethical protocols of self," dissolving this gendered structure is, I would argue, an ethical achievement that invites us to inhabit on an aesthetic level an unfamiliar subject position.[67] The sentimental can engage an ethical dimension: "precisely in the notion of moral sentiments... the ethical and aesthetic can be brought together."[68] In de Bolla's argument for a radical reexamination of the link between aesthetics and ethics, he observes that the eighteenth-century sublime continued in the political and economic theories of the mid-nineteenth century that explored relations among ethics, aesthetics, and rhetoric.[69]

Recently, John Guillory has argued that reading itself "belongs to the field of the ethical because it is a practice on the self, and because the motive of pleasure in reading contains within it the potentiality for what was known in the early modern period as 'self-improvement.'"[70] This notion of self-improvement informs Charles Altieri's analysis of literary pleasure and ethics: "in our basic practices of reading 'Literature' we respond to an invitation to explore the degree to which texts can offer states of mind so powerful and distinctive that we understand what it would mean to identify fully with them."[71] Literature, Altieri contends, requires that we are willing to experience "modes of agency and consciousness capable of making demands on how we forge identifications" that in turn shape our subjectivity.[72] These literary demands may be made in many ways, but most fundamental is the challenge of the unfamiliar, what another critic has located as the key to literary invention. This invention, according to Derek Attridge, "is a creative handling of language whereby otherness, or alterity, is brought into, or manifested within, a particular cultural field. Otherness is that which is, at a given historical moment, outside the framework provided by the culture for thinking, imagining, feeling, perceiving. . . . It is often through the old that the quality of otherness makes itself felt in an invention."[73] Literary invention "both *brings alterity into being*, into the realm of the knowable, and at the same time *is produced by alterity*."[74]

I would propose that the ongoing neglect of certain kinds of eighteenth-century poetry is due not to its aesthetic weakness (what previous generations have described as its effeminacy) but rather to its innovations—aesthetic and ethical—in representing subjectivity. Indeed, the poet's conscious self-restraint in representing the other can testify to the poet's ethos: she understands the insufficiencies of language and acknowledges the alterity beyond her. This "effeminate" poetry by women *and* men, where poetical character becomes defined as "feminine," challenges the reader to inhabit subject positions where the self improves by means of sympathy rather than conquest. In some of the most neglected poetry of the British tradition, the reader is invited to cognitive and imaginative exercises that reorder emotional, ethical, and social relations to the other.

Notes

Introduction

1. Several studies have focused almost exclusively on women poets, such as Donna Landry, *The Muses of Resistance: Laboring-Class Women's Poetry in Britain, 1739–1796* (Cambridge: Cambridge University Press, 1990); Moira Ferguson, *Eighteenth-Century Woman Poets: Nation, Class, and Gender* (Albany: State University of New York Press, 1995); Carol Barash, *English Women's Poetry, 1649–1714: Politics, Community, and Linguistic Authority* (Oxford: Clarendon Press, 1996); *Women's Poetry in the Enlightenment: The Making of a Canon, 1730–1820*, ed. Isobel Armstrong and Virginia Blain (Houndmills: Macmillan, 1999); and *Women and Poetry, 1660–1750*, ed. Sarah Prescott and David E. Shuttleton (Houndmills: Palgrave, 2003). Some analyses of gender in eighteenth-century poetry include Laura Mandell, *Misogynous Economies: The Business of Literature in Eighteenth-Century Britain* (Lexington: University Press of Kentucky, 1999); and Linda Zionkowski, *Men's Work: Gender, Class, and the Professionalization of Poetry, 1660–1784* (New York: Palgrave, 2001). Women and men poets are brought together in *Pope, Swift, and Women Writers*, ed. Donald C. Mell (Newark: University of Delaware Press, 1996); and Claudia N. Thomas, *Alexander Pope and His Eighteenth-Century Women Readers* (Carbondale: Southern Illinois University Press, 1994). Anthologies of women poets in this period include *Kissing the Rod: An Anthology of Seventeenth-Century Women's Verse*, ed. Germaine Greer, Susan Hastings, Jeslyn Medoff, and Melinda Sansone (New York: Farrar Straus Giroux, 1988); *Eighteenth-Century Women Poets: An Oxford Anthology*, ed. and intro. Roger Lonsdale (Oxford: Oxford University Press, 1989); and *British Women Poets, 1660–1800: An Anthology*, ed. and intro. Joyce Fullard (Troy, NY: Whitston, 1990).

2. Charles H. Hinnant, *The Poetry of Anne Finch: An Essay in Interpretation* (Newark: University of Delaware Press, 1994), 14.

3. David Fairer, *English Poetry of the Eighteenth Century, 1700–1789* (London: Longman, 2003).

4. Much excellent work has been done on this topic, including Mark Rose, *Authors and Owners: The Invention of Copyright* (Cambridge, MA: Harvard University Press, 1993); Kathryn Shevelow, *Women and Print Culture: The Construction of Femininity in the Early Periodical* (London: Routledge, 1989); and Martha Woodmansee, *The Author, Art, and the Market: Rereading the His-*

tory of Aesthetics (New York: Columbia University Press, 1994). On women's work in literary production see Paula McDowell, *The Women of Grub Street: Press, Politics, and Gender in the London Literary Marketplace, 1678–1730* (Oxford: Clarendon Press, 1998). See also Lisa Maruca, "Political Propriety and Feminine Property: Women in the Eighteenth-Century Text Trades," *Studies in the Literary Imagination* 34, no. 1 (Spring 2001): 79–99.

5. Sandra M. Gilbert and Susan Gubar, *The Madwoman in the Attic: The Woman Writer and the Nineteenth-Century Literary Imagination* (New Haven: Yale University Press, 1979), 51.

6. Some of my characterizations of women's poetry may recall discussions of Swift's. On Swift's exposure of poetic conventions, see Nora Crow Jaffe, *The Poet Swift* (Hanover, NH: University Press of New England, 1977), 34.

7. Thomas, *Alexander Pope and His Eighteenth-Century Women Readers*, 244.

8. On the traditional gendering of Nature as feminine, see Sherry B. Ortner, "Is Female to Male as Nature Is to Culture?," in *Woman, Culture, and Society*, ed. Michelle Zimbalist Rosaldo and Louise Lamphere (Stanford, CA: Stanford University Press, 1974), 67–88; Carolyn Merchant, *The Death of Nature: Women, Ecology, and the Scientific Revolution* (New York: Harper and Row, 1983); Kate Soper, *What is Nature? Culture, Politics and the Non-human* (Oxford: Blackwell, 1995).

9. See, for example, Londa Schiebinger, *Nature's Body: Gender in the Making of Modern Science* (Boston: Beacon Press, 1993); Christine Battersby, *Gender and Genius: Towards a Feminist Aesthetics* (Bloomington: Indiana University Press, 1989); and Carole Fabricant, "Binding and Dressing Nature's Loose Tresses: The Ideology of Augustan Landscape Design," in *Studies in Eighteenth-Century Culture*, vol. 8, ed. Roseann Runte (Madison: University of Wisconsin Press, 1979), 109–35.

10. Arne Melberg, *Theories of Mimesis* (Cambridge: Cambridge University Press, 1995), 3.

11. Raymond Williams, "Nature," in *Keywords: A Vocabulary of Culture and Society*, rev. ed. (New York: Oxford University Press, 1983), 219.

12. Arthur O. Lovejoy, "Nature as Aesthetic Norm," in *Essays in the History of Ideas* (Baltimore: Johns Hopkins University Press, 1948), 69–77.

13. Ibid., 72.

14. See Susan J. Wolfson, "Reading for Form," *Modern Language Quarterly* 61, no. 1 (March 2000): 6.

15. Laura Mandell persuasively argues that developing qualitative distinctions among "cultural artifacts can in fact disrupt a misogyny latent in critical approaches to cultural artifacts that do not distinguish good from bad literature" (*Misogynous Economies*, 11).

16. See Wolfson on how formal elements participate in "networks of social and historical conditions" ("Reading for Form," 7).

17. See especially John Sitter, *Literary Loneliness in Mid-Eighteenth-Century England* (Ithaca: Cornell University Press, 1982); Northrop Frye, "Towards Defining an Age of Sensibility," in *Eighteenth-Century English Literature: Modern Essays in Criticism*, ed. James L. Clifford (New York: Oxford University Press, 1959), 311–18; and Marshall Brown, *Preromanticism* (Stanford, CA: Stanford University Press, 1991).

18. See Dustin Griffin, *Patriotism and Poetry in Eighteenth–Century Britain* (Cambridge: Cambridge University Press, 2002).

19. The efficacy of these self-authorizing strategies parallels what Jerome J. McGann has described in Romantic studies as the force of romantic ideology. See his *The Romantic Ideology: A Critical Investigation* (Chicago: University of Chicago Press, 1983). In the early 1990s, John Bender drew attention to an "eighteenth-century ideology" that reiterated Enlightenment assumptions ("A New History of the Enlightenment?," in *The Profession of Eighteenth-Century Literature: Reflections on an Institution,* ed. Leo Damrosch [Madison: University of Wisconsin Press, 1992], 63).

20. See, for example, Helen Deutsch, *Resemblance & Disgrace: Alexander Pope and the Deformation of Culture* (Cambridge, MA: Harvard University Press, 1996); and Robert Gleckner, *Gray Agonistes: Thomas Gray and Masculine Friendship* (Baltimore: Johns Hopkins University Press, 1997).

21. Eric Rothstein, *Restoration and Eighteenth-Century Poetry, 1660–1780* (Boston: Routledge & Kegan Paul, 1981), xiii.

22. Margaret Anne Doody, *The Daring Muse: Augustan Poetry Reconsidered* (Cambridge: Cambridge University Press, 1985), 264. For her insightful analysis of women poets' approaches to the senses, see Doody, "Sensuousness in the Poetry of Eighteenth-Century Women Poets," in *Women's Poetry in the Enlightenment,* ed. Isobel Armstrong and Virginia Blain (Houndmills: Macmillan, 1999), 3–32. See also, Doody, "Women Poets of the Eighteenth Century," in *Women and Literature in Britain, 1700–1800,* ed. Viven Jones (Cambridge: Cambridge University Press, 2000).

23. Doody, *Daring Muse*, 123.

24. Cf. David G. Riede's discussion of Romantic writers' attention to questions of authority, the functions of form, and the possibilities and ethics of representation (*Oracles and Hierophants: Constructions of Romantic Authority* [Ithaca: Cornell University Press, 1991], 3).

25. On the increasing numbers of women poets, see Marlon Ross, *The Contours of Masculine Desire: Romanticism and the Rise of Women's Poetry* (New York: Oxford University Press, 1989), 3. Although Ross and others have analyzed the influence of women poets on the Romantic canon, few studies have addressed the influence of women poets on the eighteenth-century canon and the consequent changes to literary history and periodization. One of the exceptions is Richard Greene, *Mary Leapor: A Study in Eighteenth-Century Women's Poetry* (New York: Oxford University Press, 1993). On the revaluation of Romantic poetry, see, among others, Stuart Curran, "Romantic Poetry: The I Altered," in *Romanticism and Feminism,* ed. Anne K. Mellor (Bloomington: Indiana University Press, 1988), 185–207; Marlon Ross, *The Contours of Masculine Desire*; and Anne K. Mellor, *Romanticism and Gender* (New York: Routledge, 1993). See Sandra Gilbert and Susan Gubar on redrawing literary historical lines in "'But Oh! That Deep Romantic Chasm': The Engendering of Periodization," *The Kenyon Review* 13, no. 3 (Summer 1991): 74–81.

26. Laura Brown, "The Feminization of Ideology: Form and the Female in the Long Eighteenth Century," in *Ideology and Form in Eighteenth-Century Literature,* ed. David Richter (Lubbock: Texas Tech University Press, 1999), 231.

27. Here I differ with Blanford Parker's emphasis on the degree of empiricism in Augustan poetry (*The Triumph of Augustan Poetics: English Literary*

Culture from Butler to Johnson [Cambridge: Cambridge University Press, 1998]). Although I agree with his insightful argument that Augustan mimesis is "no longer circumscribed by the old binarisms of spiritual analogy against iconoclasm, or fideist against visionary poetics" (10), the use of feminine figures muddies the new empirical poetics. Certainly there is an increased attention to empirical observation, as Parker describes it, but this empiricism often depends on mythological and figurative systems as I will demonstrate in the following chapters. At their core, these systems adopt values of the feminine that reflect cultural constructs but are used to justify the "reality" of other observations.

28. Discussing the implications of Horkheimer and Adorno's work on the Enlightenment, Anthony J. Cascardi argues that myth continued to be a fundamental part of Enlightenment thinking (*Consequences of Enlightenment* [Cambridge: Cambridge University Press, 1999], 27, 31).

29. Mary Poovey, "Aesthetics and Political Economy in the Eighteenth Century: The Place of Gender in the Social Constitution of Knowledge," in *Aesthetics and Ideology*, ed. George Levine (New Brunswick, NJ: Rutgers University Press, 1994), 79–105; 89–90.

30. Roger Lonsdale, *Eighteenth-Century Women Poets: An Oxford Anthology* (Oxford: Oxford University Press, 1989), xl–xli. Citing Lonsdale's analysis, Donna Landry asserts that what "we now label 'Romanticism' was itself also a struggle in which gender ideology and competition between women and men in the literary marketplace were crucial" ("The Traffic in Women Poets," *The Eighteenth Century: Theory and Interpretation* 32 [1991]: 184).

31. Battersby, *Gender and Genius*, 3. Ann Bermingham has analyzed the fluid migration of what the era labeled *masculine* and *feminine* to labels that would devalue women as producers of culture ("Elegant Females and Gentlemen Connoisseurs: The Commerce in Culture and Self-Image in Eighteenth-Century England," in *The Consumption of Culture, 1600–1800,* ed. Ann Bermingham and John Brewer [London: Routledge, 1995], 492.

32. Shevelow, *Women and Print Culture*, 1.

33. McDowell, *Women of Grub Street*, 6.

34. See Laura L. Runge, *Gender and Language in British Literary Criticism, 1660–1790* (Cambridge: Cambridge University Press, 1997).

35. Walter Jackson Bate has described the increasing attention to the "conception of taste as non-rational," signaled by "the phrase, *je ne sais quoi*, a phrase which was given particular currency by the *Précieuses*, and which became a modish expression in both France and England by the close of the century." The word "taste" was often "synonymous with a subjective *je ne sais quoi* sentiment until almost the middle of the eighteenth century. No one denied the existence of such a sentiment" (*From Classic to Romantic: Premises of Taste in Eighteenth-Century England* [1946; repr., New York: Harper, 1961], 44). See also Robert W. Jones, *Gender and the Formation of Taste in Eighteenth-Century Britain: The Analysis of Beauty* (Cambridge: Cambridge University Press, 1998).

36. Ellen Pollak discusses the shifts in "modern strategies for conceptualizing women," including "patriarchal notions of divine-right monarchy" being supplanted by benevolism and empiricist philosophy that "evolved to accommodate the ongoing subordination of women to men in social, political, eco-

nomic, intellectual, and domestic life" (*The Poetics of Sexual Myth: Gender and Ideology in the Verse of Swift and Pope* [Chicago: University of Chicago Press, 1985], 2).

37. The conflation of poetic and social roles for the feminine appears in the era's literary marketplace. In her introduction to *Kissing the Rod*, Germaine Greer observes the conflation of romance literary conventions and gender relations in the late seventeenth-century literary marketplace, particularly as managed by John Dunton, editor of *The Athenian Mercury* (27–28).

38. John L. Mahoney, *The Whole Internal Universe: Imitation and the New Defense of Poetry in British Criticism, 1660–1830* (New York: Fordham University Press, 1985), 32.

39. The terms are those of John L. Mahoney, *Whole Internal Universe*, 32.

40. Frederick Burwick, *Mimesis and Its Romantic Reflections* (University Park: Pennsylvania State University Press, 2001), 10–11.

41. John Barrell, *English Literature in History, 1730–80: An Equal, Wide Survey* (New York: St. Martin's Press, 1983).

42. Judith Butler, *Bodies that Matter: On the Discursive Limits of "Sex"* (New York: Routledge, 1993), 3.

43. Cf. Mandell, *Misogynous Economies*, 110.

44. Zionkowski, *Men's Work*, 5.

45. Ibid., 10.

46. The instability of these terms has, of course, received repeated attention in theories of the subject.

47. Ellen Rooney, "Form and Contentment," *Modern Language Quarterly* 61, no. 1 (2000): 38–39.

48. Quoted in Heather Dubrow, "Guess Who's Coming to Dinner? Reinterpreting Formalism and the Country House Poem," *Modern Language Quarterly* 61, no. 1 (2000): 63.

49. See Ernst Cassirer, *The Philosophy of the Enlightenment*, trans. Fritz C. A. Koelln and James P. Pettegrove (1951; repr. Princeton: Princeton University Press, 1979). Cassirer describes the new view of nature that was developing even in the Renaissance and that culminated in the Enlightenment: Nature becomes an "original formative principle which moves from within. Through its capacity to unfold and take on form from within itself, nature bears the stamp of the divine" (40–41).

50. See M. H. Abrams on personification as the figure of imagination in eighteenth-century poetics in *The Mirror and the Lamp: Romantic Theory and the Critical Tradition* (New York: Oxford University Press, 1953), 288–89. Among the best discussions of personification in eighteenth-century poetry are those by Bertrand H. Bronson and Earl R. Wasserman. See Bronson, "Personification Reconsidered," *ELH: A Journal of English Literary History* 14 (September 1947): 163–77; and Wasserman, "The Inherent Values of Eighteenth-Century Personification," *PMLA* 65, part 2 (1950): 435–63. See also Clifford Siskin, "Personification and Community: Literary Change in the Mid- and Late- Eighteenth Century," *Eighteenth-Century Studies* 15, no. 4 (Summer 1982): 371–401; James J. Paxson, *The Poetics of Personification* (Cambridge: Cambridge University Press, 1994); and Jonathan Culler, "Apostrophe," *Diacritics* 7, no. 4 (1977): 59–69.

51. Lawrence Lipking describes the heightened capacity of early modern and eighteenth-century readers to respond to personifications: "the animism and anthropomorphism that a modern mythographer might attribute to ancient religions, an eighteenth-century reader took as the natural province of poets" ("The Gods of Poetry: Mythology and the Eighteenth-Century Tradition," in *Augustan Subjects: Essays in Honor of Martin C. Battestin*, ed. Albert J. Rivero [Newark: University of Delaware Press, 1997], 76–77).

52. Diana Fuss, *Identification Papers* (New York: Routledge, 1995), 2.

53. Ibid., 4, 9.

54. Consider Terry Eagleton's discussion of aesthetics as a "hybrid form of cognition which can clarify the raw stuff of perception and historical practices disclosing the inner structure of the concrete" (9). See his *The Ideology of the Aesthetic* (Oxford: Basil Blackwell, 1990), especially chapter 1, "Free Particulars," 13–30.

55. David B. Morris, *The Religious Sublime: Christian Poetry and Critical Tradition in Eighteenth-Century England* (Lexington: University Press of Kentucky, 1972).

56. Hugh Blair, *Lectures on Rhetoric and Belles Lettres*, vol. 1, ed. Harold F. Harding (Carbondale: Southern Illinois University Press, 1965), 52, 53, 54.

57. Bate, *From Classic to Romantic*, 133.

58. For Marlon Ross the gender identity of a Romantic poet is crucial: "Romantic poeticizing is not just what women cannot do because they are not expected to; it is also what some men do in order to reconfirm their capacity to influence the world in ways sociohistorically determined as masculine" (*The Contours of Masculine Desire*, 3). Margaret Doody has discussed the marked self-consciousness of Augustan canonical poets seen in their frequent references to their roles: "the visual icons used to illustrate the poet's role in the period, such as portrait frontispieces to collected works" are just one example of this self-conciousness (*Daring Muse*, 20). On Pope's consciousness of his physical deformity and its relation to his poetry see Helen Deutsch, *Resemblance & Disgrace*.

59. A word on one of the many topics I have had to leave out: satire. Although there are certainly satirical elements in many of the poems discussed in the chapters that follow, I have intentionally omitted discussing satirical poetry as a category. The importance of satire to this era requires an explanation of my omission. Much of what I analyze in the use of the muse, the landscape, and personification as well as the modes of sensibility and the sublime may be carried over, mutatis mutandis, to analyzing works such as Dryden's *MacFlecknoe*, Pope's *Dunciad*, or Swift's numerous satirical poems. But the categories of history and politics that have long driven definitions of satire in this era, more so than in defining other poetic modes and kinds, require fundamental reassessment when handled by women writers. That is a separate study in progress.

60. On the canonization and marginalization of women poets in the eighteenth century, see Richard Terry, *Poetry and the Making of the English Literary Past, 1660–1781* (Oxford: Oxford University Press, 2001). Terry describes what by the end of the eighteenth century is women poets' "enshrinement within a gender-specific canon, a canon seen as distinct, and dispensable, from the literary tradition constituted by the most celebrated male authors" (277).

61. Margaret J. M. Ezell, *Writing Women's Literary History* (Baltimore: Johns Hopkins University Press, 1993), 55. On the circulation of women's poetry, see especially Margaret J. M. Ezell, "The Posthumous Publication of Women's Manuscripts and the History of Authorship"; Kathryn R. King, "Elizabeth Singer Rowe's Tactical Use of Print and Manuscript"; and Isobel Grundy, "Lady Mary Wortley Montagu and Her Daughter: The Changing Use of Manuscripts"—all in *Women's Writing and the Circulation of Ideas: Manuscript Publication in England, 1500–1800*, ed. George L. Justice and Nathan Tinker (Cambridge: Cambridge University Press, 2002).

Chapter 1. Dryden, Pope, and the Transformation of the Muse

1. Mark Conroy, *Modernism and Authority: Strategies of Legitimation in Flaubert and Conrad* (Baltimore: Johns Hopkins University Press, 1985), 9.

2. Ernst Curtius, *European Literature and the Latin Middle Ages* (New York: Pantheon, 1953), 228.

3. Anthony, Earl of Shaftesbury, *Characteristics of Men, Manners, Opinions, Times*, ed. and notes John M. Robertson, intro. Stanley Grean, vols. 1 and 2 (Indianapolis: Bobbs-Merrill, 1964), 5, 6, 7. Shaftesbury understood the muse's role as a source of inspiration, as an object of seduction and representation, and as a figure of the reader. In his "Letter concerning Enthusiasm," addressed to Lord Sommers, Shaftesbury places the receiver of his epistle "in default of a muse" when he recounts his difficulty in composing (*Characteristics*, 1.8–9). As an author, he must search for a great man to replace the mythical muse, whose function in addition to inspiration is to provide—much more than the muse can—a companionable "presence," a community of "intimacy and freedom." That Shaftesbury defines this community in complete neglect of the burgeoning public literary marketplace makes its figurative function all the more compelling. In a strategy typical of the early eighteenth-century epistolary mode, he has replaced the sexual dynamic of artistic inspiration—the male poet's courtship of a female muse—with a relation between men that enjoys the intimacy and seduction of elite coterie poetry.

4. Clifford Siskin, "Personification and Community," 378.

5. Donald Wesling, whose definition of Augustan poetry derives chiefly from Pope, goes so far as to describe Augustan form as syntactically and mimetically authoritarian: its syntax mirrors its authoritative assumption of a universal man and a universal taste that authorizes the standards of great poetry (398). Wesling cites William Bowman Piper's analysis of the metrical form most associated with canonical Augustan poetry—the heroic couplet that aims for "supreme representational authority." See Wesling, "Augustan Form: Justification and Breakup of a Period Style," *Texas Studies in Literature and Language* 22, no. 3 (Fall 1980): 394–428. (The quotation is from William Bowman Piper, *The Heroic Couplet* [Cleveland: Case Western Reserve University Press, 1969], 435; qtd. in Wesling, 398.)

6. Steven N. Zwicker, *Lines of Authority: Politics and English Literary Culture, 1649–1689* (Ithaca: Cornell University Press, 1993), 30.

NOTES TO CHAPTER 1

7. In Howard D. Weinbrot, *Augustus Caesar in "Augustan" England: The Decline of a Classical Norm* (Princeton: Princeton University Press, 1978), however, Weinbrot provides numerous examples of Restoration and eighteenth-century writers' "rejection of Augustus" (9). In his discussion of Dryden and the label "Augustan," Maximillian E. Novak finds the term appropriate to Dryden's poetry not necessarily as it supports the political and cultural model of the Roman era, but as the poetry is responding to both the strengths and weaknesses of the Roman precedent ("Shaping the Augustan Myth: John Dryden and the Politics of Restoration Augustanism," in *Greene Centennial Studies: Essays Presented to Donald Greene in the Centennial Year of the University of Southern California*, ed. Paul J. Korshin and Robert R. Allen [Charlottesville: University Press of Virginia, 1984], 1–21, 19–20). Howard Erskine-Hill makes a similar point in *The Augustan Idea in English Literature* (London: E. Arnold, 1983), 232–33.

8. On the importance of poets in seventeenth-century politics see Zwicker, *Lines of Authority*, 15–16.

9. Doody, *Daring Muse*, chapter 1.

10. See Penelope Wilson, "Engendering the Reader: 'Wit and Poetry and Pope' Once More" In *The Enduring Legacy: Alexander Pope Tercentenary Essays*, ed. G. S. Rousseau and Pat Rogers (Cambridge: Cambridge University Press, 1988), 65.

11. See John Guillory's analysis of the complexity of poetic authority, particularly its lack of an explicitly persuasive goal, in *Poetic Authority: Spenser, Milton, and Literary History* (New York: Columbia University Press, 1983), ix.

12. "All linguistic activity . . . must have these two rhetorical poles: of usurpation and of the attempt to rectify or 'make good' that usurpation" (Conroy, *Modernism and Authority*, 6).

13. See Lipking, "Gods of Poetry," 68–86. See also Sanford Budick, *Poetry of Civilization: Mythopoeic Displacement in the Verse of Milton, Dryden, Pope, and Johnson* (New Haven: Yale University Press, 1974); Paul J. Korshin, *Typologies in England 1650–1820* (Princeton: Princeton University Press, 1982); and Leonard Barkan, *The Gods Made Flesh: Metamorphosis and the Pursuit of Paganism* (New Haven: Yale University Press, 1986).

14. Lipking, "Gods of Poetry," 72.

15. Gender could be used to deal with this problem: (1) gendered categories appeared to be outside of the politics of poetic authority and (2) these inscriptions of the feminine worked to exclude one sector of the madding crowd from a position to represent rather than be represented: women poets.

16. Harold Bloom, *The Anxiety of Influence: A Theory of Poetry* (New York: Oxford University Press, 1973), 37, 61. Bloom's attention to the sexually charged muse-poet relationship is based on his study of Romantic poets, where Bloom seems to have accepted as true the myths, or Romantic ideology, those poets used to construct their authority.

17. "The expanded reading public also included many women, who constitute virtually a separate category in readership statistics because there is historically a much less definite correlation between social class and education, reading habits, and even literacy for women than for men" (Shevelow, *Women and Print Culture*, 27).

18. Such "demotic elitism" is seen in the period's rage for compendia—blending the elitism of rationalism with the generous availability of empiricism and the desire to disseminate such information. The poetry shares this compendious urge, an urge that Bonamy Dobrée has argued can satisfy the role of epic for a culture. "The poetry from about 1720," he argues, "took all knowledge for its province and attempted a synthesis" (*English Literature in the Early Eighteenth Century, 1700–1740* [Oxford: Clarendon Press, 1959], 475). Doody relates Augustan themes and styles to the era's imperialism (17–18): Augustans "amplify the spaces poetry could cover" (*Daring Muse*, 24).

19. Zwicker, *Lines of Authority*, 26. In his preface to Gondibert, for example, Davenant attempts to replace inspiration with wit: "this is a major piece of aesthetic legislation, and it is eagerly taken up by Hobbes" (22–23).

20. Ibid., 23, 29.

21. Ibid.

22. The volume, argues Zwicker, "reinforces the royalist poetics of wit. . . . Those who celebrated monarchy were not willing to allow the politics of the saints to exclude them from the precincts of sacred authority" (ibid., 29). The resulting sublimity made a far greater impact on Cowley's literary successors in his imitations of Pindar than in his unfinished religious epic, *Davideis*.

23. See Stella P. Revard, "The Seventeenth-Century Religious Ode and Its Classical Models," in *"Bright Shootes of Everlastingnesse": The Seventeenth-Century Religious Lyric*, Essays in Seventeenth-Century Literature, vol. 2, edited by Claude J. Summers and Ted-Larry Pebworth (Columbia: University of Missouri Press, 1987). "For Cowley," argues Revard, "Pindar is a poetical and not a religious model" (189).

24. All quotations of Cowley's poetry are from *Poems: Miscellanies, The Mistress, Pindarique Odes, Davideis, Verses written on Several Occasions*, ed. A. R. Waller (Cambridge: Cambridge University Press, 1905).

25. Poetry of the religious sublime is not included among the hallmarks of Augustan literary achievement because its tone departs from that of the canonical Augustan voice of urbane conversation and public argument. The religious sublime's non-Augustan tone results from its conscious struggle with sources of inspiration, thus drawing attention to the problem of accessing and representing truth, instead of asserting unproblematic representation.

26. Milton's invocations provided a model to succeeding generations of poets, especially his invocation to light (Marjorie Hope Nicolson *Newton Demands the Muse: Newton's* Optics *and the Eighteenth-Century Poets* [Princeton: Princeton University Press, 1946], 40).

27. Although the poet suggests a sexual dimension to his relationship with the muse, the sexuality conforms to Judeo-Christian doctrine; see Noam Flinker, "Courting Urania: The Narrator of *Paradise Lost* Invokes His Muse," in *Milton and the Idea of Woman*, ed. Julia M. Walker (Urbana: University of Illinois Press, 1988), 86–99. According to John T. Shawcross, the union between man and God in *Paradise Lost* is expressed through the metaphor of sexual intercourse, a metaphor that underlies Milton's invocations ("The Metaphor of Inspiration in *Paradise Lost*," in *Th'upright Heart and Pure; Essays on John Milton Commemorating the Tercentenary of the Publication of* Paradise Lost, ed. Amadeus P. Fiore [Pittsburgh: Duquesne University Press, 1967], 75–76).

All quotations of Milton's poetry are from *Complete Poems and Major Prose*, ed. Merritt Y. Hughes (New York: Macmillan, 1957).

28. That Christian writers adopted the spiritually handicapping Muse suggests the power of the figure in the writers' imagination. Christian poets occasionally adopted a classical precedent for replacing the muse: some poets of antiquity invoked Zeus, whom Christian poets could easily replace with their Christian God (Curtius, *European Literature*, 233). See Curtius for a survey of the tradition of tension between Christian poets' pagan and Christian allegiances (228–46). According to Lily B. Campbell, Urania was assigned the territory of Christian epic in the sixteenth century ("The Christian Muse," *Huntington Library Bulletin* 8 [1935]: 36–37).

29. "Of the great epic poets in Western literature," argues Walter Schindler, "Milton seems most conscious of the imaginative possibilities inherent in the formulas of invocation and aspires most vigorously to realize them" (*Voice and Crisis: Invocation in Milton's Poetry* [Hamden, CT: Archon Books, 1984], 11).

30. The poet revisits the divine,

> now with bolder wing,
> Escap't the *Stygian* Pool, though long detain'd
> In that obscure sojourn, while in my flight
> Through utter and through middle darkness borne
> With other notes than to th' *Orphean* Lyre
> I sung of *Chaos* and *Eternal Night*,
> Taught by the heav'nly Muse to venture down
> The dark descent, and up to reascend,
> Though hard and rare: thee I revisit safe,
> And feel thy sovran vital Lamp; but thou
> Revisit'st not these eyes, that roll in vain
> To find thy piercing ray, and find no dawn....
>   (3.13–24)

31. Milton establishes his authority through his body's relation to God as light: although the poet cannot see, he feels the warmth of God's "sovran vital Lamp." The poet's body is analogous to cosmic bodies, his eyes, like lost planets, "that roll in vain / To find thy piercing ray," but this body achieves the authority of pathos in its self-proclaimed blindness.

32. Dobrée, *English Literature*, 3.

33. James Anderson Winn, *"When Beauty Fires the Blood": Love and the Arts in the Age of Dryden* (Ann Arbor: University of Michigan Press, 1992), 20.

34. Mark Van Doren, *The Poetry of John Dryden* (New York: Harcourt, Brace), 1920.

35. All quotations of Dryden's poetry are from the multivolume *Works of John Dryden* (Berkeley: University of California Press).

36. Winn, *"When Beauty Fires the Blood,"* 8.

37. Zwicker, *Lines of Authority*, 92.

38. Ibid., 92–93.

39. The poem has a "pleasant haze of scriptural sanctity that Dryden casts over sexual abundance and indiscretion" (ibid., 132).

40. Winn, *"When Beauty Fires the Blood,"* 83.

41. Ibid., 83. He quotes the relevant passage in Dryden's Virgil:

> His dauntless heart wou'd fain have held
> From weeping, but his eyes rebell'd.
> Perhaps the Godlike Hero in his breast
> Disdain'd, or was asham'd to show
> So weak, so womanish a woe,
> Which yet the Brother and the Friend so plenteously confest.
>
> (273–78)

According to Winn, seventeenth-century readers regarded classical and biblical references to homosexual affection as a "powerful and acceptable way of indicating intense friendship" (84).

42. Susan Staves suggests that "the late seventeenth century's interest in women was aroused by the usefulness of seeing women as models for men. As the culture became more a bourgeois culture of men who rejected the personal use of violence, where better to look for examples of how people manage without violence than among women?" (*Players' Scepters: Fictions of Authority in the Restoration* [Lincoln: University of Nebraska Press, 1979], 186).

43. Arthur W. Hoffman discusses Killigrew's role as muse and compares Dryden's combination of classical and Christian elements with Milton's muse in book 1 of *Paradise Lost* (*John Dryden's Imagery* [Gainesville: University of Florida Press, 1962], 122–23).

44. Consider, for example, the sing-song praise in Dryden's description of Killigrew's pastoral paintings:

> Her Pencil drew, what e're her Soul design'd,
> And oft the happy Draught surpass'd the Image in her Mind:
> The *Sylvan* Scenes of Herds and Flocks,
> And fruitful Plains and barren Rocks,
> Of shallow Brooks that flow'd so clear,
> The Bottom did the Top appear;
> Of deeper too and ampler Flouds,
> Which as in Mirrors, shew'd the Woods;
> Of lofty Trees with Sacred Shades,
> And Perspectives of pleasant Glades.
>
> (106–15)

45. See, for example, David M. Vieth, "Irony in Dryden's Ode to Anne Killigrew," *Studies in Philology* 62 (1965): 91–100; and A. D. Hope, "Anne Killigrew, or the Art of Modulating," in *Dryden's Mind and Art*, ed. Bruce King (Edinburgh: Oliver and Boyd, 1969), 99–113.

46. Winn, *"When Beauty Fires the Blood,"* 90. Winn sees the tone as a result of Dryden's various relationships with Killigrew: "he is a professional, she an amateur (as in the poem to Howard); he is an old master, she a young beginner (as in the elegy for Oldham); . . . he is a poet sensitive to the beauty of painting, but convinced of the superiority of poetry (as in the later poem to Kneller); he is a survivor grieving for the dead (as in the elegies for Hastings, Oldham, Charles II, and the Countess of Abingdon)" 96.

47. Hoffman, *John Dryden's Imagery*, 102–3. Jean H. Hagstrum describes Dryden's use of baroque imagery in many of his poems (*The Sister Arts: The Tradition of Literary Pictorialism and English Poetry from Dryden to Gray* [Chicago: University of Chicago Press, 1958], 197).

48. Certainly many elegies served their poets as something other than a recollection of the dead, among the most memorable uses of elegy for other purposes are Donne's *Anniversaries* and Milton's *Lycidas*.

49. *Works of John Dryden*, 3.230.

50. Ibid., 3.232.

51. Ibid., 3.233.

52. Ibid.

53. Ibid.

54. Ibid., 3.231.

55. Winn, *"When Beauty Fires the Blood,"* 57.

56. David Bruce Kramer, *The Imperial Dryden: The Poetics of Appropriation in Seventeenth-Century England* (Athens: University of Georgia Press, 1994), 132–33. Kramer has discussed the shift in Dryden's representation of his poetic persona from a manly, aggressive persona during his period as poet laureate, to an effeminate, defeated persona with the Glorious Revolution of 1688 (5).

57. Maynard Mack remarks in his essay "The Muse of Satire" that it is "not without significance, it seems to me, that though Pope, following the great victories of naturalism in the seventeenth century, had to make do with a minimum of mythology and myth, he never discarded the Muse, either the conception or the term" (*Collected in Himself: Essays Critical, Biographical and Bibliographical on Pope and Some of His Contemporaries* [Newark: University of Delaware Press, 1982], 57).

58. Pope's trajectory toward the epic was complemented by two digressions into the religious sublime, "The Messiah" (1712) and *Eloisa to Abelard* (1717). Unlike Milton's and Cowley's uses of the muse, however, Pope's humanizes and historicizes the muse in ways that parallel his use of the muse in his more representative works. "The Messiah" includes the muses, but subordinates them by focusing on the poetic ability of the prophet Isaiah. Usually, however, it is a man of England rather than a Hebrew prophet. Through the epistolary form of *Eloisa to Abelard*, Pope avoids labeling a source of religious-sublime authority. He expresses his religious and irreligious transports through Eloisa's voice, based on authentic letters. The mode of address—an epistle to her former lover and spiritual guide Abelard—allows the poet to avoid invoking the muse.

59. Carole Fabricant, "Defining Self and Others: Pope and Eighteenth-Century Gender Ideology," *Criticism* 39, no. 4 (1997): 506. She compares Swift's and Pope's attitudes toward the politics of representation: "Whereas Swift's writings offer a continuing critique of the political implications of representation, Pope's linguistically and aesthetically exploit the latter while mystifying or naturalizing the consequences of its operations in terms of power relationships" (506).

60. David Fairer, *Pope's Imagination* (Manchester: Manchester University Press, 1984).

61. Deutsch, *Resemblance & Disgrace*, 41.

62. As a Catholic denied access to "formal classical education, political involvement, or the possession of property within London" and his difficult physical problems, Pope could be seen as occupying a "feminized" position (Catherine Ingrassia, *Authorship, Commerce, and Gender in Early Eighteenth-Century England: A Culture of Paper Credit* [Cambridge: Cambridge University Press, 1998], 45).

63. Valerie Rumbold, *Women's Place in Pope's World* (Cambridge: Cambridge University Press, 1989).

64. To John Caryll, 5 Dec 1712, in Correspondence, 1.163, qtd. in Dustin Griffin, "The Visionary Scene: Vision and Allegory in the Poetry of Pope," in *Enlightening Allegory: Theory, Practice, and Contexts of Allegory in the Late Seventeenth and Eighteenth Centuries*, ed. Kevin L. Cope (New York: AMS Press, 1993), 326.

65. Walter Schindler rightly observes that both ancient classical and English poetry hold many examples of invocations of the muse outside of the epic (*Voice and Crisis*, 1–2).

66. All quotations from Pope are from the Twickenham edition.

67. *Poems of Alexander Pope*, 5.59.

68. Ibid., 5.88.

69. Patricia Meyer Spacks, *An Argument of Images: The Poetry of Alexander Pope* (Cambridge, MA: Harvard University Press, 1971), 29.

70. Ibid., 31.

71. See Ingrassia's discussion of "Dulness the woman": "Dulness symbolizes Pope's escalating fear of a pervasive 'feminization' that threatens to permeate nearly every aspect of English culture" (*Authorship, Commerce, and Gender*, 48).

72. Ellen Pollak, *The Poetics of Sexual Myth: Gender and Ideology in the Verse of Swift and Pope* (Chicago: University of Chicago Press, 1985), 12.

73. All quotations from Swift are from *The Complete Poems*, ed. Pat Rogers (New Haven: Yale University Press, 1983).

74. See Pollak's discussion of this "famous cryptic stanza" (*Poetics of Sexual Myth*, 130).

Chapter 2. Speaking Objects: Women Poets and the Muse

1. Dorothy Mermin, "Women Becoming Poets: Katherine Philips, Aphra Behn, Anne Finch," *English Literary History* 57, no. 2 (1990): 335–55, 349.

2. Anne Freadman, "Poeta (1st dec., n., fem.)," *Australian Journal of French Studies* 16, no. 2 (1972): 152.

3. For an early account of the woman as Other and the man as Subject see Simone de Beauvoir, *The Second Sex*, trans. and ed. H. M. Parshley (New York: Vintage, 1989).

4. See Joanne Feit Diehl, "'Come Slowly—Eden': An Exploration of Women Poets and Their Muse," *Signs* 3, no. 3 (1978): 572–87. Mary K. DeShazer analyzes the muse in the poetry of Louise Bogan, H. D., May Sarton, Adrienne Rich, and Audre Lorde in *Inspiring Women: Reimagining the Muse* (New York: Pergamon, 1986). See also Pamela Di Pesa, "The Imperious Muse: Some Observations on Women, Nature, and the Poetic Tradition," in *Feminist Criticism: Essays on Theory, Poetry, and Prose*, ed. Cheryl L. Brown and Karen Olson (Metuchen, NJ: Scarecrow Press, 1978), 59–68. The greatest lyric poet of the classical era was a woman whose art foregrounded an intense relationship with the muses, one that critics have seen as religious, erotic, or both (Bruno Gentili, *Poetry and Its Public in Ancient Greece: From Homer to the Fifth Century* [Bal-

timore: Johns Hopkins University Press, 1988], 79, 86). Sappho herself, though considered the greatest ancient lyric poet, has served a "glaringly muse-like" role in the western poetic tradition; her role as an inspiring silent one found "an apparent objective correlative in the fact that most of her poetry was thought to be lost" (Freadman, "Poeta," 156). For a history of Sappho's place in western European (predominantly French) literature, see Joan DeJean's *Fictions of Sappho, 1546–1937* (Chicago: University of Chicago Press, 1989).

5. Hinnant, *Poetry of Anne Finch*, 32.

6. John L. Mahoney, *The Whole Internal Universe*, 32.

7. Ibid., 32. Mahoney argues that as early as Dryden we find some versions of a mimesis of "the inner life, the passions, the imaginings of human beings" (151).

8. See Gunter Gebauer and Christoph Wulf, *Mimesis: Culture, Art, Society*, trans. Don Reneau (Berkeley: University of California Press, 1992), 3.

9. Barash's larger concern in her book *English Women's Poetry, 1649–1714* includes ways in which English women poets "tended to figure their relationship to writing (and to other women) as part of the larger question of their relationship to political legitimacy" (5).

10. Catherine Gallagher, "Embracing the Absolute: The Politics of the Female Subject in Seventeenth-Century England," *Genders* 1 (Spring 1988): 25.

11. Mary J. Carruthers has examined how Adrienne Rich, Audre Lorde, Judy Grahn, and Olga Broumas use the muse to locate their poetic authority in a new myth based on "a meeting of familiars" ("The Re-Vision of the Muse," *The Hudson Review* 36, no. 2 [1983]: 296).

12. In "The Sapphic-Platonics of Katherine Philips, 1632–1664" (*Signs* 15, no. 1 [Autumn 1989]: 34–60), Harriette Andreadis discusses Philips's use of "cavalier conventions of platonic heterosexual love, with their originally platonic and male homoerotic feeling . . . to describe her relations with women" (37). On the erotic implications of female friendship in Philips's poetry see Arlene Stiebel, "Subversive Sexuality: Masking the Erotic in Poems by Katherine Philips and Aphra Behn," in *Renaissance Discourses of Desire*, ed. Claude J. Summers and Ted-Larry Pebworth (Columbia: University of Missouri Press, 1993), 223–36. All quotations from Philips are from *Poems* (1667).

13. In *English Women's Poetry, 1649–1714*, Carol Barash argues that Philips's "Society of Friendship" originated as a literary and political symbol of royal allegiance during the interregnum (56).

14. Philips, *Poems*, 102.

15. Elaine Hobby describes Philips's definition of female friendship as based on a notion of similitude—"that women friends are so alike that they mirror one another" (*Virtue of Necessity: English Women's Writing, 1649–88* [Ann Arbor: University of Michigan Press, 1989], 138).

16. Winn, *"When Beauty Fires the Blood,"* 420.

17. For Aphra Behn, whose outspoken and at times racy poetry would often be cited as the counterpart to that of Philips, the muse was less pivotal to her articulation of a poetic self. Indeed, as I argue in chapter 3, Behn is often interested in poetic representation as a means of *eluding* self-representation. She performs this most ingeniously in her less formal poems, where invocations of the muses would be superfluous. Relying heavily on pastoral dialogue in many of her poems, Behn plays with personas to establish her poetic authority—per-

haps a fitting approach for a writer who worked in a variety of genres, especially drama. Readers will recall her preface to *The Luckey Chance* (1686), where "All I ask, is the Priviledge for my Masculine Part the Poet in me, (if any such you will allow me) to tread in those successful Paths my Predecessors have so long thriv'd in, to take those Measures that both the Ancient and Modern Writers have set me, and by which they have pleas'd the World so well. If I must not, because of my Sex, have this Freedom, but that you will usurp all to your selves; I lay down my Quill" (*The Works of Aphra Behn*, vol. 7., ed. Janet Todd [Columbus: Ohio State University Press, 1996], 217). Behn relied most on the muse in her elegies, for example, "On the Death of the late Earl of Rochester" and "On the Death of E. Waller, Esq." and in her poems on affairs of state, including "A Pindarick Poem on the Happy Coronation of His Most Sacred Majesty James II" and "A Congratulatory Poem to her Sacred Majesty Queen Mary, upon Her Arrival in England." In these formal, public poems, the muse stands in as Behn's public poetic self to mediate her political claims.

18. Qtd. from Greer and others, *Kissing the Rod,* 204–5.

19. On the decline of even Philips's reputation, see Paula Loscocco, "'Manly Sweetness': Katherine Philips among the Neoclassicals," *The Huntington Library Quarterly* 56, no. 3 (Summer 1993): 259–79.

20. Ibid., 269.

21. Barash discusses the "real gynocentric rituals" at Mary of Modena's court that encouraged her female entourage to participate as actors and writers (*English Women's Poetry,* 15).

22. All quotations from Killigrew are from *Poems (1686) by Mrs. Anne Killigrew*, intro. Richard Morton (Gainesville: Scholars' Facsimiles and Reprints, 1967).

23. Her interests in both poetry and painting fed each other, her paintings often serving as illustration to her poems and her poems serving as ekphrases to her paintings (e.g., "St. John Baptist Painted by her self . . . ," and "On a Picture Painted by her self, representing two Nimphs of Diana's"). Her skill as a painter is suggested not only by her self-portrait but by the status of those who sat for her: James, Duke of York, and Mary of Modena.

24. Killigrew, *Poems,* 5.

25. In this championing of virtue, Killigrew participates in an increasing trend of Restoration and eighteenth-century women writers who assert their virtue in contrast to what had been a more vehement public engagement during the interregnum (Hobby, *Virtue of Necessity*, 18). See Carol Barash on the *femme forte* tradition, *English Women's Poetry*, 32–40.

26. This model of Christian sacrifice is common in poetry of the religious sublime (cf. Romans 12.1: "present your bodies a living sacrifice, holy, acceptable unto God, which is your reasonable service").

27. The woman writer risked a scandalous reputation simply by writing, as has been amply established elsewhere. Women poets' relationships with their muses had already been stigmatized as "sexually ambiguous and contemptible," as Frances Teague recounts in "Early Modern Women and 'the muses ffemall,'" in *"The Muses Females Are": Mary Moulsworth and Other Women Writers of the English Renaissance*, ed. Robert C. Evans and Anne C. Little (West Cornwall, CT: Locust Hill Press, 1995), 173–79, 175.

28. Ovid, *Metamorphoses*, vol. 1, trans. by Frank Justus Miller, Loeb Classical Library (Cambridge, MA: Harvard University Press, 1984).

29. Barash makes a similar point: "Apollo has not metaphorically raped the speaker, as Straub argues; rather her belief in her own writing has caused her to imagine the myth from the male poet's point of view: Daphne has not been raped but 'transform'd' into the laurel branch to crown the conceited female Petrarchan poet" (*English Women's Poetry*, 166). See also Barash's discussion of Killigrew's "many metamorphic narratives" (157).

30. The violent eroticism of Apollo's aesthetic power over Daphne is underscored when Killigrew elaborates on the element of seduction as she claims her innocence in reference to Cupid (and as Dryden will also claim for her in his reference to Cupid):

> The Learn'd in Love say, Thus the Winged Boy
> Does first approach, drest up in welcome Joy;
> At first he to the Cheated Lovers sight
> Nought represents, but Rapture and Delight . . .
>
> (25–28)

31. In her analysis of Killigrew's "Upon the saying that my Verses" and Pope's *Arbuthnot*, Kristina Straub also identifies Killigrew's images of rape. Killigrew, according to Straub, turns this attack back on her reader in "an attempt to force her readers to recognize their own complicity in her victimization" ("Indecent Liberties with a Poet: Audience and the Metaphor of Rape in Killigrew's 'Upon the saying that my Verses' and Pope's *Arbuthnot*," *Tulsa Studies in Women's Literature* 6 [1987]: 30).

32. Prophecy was a mode particularly amenable to women writers in this period. According to Hobby, between 1649 and 1688, "well over half the texts published by women . . . were prophecies. It was precisely the stereotypes of women as irrational creatures that gave them authority as vessels of divine messages" (*Virtue of Necessity*, 26). In the role of prophet, women could not only be pardoned for speaking but could be seen as required to speak as an organ of God. See Barash, *English Women's Poetry*, 30.

33. See Barash on the uses of Cassandra to represent women writers and political actors in the Restoration court (*English Women's Poetry*, 153).

34. Paula Loscocco rightly observes examples in Dryden's poem where he "draws deliberate attention to the ways in which he separates Killigrew from her natural gender," a separation, Loscocco argues, that Dryden must make in order to praise Killigrew in a literary climate that is increasingly devaluing "terms associated in any way with women and femininity" ("Manly Sweetness," 268). Dryden participates in this devaluation on a subtler level, however, by granting Killigrew a moral authority that eclipses her poetic authority.

35. Killigrew also died much earlier than did Finch.

36. I am deeply indebted to Charles H. Hinnant's comprehensive study *The Poetry of Anne Finch*. Although my interpretive emphases vary from his, my argument is compatible with Hinnant's general assertion that Finch's achievement "lies in taking over poetic forms and tropes that had hitherto largely been employed by men and giving those poetic forms and tropes an ironic and subversive twist by speaking through them as a woman" (32). Barbara McGovern has also described Finch's positive response to "[w]riting from a marginal posi-

tion in her social and literary milieu" in *Anne Finch and Her Poetry: A Critical Biography* (Athens: University of Georgia Press, 1992), 5. According to McGovern, Finch "often viewed her exclusion from masculine traditions as a challenge to her creativity, rather than a repression of it" (5). See also: Jean Mallinson, "Anne Finch: A Woman Poet and the Tradition," in *Gender at Work: Four Women Writers of the Eighteenth Century*, ed. Ann Messenger (Detroit: Wayne State University Press, 1990), 45; Ann Messenger, "Publishing without Perishing: Lady Winchilsea's *Miscellany Poems* of 1713," *Restoration* 5 (1981): 27–37; Thomas F. Bonnell, "Collins, Lady Winchilsea, and the Pursuit of the Muse," in *Teaching Eighteenth-Century Poetry*, ed. Christopher Fox (New York: AMS Press, 1990), 273–89; and Jean Ellis D'Alessandro, "Anne Countess of Winchilsea and the Whole Duty of Woman: Socio-Cultural Inference in a Reading of 'The Introduction,'" *Lingue del Mondo* 52, no. 5/6 (1988): 9–15.

37. As more and more English women entered the literary market in the Restoration and eighteenth century, poets such as Dryden, Pope, and Thomson developed a tropological paradigm in which the poet gendered as masculine proves his mimetic powers by feminizing the objects he represents.

38. Unless otherwise indicated, all quotations from Finch are from *The Poems of Anne Countess of Winchilsea*, ed. Myra Reynolds (Chicago: University of Chicago Press, 1903). For another clash with classical sources of inspiration, see, for example, Finch's "To Mr. F. Now Earl of W" (20).

39. Ibid., 7.

40. Having announced her rejection by the classical god of poetry, in another poem Finch moves on to her rejection of this god. She satirizes Apollo's indifference to women poets, and, in turn, the indifference of the poetic tradition to women poets, in "The Circuit of Apollo." In his visit to Kent, where he saw that "most that pretended to Verse, were the Women" (4), he vows to award the laurel to "she that writt best" (6). Casting Apollo's judgment in the mold of Paris's judgment of the most beautiful goddess, Finch suggests the extent to which aesthetic standards for women writers are often sexual standards. Because Apollo fears that the contestants may be jealous if he declares one woman the winner (such is the stereotype of female jealousy), he decides to divide the bays among the four, thus abandoning any real consideration of their qualities as artists.

41. Pat Rogers notes that "in a letter of 12 January 1712 Swift writes, 'I amuse myself sometimes with writing verses to Mrs Finch,' and these are the only extant lines which fit the description" (*Jonathan Swift: The Complete Poems*, ed. Pat Rogers [New Haven: Yale University Press, 1983], 631).

42. Reynolds, *Poems*, 6.

43. McGovern, *Anne Finch*, 72.

44. Reynolds, *Poems*, 32.

45. Ibid., 23.

46. *The Complete Poetry*, ed. and intro. John T. Shawcross (New York: New York University Press, 1968), 88.

47. The epistolary mode exploits this construction of a receptive reader whose ties to the writer are social, sentimental, and lettered. The most familiar example is Pope's *Essay on Man*, which preserves the frame of an epistle to Bolingbroke and allows Pope to formulate his poetic worth in terms of Bolingbroke's approving reception.

48. Indeed, her favorite poetic kind has been regarded as one of the lowest: the fable. See Hinnant on the complexity of Finch's fables (*Poetry of Anne Finch*, 167).

49. Reynolds, *Poems*, 46.

50. See Hinnant's discussion of the poem's critique of seventeenth-century verbal extravagance and its reliance, instead, on tautology (*Poetry of Anne Finch*, 81).

51. According to Hinnant, "the imperatives of friendship, which seem to abolish absence and loss, here disclose a dichotomy between utterance and intention that no profession of love can bridge" (*Poetry of Anne Finch*, 81).

52. In *English Women's Poetry*, Barash analyzes friendship in English women's poetry as a "trope of political cohesion and stability" (15).

53. Sir Philip Sidney, *The Poems*, ed. William A. Ringler, Jr. (Oxford: Clarendon Press, 1962), 182. By permission of Oxford University Press.

54. Murray Krieger, "Presentation and Representation in the Renaissance Lyric: The Net of Words and the Escape of the Gods," in *Mimesis: From Mirror to Method, Augustine to Descartes*, ed. John D. Lyons and Stephen G. Nichols, Jr. (Hanover, NH: University Press of New England, 1982), 122.

55. For example, when Pope in *An Essay on Man* invites Bolingbroke to survey the map of mankind, his use of visual images establishes the poet's grasp of the abstraction "mankind." For Pope the differences, the gradations between elements and beings, in the Great Chain require the poet to make categorical distinctions. The poet and the reader may identify through shared comprehension of the differences within this Great Chain; hence, the rhetorical and existential collapses seen in Finch's view of writing and being may look like mimetic failures in relation to Pope's poetics.

56. Hinnant argues that Finch was highly reflective about her art, in particular defining her poetry "against the repertory of gender identifications available in her culture" (*Poetry of Anne Finch*, 38).

57. See Barash, *English Women's Poetry*, and Barbara McGovern, "Finch, Pope, and Swift: The Bond of Displacement" in *Pope, Swift, and Women Writers*, ed. Donald C. Mell (Newark: University of Delaware Press, 1996), 105–24.

58. Barash, *English Women's Poetry*, 260, 261.

59. Ibid., 261.

60. See Gebauer and Wulf on a mimesis that "produces an otherwise unattainable proximity to objects and is thus a necessary condition of understanding" (*Mimesis*, 2–3).

61. Greer and others, *Kissing the Rod*, 27.

62. Ibid.

63. Kathryn R. King, "Elizabeth Singer Rowe's Tactical Use of Print and Manuscript," in *Women's Writing and the Circulation of Ideas: Manuscript Publication in England, 1550–1800*, ed. George L. Justice and Nathan Tinker (Cambridge: Cambridge University Press, 2002), 160–63.

64. This tradition bolstered the developing stereotype of women as vessels of moral and spiritual authority, part of a larger project of the reformation of manners and the cult of virtue. See David Morse, *The Age of Virtue: British Culture from the Restoration to Romanticism* (Houndmills, UK: Macmillan, 2000).

65. A "bright ethereal youth" (25) appears in the role of a seductive male muse whose "florid bloom," "lovely brows," and "radiant hair" enchant the dreamer (28, 29, 30). He tells her to reject the nonreligious poetry of her past: "To Heav'n, nor longer pause, devote thy songs, / To Heav'n the muse's sacred art belongs" (36–37).

66. All quotations from Rowe are from *The miscellaneous works, in prose and verse, of Mrs. Elizabeth Rowe*, 2 vols. (London, 1749).

67. This fountain connects the poet with the divine source as well as with the poetic source as the image recalls the pagan Pierian springs. Figuring herself as the bathing worshipper, Rowe deftly calls on classical mythological narratives where nymphs are to be found in the greatest intimacy. But Rowe leaves these classical associations to be lightly inferred to avoid disturbing the Christian content. The poet is also careful to convey this erotically charged contact with the divine in terms that invoke sexuality and resurrection, when desires "die away / In endless plenty" (5–6).

68. Repeatedly in her oeuvre, Rowe complains of the difficulty of expressing such devotion, but repeatedly her passion overwhelms rational reticence. When she does call on the muses, as in soliloquy 40, Rowe, like Milton, requests divine not pagan aid:

> I Call not you that on *Parnassus* sit,
> And by the flow'ry banks of *Helicon*,
> Circle your brows with fading coronets;
> While some romantic hero you adorn
> With lying epithets, and airy praise:
> Or some fantastic lover's fate rehearse
> In notes that with a soft, inticing art,
> A charming, but pernicious magic draw
> The chastest minds from virtue's sacred paths.
> (1–9)

69. On Jane Barker's revisions of the muse, see Kathryn R. King, "Jane Barker, *Poetical Recreations*, and the Sociable Text," *ELH* 61, no. 3 (1994): 551–70.

70. The description of Leapor is from Roger Lonsdale, *Eighteenth-Century Women Poets*, 194. All quotations from Leapor are from *Poems upon Several Occasions. By the Late Mrs. Leapor*, 2 vols. (London: J. Roberts, 1748, 1751).

Chapter 3. Gender and Order in the Prospect

1. The prospect poem first gained prominence in the events that led up to the Civil War and in response to land enclosure policies. In the decades following the Restoration, the prospect continued to be used to order political power and the poet's place in a growing literary marketplace. With mounting anxiety over poetic property, an anxiety that would be addressed in part by copyright legislation, the prospect was the site in which to claim poetic territory. Cf. Martha Woodmansee, "The Genius and the Copyright: Economic and Legal Conditions of the Emergence of the 'Author,'" *Eighteenth-Century Studies* 17, no. 4 (Summer 1984): 425–48.

2. Robert Aubin, *Topographical Poetry in XVIII–century England* (New York: Modern Language Association, 1936), 35. According to Ralph Cohen, the prospect view in particular permitted Augustan poets to relate "inherited poetic features" to "scientific spatial assumptions, to philosophical assumptions regarding the acquisition of knowledge by experience, experiment and observation, and to religious assumptions that connect local observation with God's presence in infinity" ("The Augustan Mode in English Poetry," *Eighteenth-Century Studies* 1, no. 1 [September 1967], 9).

3. James Turner asserts that the "central ideological fact of rural literature" is that "it succeeds as description the more it approaches identity with the world of rural production, but it is meaningful *as literature* precisely because it is not that world, because it triumphs over and obliterates it" (*The Politics of Landscape: Rural Scenery and Society in English Poetry, 1630–1660* [Cambridge, MA: Harvard University Press, 1979], 195). John Barrell's study emphasizes the aggressive qualities of the poetic ordering of landscape, which did not represent "the needs of the people who had created it" (*The Idea of Landscape and the Sense of Place, 1730–1840. An Approach to the Poetry of John Clare* [Cambridge: Cambridge University Press, 1972], 58–59). See also Barrell, *English Literature in History*. Anthony Low focuses on landscape poetry from the perspective of England's agricultural revolution and its influence on the development of georgic poetry in England (*The Georgic Revolution* [Princeton: Princeton University Press, 1985]). Rachel Crawford analyzes how changes in Britain's class structure contributed to changing ideas of representational space, property, and literary forms (*Poetry, Enclosure, and the Vernacular Landscape* [Cambridge: Cambridge University Press, 2002], 17). For a wide-ranging analysis of landscape, see *Landscape and Power*, ed. and intro. W. J. T. Mitchell (Chicago: University of Chicago Press, 1994).

4. See Carole Fabricant, "The Aesthetics and Politics of Landscape in the Eighteenth-Century," in *Studies in Eighteenth-Century British Art and Aesthetics*, ed. Ralph Cohen (Berkeley: University of California Press, 1985), 49–81; and Jacqueline Labbe, *Romantic Visualities: Landscape, Gender, and Romanticism* (New York: St. Martin's Press, 1998). On the long-standing feminization of Nature in Western culture, see Carolyn Merchant, *The Death of Nature*, and Kate Soper, *What is Nature?*

5. Jacqueline Labbe, *Romantic Visualities*, ix.

6. Turner, *Politics of Landscape*, 44. In his study of the images he calls *Topographia* Turner finds that they appear most frequently from 1630 to 1660 in part because of fears "that property in land would be swept away by rural insurrection" (7).

7. Clément Rosset, *L'anti-nature: Éléments pour une philosophie tragique* (Paris: Presses universitaires de France, 1973), 14–15.

8. Paul de Man has analyzed how "so often in Romantic poetry, the landscape replaces the muse" (*The Rhetoric of Romanticism* [New York: Columbia University Press, 1984], 125). Invoking the landscape rather than the muse was a convention already established in Augustan poetry, but neither in Augustan nor Romantic poetry can we strictly say "the landscape *replaces* the muse" but rather that it assimilates the muse's qualities.

9. The muse lingered by name as a companion of the poet, in some poems accompanying the surveyor, not unlike Wordsworth's listening sister in "Lines

Composed a Few Miles Above Tintern Abbey." In other poems, the muse's ability to travel served the stationary poet in wide-ranging descriptions of landscapes, a convention so common that by 1789 a writer for the *Gentleman's Magazine* complained that "readers have been used to see the Muses labouring up ... many hills since Cooper's and Grongar, and some gentle Bard reclining on almost every mole-hill" (58:151). Qtd. in C. V. Deane, *Aspects of Eighteenth-Century Nature Poetry* (Oxford: Basil Blackwood, 1935), 109n.

10. Cf. Lipking's argument that well before the Romantic era, poets had turned "from convention and allusion to psychology" ("Gods of Poetry," 76).

11. Tim Fulford, *Landscape, Liberty and Authority: Poetry, Criticism and Politics from Thomson to Wordsworth* (Cambridge: Cambridge University Press, 1996), 5.

12. Crawford, *Poetry, Enclosure, and the Vernacular Landscape*, 72.

13. These opening lines, observes Brendan O Hehir, echo a "rejection-of-the-Muses topos" seen in Horace, Ovid, and other ancient poets. Denham varies the topos significantly, however, by focusing on the elevation of the poet's own powers. See *Expans'd Hieroglyphicks: A Critical Edition of Sir John Denham's Coopers Hill* (Berkeley: University of California Press, 1969), 179–80. All quotations from Denham are from O Hehir's edition of the B text, draft 4 (1655; 1668).

14. The poet thus imitates Charles I's ability to move the court:

> And as Courts make not Kings, but Kings the Court,
> So where the Muses & their train resort,
> *Parnassus* stands; if I can be to thee
> A Poet, thou *Parnassus* art to me.
>
> (5–8)

The transfer of powers from the muses to the land and its poet is an essential image because the stability of the land—that is, the nation—is at stake. Ironically, part of what Denham attempts to legitimate is the very authority of Charles's government based on a notion of the mobility of the court, particularly as it followed him to Oxford.

15. The fluctuations of vision and power require the judgment of the King's gaze:

> Under his proud survey the City lies,
> And like a mist beneath a hill doth rise;
> Whose state and wealth the business and the crowd,
> Seems at this distance but a darker cloud:
> And is to him who rightly things esteems,
> No other in effect than what it seems.
>
> (25–30)

16. O Hehir argues that in the "B" text "the river can no longer convincingly be regarded as an emblem of the specifically kingly power" (*Expans'd Hieroglyphics*, 241). Rather, it is an "emblem of sheer power, the energy contained within a state" (252). Earl R. Wasserman interprets the invocation of the Thames as formulating the "*concordia discors* of the total state" (*The Subtler Language: Critical Readings of Neoclassic and Romantic Poems* [Baltimore: Johns Hopkins University Press, 1959], 69).

17. The river's masculine identity derives from the classical figuration of the river as male god.

18. Butler, *Bodies that Matter*, 3.

19. Addison, *The Spectator,* no. 412 (Oxford edition, 3.540–42). All quotations from Addison are from *The Spectator*, ed. and intro. Donald F. Bond, 5 vols. (Oxford: Clarendon Press, 1965). By permission of Oxford University Press.

20. Mary Poovey discusses Addison's conversion of the gaze from "leisured gentlemen" to men of the middle class. See her "Aesthetics and Political Economy," 84.

21. In no. 465 of *The Spectator*, where the Ode appears, Addison asserts that "The Supream Being has made the best Arguments for his own Existence, in the Formation of the Heavens and the Earth, and these are Arguments which a Man of Sense cannot forbear attending to, who is out of the Noise and Hurry of Human Affairs" (Oxford edition, 4.144–45).

22. Susan Staves, *Married Women's Separate Property in England, 1660–1833* (Cambridge, MA: Harvard University Press, 1990), 4.

23. Both Turner and John Barrell have recounted how the poet's class is an integral part of his access to topographical prospects. But both critics fail to point out that the mobility and panorama of topographical poetry excluded not only the laboring class but also women of all classes. While some affluent women had opportunities to travel, we rarely see in their poetry the use of a prospect from which contemporary politics and religion and history may be ordered. According to Barrell, mobility is fundamental to the poet's control over the landscape (*The Idea of Landscape*, 63).

24. Reynolds, *Poems*, 9.

25. Labbe argues that whereas the eighteenth-century man is conditioned to resent a restricted view of the land, "the body, and vision, of a woman 'should' welcome it as her natural environment" (*Romantic Visualities*, ix).

26. See Lonsdale's brief biographical sketch in *Eighteenth-Century Women Poets*, 141.

27. Addison, *The Spectator,* 3.399.

28. Quoted from Adams, *Miscellany Poems. By Mrs Jane [sic] Adams*, 188–89.

29. See Labbe's discussion of the garden's figurative role in conduct books for women in the late eighteenth century: "the garden figures the very precepts those conduct books seek to inculcate: domestic retirement, decoration, the promise of (properly confined) fertility, quiet, soothing pleasure" and utility (*Romantic Visualities*, 78).

30. Staves, *Married Women's Separate Property*, 227. See also Gillian Skinner on women's access to property in the eighteenth century, which she describes as possible but extremely limited ("Women's Status as Legal and Civic Subjects: 'A Worse Condition than Slavery Itself?,'" in *Women and Literature in Britain, 1700–1800*, ed. Viven Jones [Cambridge: Cambridge University Press, 2000]).

31. The Bathurst of the title is Allen, first Baron Bathurst (1684–1775).

32. All quotations from Montagu are from *Essays and Poems and* Simplicity, a Comedy, ed. Robert Halsband and Isobel Grundy (Oxford: Clarendon Press, 1993), 242–44. By permission of Oxford University Press.

33. Eighteenth-century poets frequently used the "storied urn" and images of sculpture to "express genuine and deep emotions" (Rachel Trickett, "The Augustan Pantheon: Mythology and Personification in Eighteenth-Century Poetry," *Essays and Studies* 6 [1953]: 83).

34. Montagu may well have been familiar with Jonathan Swift's "Verses Wrote in a Lady's Ivory Table-Book" (w. probably 1698; pub. 1711); her poem may deliberately revise Swift's imagery of the woman as a book to be written upon. Swift's poem figures the woman's vagina as the leaves of the book accessible to the male visitor, whose penis can "blot it out" and "Clap his own nonsense in the place." If Montagu's poem counters Swift's in particular, the woman as feeling self has replaced Swift's woman as corporeal object.

35. See Robert A. Erickson, *The Language of the Heart, 1600–1750* (Philadelphia: University of Pennsylvania Press, 1997), 16. "The 'tables of the heart' and the writing on these tables," notes Erickson, "is an important recurring image in Proverbs, the prophetic writings, and the epistles of St. Paul" (16).

36. Leapor, *Poems*, 2.111–22.

37. *The Woman's Labour* [and Stephen Duck's *The Thresher's Labour*], intro. Moira Ferguson, Augustan Reprint Society, publication 230 (Los Angeles: William Andrews Clark Memorial Library, 1985), 15.

38. Carole Fabricant, *Swift's Landscape* (Baltimore: Johns Hopkins University Press, 1982), 198.

39. Ibid., 198. Fabricant defines Swift's landscapes as "an all-encompassing ideological landscape . . . linked to prevailing social and economic conditions" (1). She argues compellingly that Swift's attention to *Irish* land made him show "an indifference toward or a contempt of prospects" (174).

40. On pastoral as a kind hospitable to women poets, see Elizabeth V. Young, "Aphra Behn, Gender, and Pastoral," *SEL: Studies in English Literature* 33, no. 3 (1993): 523–43.

41. Although her poetry's sexual imagery does not approach the graphic violence of Rochester's, it does assert the sexuality of women and men to a degree unusual for a seventeenth-century woman poet. Her poetic and personal reputation suffered, especially as the era's sexual codes grew more restrictive.

42. That the tree is a reversal of Daphne's transformation is a point also made by Alvin Snider in "Cartesian Bodies," *Modern Philology* 98, no. 2 (November 2000): 318.

43. Snider discusses this poem in the context of Cartesian theories of agency and bodies. Behn, observes Snider, "invests nature with a kind of agency at the same time that she renders the human body in terms both eroticized and mechanistic" (ibid., 302).

44. All quotations from Behn are from *The Works of Aphra Behn*, 6 vols., ed. Montague Summers (London: W. Heinemann, 1915).

45. On this tree as a "witty trope of hermaphroditic sexuality, indefinite sexual identity, and slippery gender" see Roberta C. Martin, "'Beauteous wonder of a different kind': Aphra Behn's Destabilization of Sexual Categories," *College English* 61, no. 2 (November 1998): 192–210. See also Elizabeth V. Young's analysis of the tree's androgyny ("Aphra Behn," 525–28).

46. The commodification of women's beauty and its figuration as treasure is a commonplace of feminist cultural materialist readings.

47. Significantly, the female lover who wantoned beneath the juniper tree's limbs is the one who cuts down the tree as an act of pity when the lovers no longer visit its covering branches.

48. Behn flaunts the translatability of figurative language by mixing pagan and Christian vocabularies, making the profane sound sacred.

49. Seen as a translation of the Apollo/Daphne plot, the tree is an arboreal Daphne granted speech through personification. Like Daphne, the tree can claim sexual purity through its objectified condition. Unlike Apollo, who makes the tree into a symbol of his artistic power, Behn's female lover makes the tree into an instrument of her social power, specifically, the protection of her reputation.

50. I am indebted to Kathryn R. King for this observation.

51. See Rachel Crawford's analysis of Behn's uses of the bower motif and *hortus conclusus* in "Troping the Subject: Behn, Smith, Hemans and the Poetics of the Bower," *Studies in Romanticism* 38, no. 2 (Summer 1999): 249–79.

52. On the role of disguise in Behn's poetry see Paul Salzman, "Aphra Behn: Poetry and Masquerade," in *Aphra Behn Studies*, ed. Janet Todd (Cambridge: Cambridge University Press, 1996), 109–29.

53. Summers, *Works of Aphra Behn*.

54. While Dryden does not use gendered landscapes and abstractions as extensively as Denham, Pope, or Thomson, these images help define his concern with reordering Restoration history. Dryden's gendered landscapes and abstractions support his elevation of history as poetic material and establish political "truth" through the fiction of gendered Nature. Readers will recall his use of feminine imagery to assert the submission of the English people to the king's masculine power in *Astraea Redux* (230–33). As many critics have observed, *Absalom and Achitophel* depends on overt and embedded sexual paradigms which Dryden exploits precisely for their thematic relevance to the succession crisis. Using conventional biblical descriptions of feminine lands and nations, Dryden confers spiritual largess onto Charles II's promiscuity (7–10). Absalom's innate goodness and abuse by Shaftesbury are conveyed by Dryden's use of the primordial biblical landscape: "In him alone, 'twas Natural to please. / His motions all accompanied with grace; / And *Paradise* was open'd in his face" (28–30) (*The Works of John Dryden*, vol. 2, *Poems 1681–1684*, ed. H. T. Swedenberg, Jr., and Vinton A. Dearing [Berkeley: University of California Press, 1972], 3–36). This description of Absalom's feminine innocence supports Dryden's polarization of Achitophel as satanic tempter and Absalom as the impressionable Eve of Milton's epic.

55. See Deutsch, *Resemblance & Disgrace*, 86.

56. See Valerie Rumbold on how Pope's "religion, politics, and illness" barred him from "the full enjoyment of the privileges reserved for men in his society" (*Women's Place*, 2). Deutsch argues that "precisely because the poet rents but neither owns, inherits, nor speculates, he is able to take true possession of an interior property in himself, a property he proudly marks with the sign of his literary labor" (*Resemblance & Disgrace*, 87). That cultural notions of property would increasingly shift from land to "paper credit," as Ingrassia has argued (*Authorship, Commerce, and Gender*) may in part account for other writers' focus on a property in the self.

57. Ibid., 108.

58. On the centrality of mercantile metaphors to Pope's poetry, see David B. Morris, *Alexander Pope: The Genius of Sense* (Cambridge, MA: Harvard University Press, 1984).

59. George Granville, Lord Lansdowne.

60. See Clément Rosset, *L'anti-nature*, 14.

61. The setting can also allow Pope to indirectly point to evidence of monarchical abuse, seen, for example, in the "levell'd Towns with Weeds lie cover'd o'er" and the "Heaps of Ruin" over which "stalk'd the stately Hind" (lines 67, 70), while containing them within the narrative of Lodona.

62. For a detailed discussion of the symbolic and historical associations among Lodona, Queen Anne, and Queen Elizabeth, see Vincent Carretta, *The Snarling Muse: Verbal and Visual Satire from Pope to Churchill* (Philadelphia: University of Pennsylvania Press, 1983), 1–19.

63. Pope's myth blends three ancient ones: Apollo's chase of Daphne, Pan's chase of Syrinx, and Alpheus's chase of Arethusa.

64. Earl Wasserman has discussed in detail the political implications of the Lodona myth. Arguing that the poem's primary theme is "the War and the Peace of Utrecht as seen from a Tory perspective," Wasserman finds that Lodona's extravagance symbolizes England's excessive involvement beyond its national boundaries (*The Subtler Language: Critical Readings of Neoclassic and Romantic Poems* [Baltimore: Johns Hopkins University Press, 1959], 135–36). In this set of political references, the poet keeps the peace.

65. Although Vincent Carretta convincingly argues that "Pope defends Anne and the Stuart succession by portraying them as the result and reiteration of previous British history" (*Snarling Muse*, 18), in his neglect of the poem's gender politics Carretta fails to point out Pope's defense of a masculine order that circumscribes the queen.

66. For eighteenth-century poets, the view of a landscape inverted in water would allow "scope for at least implied puns on 'reflections': merely exterior impressions—descriptive images—slide into imaginative ideal dramas—mental images" (John Dixon Hunt, *The Figure in the Landscape: Poetry, Painting, and Gardening During the Eighteenth Century* [Baltimore: Johns Hopkins University Press, 1976], 182). Passages in which someone gazes into reflecting water often allude to the Narcissus myth: "The popularity of this myth of introspection, self-knowledge and dialogue with nature ... allowed poets to allude to it as an easy image of meditation, promoted and answered or not by natural surroundings" (227).

67. According to Wasserman, Lodona is primarily important for her political significance, but as a mirror of Nature, "the transformation of Lodona and the transforming action of poetry are parallel events" (*Subtler Language*, 153).

68. Brean S. Hammond suggests that given Pope's abiding interest in the theme we might call him the "poet of friendship" (*Pope and Bolingbroke: A Study of Friendship and Influence* [Columbia: University of Missouri Press, 1984], 1).

69. Barrell describes the usefulness of Bolingbroke in Pope's treatment of the landscape: "It is as a man of landed property that Bolingbroke, an adherent to the country party to which the disinterested virtues of the country gentle-

man were particularly apparent, can 'expatiate free' (and with him, by association, Pope) 'o'er all this scene of Man'—can grasp the 'plan', the design of the landscape" (*English Literature in History*, 36).

70. In "The Design," which precedes the poem, Pope claimed it was much easier for him to write this in verse rather than prose: "I chose verse, and even rhyme," he explains, "for two reasons. The one will appear obvious; that principles, maxims, or precepts so written, both strike the reader more strongly at first, and are more easily retained by him afterwards: The other may seem odd, but is true, I found I could express them more *shortly* this way than in prose itself" (*Poems*, 3.7–8). Perhaps the condensation that he claimed the verse form gave his thoughts is related to the greater density of figurative language tolerated in poetry.

71. See Claudia Thomas's analysis of Elizabeth Carter's "In Diem Natalem," parts of which revise *An Essay on Man* (*Alexander Pope*, 212).

72. See Mack's introduction to the poem for a discussion of its relation to deistic philosophy, *An Essay on Man*, ed. and intro. Maynard Mack, vol. 3, part 1, *The Poems of Alexander Pope* (London: Methuen; New Haven: Yale University Press, 1959).

73. Although Pope depends on personified feminine Nature as the primary objective correlative for his argument, he enlists many feminine personifications to explain the mind and heart of man, including Imagination (2.143), Science ("First strip off all her equipage of Pride" [2.44]), Reason ("weak queen" [2.150]), Tyranny (3.249–56), Fortune (she "her gifts may variously dispose" [4.67]), and Virtue.

74. Pope, *Poems*.

75. Patricia Meyer Spacks, *An Argument of Images: The Poetry of Alexander Pope* (Cambridge, MA: Harvard University Press, 1971), 42, 43. Her analysis of the beginning of *An Essay on Man* highlights the importance of vision to Pope's argument: "When the poet invites Bolingbroke to 'beat this ample field' (1.9), the entire 'scene of Man' (5), to examine the ways 'Of all who blindly creep, or sightless soar' (12), the difference between his own capacity for perception and the blindness of those who are its object is real and vivid" (81).

76. See Harry M. Solomon, *The Rape of the Text: Reading and Misreading Pope's Essay on Man* (Tuscaloosa: University of Alabama Press, 1993): for Pope the self is "an interpretive impasse, source of opposing and incompatible perspectives" (64).

77. In Pope's conclusion of the *Essay* his warm conversational tone toward Bolingbroke reinforces the *Essay*'s last major argument: that self-love can lead to love of others.

78. Applicable to *An Essay on Man* are John Dixon Hunt's remarks on Pope's Imitations of Horace: "The intricacies of communion between friends and equals . . . need the sympathetic surroundings of an equally subtle landscape" (*Figure in the Landscape*, 78).

79. Hammond, *Pope and Bolingbroke*, 45.

80. The word *genius* serves different notions of poetic privilege in Augustan, post-Augustan, and Romantic poetry. On the transformation from *genius* as outside to inside the artist, see Ken Frieden, "The Eighteenth-Century Introjection of Genius," in *Genius and Monologue* (Ithaca: Cornell University Press,

1985), 66–83. For Pope and many Augustans *genius* signified a *genius loci*, which, Barrell observes, imposes on the landscape "an alien structure of aesthetic form, of classical association, . . . even before its individuality is consulted" (*Idea of Landscape*, 60). According to Mack, for Pope the "'genius of the place' . . . embodies that intuition of a mysterious life in things" (*The Garden and the City: Retirement and Politics in the Later Poetry of Pope, 1731–43* [Toronto: University of Toronto Press, 1969], 24). For a wide-ranging discussion of the significance of genius as masculine, see Christine Battersby, *Gender and Genius*.

81. Hammond, *Pope and Bolingbroke*, 13.

Chapter 4. The Voice of Nature and the Poet's Labor

1. The etymology of the older term, *prosopopeia*, still used in English as an alternate form of personification is suggestive: the Greek *prosopon* and *poiein* mean to make a person, face, or mask. Although the terms are often used interchangeably in English, Pierre Fontanier supports a distinction between them (*Les Figures du Discours*, intro., Gérard Genette [Paris: Flammarion, 1977], 111, 404).

2. Cf. Ernst Cassirer's summary of the new view of nature that was developing in the early modern period: "Nature is more than mere creation; it participates in original divine essence because the divine power pervades nature itself. The dualism between creator and creation is thus abolished. Nature as that which is moved is no longer set over against the divine mover; it is now an original formative principle which moves from within. Through its capacity to unfold and take on form from within itself, nature bears the stamp of the divine" (*Philosophy of the Enlightenment*, 40–41).

3. Lipking describes the intense sensory effects of personification mostly lost on modern readers: "between the Renaissance and the Romantics, an ability to conjure up the figure was the sign of poetic genius; it went beyond rhetoric to suggest an encounter with the divine" ("Gods of Poetry," 76–77).

4. The troping action in which Nature includes and generates other Nature(s) corresponds to a feature of Nature that fascinated many in the eighteenth century: its movement; see Hagstrum, *Sister Arts*, 255. Among the best discussions of personification in eighteenth-century poetry are those by Bronson and Wasserman. See Bertrand H. Bronson, "Personification Reconsidered" and Earl R. Wasserman, "Inherent Values."

5. Addison, *The Spectator* 3.573.

6. Hagstrum, *Sister Arts*, 267. The capacity to visualize and give an ontological dimension to poetic description was eventually labeled by Henry Home, Lord Kames, as "ideal presence" in his *Elements of Criticism* (1762). Ideal presence manifests itself when the reader can "conceive every incident as passing in his presence, precisely as if he were an eyewitness" (quoted in Eric Rothstein, *Restoration and Eighteenth-Century Poetry*, 69). See also Wallace Jackson, *Immediacy: The Development of a Critical Concept from Addison to Coleridge* (Amsterdam: Rodopi, 1973): "the new doctrine [of immediacy] emphasized not the mimetic-reflective powers of the artist, but rather the special quality possessed

by the highest genius for taking us directly into the ambience of his invention and causing us to experience it immediately" (6).

7. See John Sitter's analysis of the significance of feminine personifications in eighteenth-century poetry (*Literary Loneliness in Mid-Eighteenth-Century England* [Ithaca: Cornell University Press, 1982], esp. 130–36.

8. See Suvir Kaul's discussion of John Locke and Edward Young on the self as property in *Thomas Gray and Literary Authority: A Study in Ideology and Poetics* (Stanford, CA: Stanford University Press, 1992), 37–38. Kaul argues that the "metaphysics of identity and property is the ideological telos of many eighteenth-century discussions of Authority. Underlying such claims is ultimately Locke's 'property-centered' definition of the political and existential subject" (37–38).

9. Jean Mallinson has discussed the importance of the bird in Finch's poetry, where "the bird often occurs in figures of speech about herself" ("Anne Finch," 70).

10. Reynolds, *Poems*, 51 and 267.

11. Merchant, *Death of Nature*, 253–54. One of vitalism's proponents, *another* Anne Finch in her study *The Grounds of Natural Philosophy* (1668), "took the materialist stance that motion was inherent in matter and that nature was self-knowing and perceptive" (271). See also Pamela K. Gilbert, "The 'Other' Anne Finch: Lady Conway's 'Duelogue' of Textual Selves," *Essays in Arts and Sciences* 26 (October 1997): 15–26.

12. On the imagery of "shades" in Finch see Ruth Salvaggio, *Enlightened Absence: Neoclassical Configurations of the Feminine* (Urbana: University of Illinois Press, 1988), 108–13; and Jean Ellis D'Alessandro, "Anne Countess of Winchilsea and the Whole Duty of Woman." Unless otherwise indicated, all quotations from Finch are from Reynolds's edition.

13. Reuben A. Brower, "Lady Winchilsea and the Poetic Tradition of the Seventeenth Century," *Studies in Philology* 42 (January 1945): 73.

14. Hinnant, *Poetry of Anne Finch*, 42.

15. According to the second edition of the *Oxford English Dictionary* (1989), among the definitions of *rage* that would have been current for Finch are "a vehement passion" and "poetic or prophetic enthusiasm or inspiration."

16. Hinnant interprets this poem as focusing on the "inadequacy of outward perception" that accompanies "a deeper sense of the inadequacy of human language" (*Poetry of Anne Finch*, 155).

17. Quotations from this poem are from *The Anne Finch Wellesley Manuscript Poems. A Critical Edition*, ed. Barbara McGovern and Charles H. Hinnant (Athens: University of Georgia Press, 1998), 31.

18. Laurence Eusden (1688–1730) was "a much ridiculed versifier who was appointed poet laureate in 1718" (McGovern and Hinnant, *Wellesley Manuscript Poems*, 155). Targeting Eusden in particular, Finch may be obliquely attacking his condescension toward women readers and writers. See Barbara M. Benedict's discussion of Eusden's "On a Dispute with a Gentleman about the Excellence of some of Mr. *Dryden*'s Writings; when a Lady, being ask'd her Opinion, blam'd them" (*Making the Modern Reader: Cultural Mediation in Early Modern Literary Anthologies* [Princeton: Princeton University Press, 1996], 122).

19. Finch's class position was an extremely complicated and compromised one because of her husband's status as a nonjuror.

20. David Fairer and Christine Gerrard note that Dyer's focus on a "landscape shaped by memory and personal meaning rather than one constructed to yield a consistent political reading" diverges from the prospects of Denham and Pope (*Eighteenth-Century Poetry: An Annotated Anthology* [Oxford: Blackwell, 1999], 228).

21. All quotations from Dyer are from *Poems. By John Dyer, L. L. B. Viz. I. Grongar Hill. II. The Ruins of Rome. III. The Fleece, in Four Books* (London, 1761).

22. As in Dyer's "Grongar Hill," Joseph Warton's "The Enthusiast" (written 1740, published 1744) elevates sensory over proprietary relations to Nature:

> Yon shepherd idly stretch'd on the rude rock,
> List'ning to dashing waves, and sea-mew's clang
> High-hovering o'er his head, who views beneath
> The dolphin dancing o'er the level brine,
> Feels more true bliss than the proud admiral,
> Amid his vessels bright with burnish'd gold
> And silken streamers, though his lordly nod
> Ten thousand war-worn mariners revere.
>
> (66–73)

For Warton entering Nature's secret retreats brings wisdom and virtuous eroticism (15–25). The enthusiastical relation to Nature depends on a sexualized narrative, which John Sitter has analyzed in *Literary Loneliness* (esp. chapter 4). Warton's Enthusiast must be embraced by Nature and listen to her voice, as Shakespeare did. (Quotation of "The Enthusiast" is from *The Three Wartons: A Choice of Their Verse*, ed. Eric Partridge [London: Scholartis Press, 1927]).

23. On William Wordsworth's evaluation of Thomson and Finch see Germaine Greer, "Wordsworth and Winchilsea: The Progress of an Error," in *The Nature of Identity*, ed. William Weathers (Tulsa, OK: University of Tulsa, 1981), 1–13. On Thomson's relation with the Countess of Hertford, see Helen Sard Hughes, *The Gentle Hertford: Her Life and Letters* (New York: Macmillan, 1940); and James Sambrook, *James Thomson, 1700–1748: A Life* (Oxford: Clarendon Press, 1991), esp. 61–65. McGovern discusses Finch's friendship with the Countess of Hertford (*Anne Finch*, 114–15).

24. W. B. Hutchings, "'Can Pure Description Hold the Place of Sense?': Thomson's Landscape Poetry," in *James Thomson: Essays for the Tercentenary*, ed. Richard Terry (Liverpool: Liverpool University Press, 2000), 49.

25. In *Summer* Dodington, Thomson's "youthful Muse's early friend" (21), possesses feminine and masculine features that resemble a variety of masculine and feminine personifications in the iconographical tradition: the feminine "graces," masculine "light of mind," feminine "tenderness of heart," masculine "Genius," and feminine "wisdom" (22–24). All quotations from Thomson are from *The Seasons and The Castle of Indolence*, ed. James Sambrook (Oxford: Clarendon Press, 1972).

26. Immediately preceding this invocation is another layer of invocation typical of Thomson's allegiance to nature. He invokes a muse who receives an invocation from the natural world:

> As rising from the vegetable world
> My theme ascends, with equal wing ascend,
> My panting Muse; and hark, how loud the woods
> Invite you forth in all your gayest trim.
>
> (*Spring* 572–75)

27. See Patricia Meyer Spacks's analysis of Thomson's description: "in spite of his insistence that he is offering us something to 'see' . . . Thomson controls his descriptive passage through idea, a sense of pattern, rather than through visual detail" (*The Poetry of Vision: Five Eighteenth-Century Poets* [Cambridge, MA: Harvard University Press, 1967], 19).

28. The variety of objects invoked—Nature, the muse, Milton, Newton and his optical theories, God, the sun, Dodington—allows the construction of a variety of poetic selves, thus expressing Nature's and the poet's multiplicity. The poem's multiple sources of inspiration parallel its lack of thematic subordination, which Boswell claimed Johnson found to be its "great defect" (James Boswell, *Life of Johnson*, ed. R. W. Chapman [Oxford: Oxford University Press, 1970], 456).

29. Hagstrum considers "pictorialized natural personification" Thomson's "central formal element in rendering landscape" (*Sister Arts*, 257).

30. See Alan McKillop's "Description and Science" (43–88) in *The Background of Thomson's* Seasons for a discussion of Thomson's combination of scientific, philosophical, religious, and poetic vocabulary.

31. Cf. W. B. Hutchings's argument that "Thomson engages an aesthetic which is formal and linguistic in the attempt to create a poem which matches the very aesthetic of its subject" ("'Can Pure Description,'" 53).

32. Decades later, in 1777, Joseph Priestley was to describe the vividness of the reader's encounter with a "*serious* personification": "the mind is under a temporary deception, the personification is neither made nor helped out by the speaker, but it obtrudes itself upon him; and, while the illusion continues, the passions are as strongly affected, as if the object of them really had the power of thought." From *A Course of Lectures on Oratory and Criticism*, quoted in Wasserman, "Inherent Values," 442.

33. On images of circulation in the body, see Robert A. Erickson, *The Language of the Heart,* 10.

34. See Michael Riffaterre's discussion of prosopopeia and his incorporation of Paul de Man's remarks on the trope: "the symmetrical structure of prosopopeia entails that, by making the dead speak; the living are struck dumb. . . : either the subject will take over the object, or it will be penetrated by the object" ("Prosopopeia," *Yale French Studies* 69 [1985]: 112).

35. Finding a *locus amoenus* "on the dark-green grass, beside the brink / Of haunted stream that by the roots of oak / Rolls o'er the rocky channel," the poet imitates the position of a river god, a position that infuses him with song: he lies "at large / And sing[s] the glories of the circling year" (*Summer,* 11–14).

36. "Deist or not, Thomson saw himself as a devotional poet with the highest imaginable artistic and didactic purposes" (Sambrook, Introduction, xiv).

37. Fredric V. Bogel describes the first half of the century as focused on "ways and modes of knowing" whereas the second half of the century focuses

on "the kinds of being—and the force of being—that our world, our experience, other people, and we ourselves are felt to have" (*Literature and Insubstantiality in Later Eighteenth-Century England* [Princeton: Princeton University Press, 1984], 4).

38. The topographical view was substantially obscured earlier in the eighteenth century with the emergence of graveyard poetry such as Thomas Parnell's *Night Piece on Death* (1722) (George Sherburn and Donald F. Bond, *The Restoration and Eighteenth Century, 1660–1789*, vol. 3, *A Literary History of England*, ed. Albert C. Baugh, 2nd ed. [London: Routledge & Kegan Paul, 1967], 947).

39. All quotations from Collins are from *Thomas Gray and William Collins: Poetical Works*, ed. Roger Lonsdale (1977; repr. Oxford: Oxford University Press, 1985). By permission of Oxford University Press.

40. Paul Sherwin, *Precious Bane: Collins and the Miltonic Legacy* (Austin: University of Texas Press, 1977), 119.

41. Ibid.

42. Cf. Bogel's observation that "Collins' moments of encounter are subtly pervaded by the ambiguity of presence and absence that resides in the structure of the invocation" (*Literature and Insubstantiality*, 89).

43. "An enclosed, inviolate garden; in spiritual and exegetical tradition, the symbol of the soul, the Church, or the virginity of Mary"; see its ancient referent in the Song of Solomon 4.12 (*OED* 7.412).

44. I identify the "Youth of Morn" as a poet-Apollo-sun figure, despite several critics' arguments that the youth is only one of these. In *The Romantic Sublime: Studies in the Structure and Psychology of Transcendence* (Baltimore: Johns Hopkins University Press, 1976), Thomas Weiskel convincingly argues for a multiple identification (141).

45. Martin Price has described the sublime poet's typical movement to a "sacred precinct" as "an appeal to otherness" ("The Sublime Poem: Pictures and Powers," *The Yale Review* 58 [1968]: 199, 200).

46. Cf. Earl Wasserman's analysis of the poet's relation to external objects: Collins countered the empirical epistemology that dominated his era, aspiring instead to a "visual experience of the abstract and the universal as something directly and fully given to his fancy without the mediation of prior sensory experience of them as particulars" ("Collins' 'Ode on the Poetic Character,'" *English Literary History* 34 [1967]: 100).

47. Henry Weinfield, *The Poet without a Name: Gray's Elegy and the Problem of History* (Carbondale: Southern Illinois University Press, 1991), 64.

48. Ibid., 65.

49. Cf. William Empson, *Some Versions of Pastoral* (London: Chatto & Windus, 1935), 4–5. According to Kaul, "Gray can also be located (though in a qualified manner) in this shift from the 'gentleman-author' to the 'man of letters,' a sort of professional of society" (*Thomas Gray and Literary Authority*, 9).

50. Robert Gleckner describes the darkness in the *Elegy* as figuring the death of Gray's friend Richard West as well as Gray's psychological and emotional condition (*Gray Agonistes*, 128). Kaul has observed the many "ironies of Gray's rewriting of the prospect," including that the "'vision' of the poet-figure is circumscribed by the absence of light" (*Thomas Gray and Literary Authority*,

129). All quotations from Gray are from Londsdale, *Thomas Gray and William Collins*. By permission of Oxford University Press.

51. See Herbert W. Starr's "'A Youth to Fortune and to Fame Unknown': A Reestimation," Frank H. Ellis's "Gray's *Elegy*: The Biographical Problem in Literary Criticism," Morse Peckham's "Gray's 'Epitaph' Revisited," and John H. Sutherland's "The Stonecutter in Gray's 'Elegy'"—all in *Twentieth-Century Interpretations of Gray's* Elegy: *A Collection of Critical Essays*, ed. Herbert W. Starr (Englewood Cliffs, NJ: Prentice-Hall, 1968).

52. Weinfield, *Poet without a Name*, 141.

53. This passage prompted William Empson's often-cited analysis of the poem's "latent political ideas": "What this means, as the context makes clear, is that eighteenth-century England had no scholarship system.... This is stated as pathetic, but the reader is put into a mood in which one would not try to alter it" (*Some Versions of Pastoral*, 4).

54. Kaul, *Thomas Gray and Literary Authority*, 122.

55. John Guillory, *Cultural Capital: The Problem of Literary Canon Formation* (Chicago: University of Chicago Press, 1993), 110. "It is in this sense," Guillory continues, "that the poem meditates on the process of what we call canon formation, by projecting onto the figure of the peasant a certain pleasure in the very nonexistence of poems by the 'mute, inglorious Milton.' The very conditions enabling literary production can thus be reexperienced as morally inferior to the conditions which constrain production," 110–11.

56. Of course all writers of their own epitaphs objectify themselves, but not always in the role of speaker.

57. This feminized worth is also attributed to Shakespeare in Gray's *The Progress of Poesy* (1757): "before his infant eyes would run / Such forms, as glitter in the Muse's ray / With orient hues, unborrow'd of the Sun" (118–20). In previous stanzas, the muse symbolized the spirit of poetry as it moves from Greece to Rome and to England. Interestingly, Gray's note to stanza 2.2, which describes the Muse's travels in the remote lands, describes her as "poetic Genius"—a personification that was conventionally masculine. That Gray wants this Genius feminine in his verses is underscored by engaging the muse in an aesthetic dalliance with savage poets: "She deigns to hear the savage Youth repeat / In loose numbers wildly sweet / Their feather-cinctured Chiefs, and dusky Loves" (60–62).

58. Gleckner, *Gray Agonistes*, 132, citing Rogers, *The Augustan Vision* (London: Wiedenfeld & Nicholson, 1974), 138. Bogel, *Literature and Insubstantiality*, 41.

59. Kaul, *Thomas Gray and Literary Authority*, 147.

60. Ibid., 131.

61. Ibid.

62. Guillory, *Cultural Capital*, 114.

63. The poem may be seen as a particular challenge to Thomson's "Winter" of *The Seasons*.

64. Leapor, *Poems on several Occasions*, vol. 1.

65. Cf. Yearsley's "Clifton Hill," which is also set in winter. Mary Waldron argues that "the poem may at first look rather like a plea for the poor and oppressed, but it is not really so. As is usual Yearsley sees herself rather as a go-

between, a messenger; she identifies strongly with the educated, literary reading public although her life has led her among scenes that such people can never know at first hand. In this way she distances herself from her subjects" (*Lactilla, Milkwoman of Clifton: The Life and Writings of Ann Yearsley, 1753–1806* [Athens: University of Georgia Press, 1996], 108).

66. Lipking, "Gods of Poetry," 79. See Siskin, "Personification and Community," 374, 378, 379.

67. Doody, *The Daring Muse*, 166.

68. Bogel, *Literature and Insubstantiality*, 207–8.

69. Emmanuel Levinas, Entre Nous*: On Thinking-of-the-Other*, trans. Michael B. Smith and Barbara Harshav (New York: Columbia University Press, 1998), 10. According to Levinas, "the Face is definitely not a plastic form like a portrait; the relation to the Face is both the relation to the absolutely weak—to what is absolutely exposed, what is bare and destitute, the relation with bareness and consequently with what is alone and can undergo the supreme isolation we call death—and there is, consequently, in the Face of the Other always the death of the Other and thus, in some way, an incitement to murder, the temptation to go to the extreme, to completely neglect the other—and at the same time (and this is the paradoxical thing) the Face is also the 'Thou Shalt not Kill'" (104).

Chapter 5. The Nightingale's Breast against the Thorn

1. Morris, *Religious Sublime*, 155.

2. Ibid., 155–56.

3. G. J. Barker-Benfield, *The Culture of Sensibility: Sex and Society in Eighteenth-Century Britain* (Chicago: University of Chicago Press, 1992), xvii.

4. Ibid.

5. Ibid.

6. Ibid., xvii–xviii. Barker-Benfield argues that sensibility feminizes culture. On sensibility as a masculinizing process, see Claudia L. Johnson, *Equivocal Beings: Politics, Gender, and Sentimentality in the 1790s, Wollstonecraft, Radcliffe, Burney, Austen* (Chicago: University of Chicago Press, 1995); and Julie Ellison, *Cato's Tears and the Making of Anglo-American Emotion* (Chicago: University of Chicago Press, 1999).

7. Janet Todd, *Sensibility: An Introduction* (London: Methuen, 1986), 3.

8. William A. Sessions, "Abandonment and the English Religious Lyric in the Seventeenth Century," in *"Bright Shootes of Everlastingnesse": The Seventeenth-Century Religious Lyric*, Essays in Seventeenth-Century Literature, vol. 2, ed. Claude J. Summers and Ted-Larry Pebworth (Columbia: University of Missouri Press, 1987), 5–7.

9. Joseph Warton, *An Essay on the Writings and Genius of Pope 1756–1782*, 2 vols, Popeiana 18 (New York: Garland Publishing, 1974), 1.x. I thank David B. Morris for leading me to Warton's distinction.

10. We may liken this character of representation to what Tom Huhn describes as the "occlusion of *imitation*," which, he argues, commences "sometime around the beginning of the eighteenth century, although it takes nearly a cen-

tury for the substantive import of the word to be evacuated" ("Burke's Sympathy for Taste," *Eighteenth-Century Studies*, 35, no. 3 [2002]: 379). Huhn's essay focuses on how in Burke's *Enquiry* "sympathy comes to displace and thereby extend what mimesis previously had achieved as mere imitation" (380).

11. See Weiskel, *The Romantic Sublime*.

12. Edmund Burke, *A Philosophical Enquiry into the Origin of our Ideas of the Sublime and Beautiful,* ed. and intro. Adam Phillips (Oxford: Oxford University Press, 1990), 59.

13. See R. F. Brissenden, *Virtue in Distress: Studies in the Novel of Sentiment from Richardson to Sade* (New York: Harper & Row, 1974).

14. According to Pipkin, many twentieth-century Romantic scholars have focused on examples of the "mythic identity of the self-begotten male poet and his ability, as Weiskel puts it, to 'transcend the human'" ("The Material Sublime of Women Romantic Poets," *Studies in English Literature* 38 [1998]: 598). The example that epitomizes this sublime is the Mount Snowdon episode of Wordsworth's *The Prelude* (Bk. 13, 1805) (Pipkin, "Material Sublime," 598).

15. John Baillie, *An Essay on the Sublime (1747)*, The Augustan Reprint Society, no. 43 (Los Angeles: William Andrews Clark Memorial Library, 1953), 4.

16. Ibid.

17. Ibid., 19–20.

18. Ibid., 23.

19. Blair, *Lectures on Rhetoric*, 52, 53, 54.

20. From Lonsdale, Introduction, 461.

21. Cf. Pipkin's discussion of Frances Reynolds's *An Enquiry concerning the Principles of Taste, and of the Origin of Our Ideas of Beauty, etc.* (1785; rpt. Los Angeles: Augustan Reprint Society, 1951). Pipkin remarks that Reynolds's religious sublime reflects that even in 1785 "there are still versions of sublimity in circulation that involve neither transcendence of the human mind nor the usurpation of nature's powers" ("Material Sublime," 607–8).

22. Ashfield and de Bolla, *The Sublime*, 197.

23. Adam Smith, *The Theory of Moral Sentiments*, ed. Knud Haakonssen (Cambridge: Cambridge University Press, 2002), 176.

24. Ibid.

25. Sitter, *Literary Loneliness*, chapter 3 and esp. 96–97.

26. All quotations from Watts are from *Miscellaneous Thoughts in Prose and Verse, on Natural, Moral, and Divine Subjects . . . .* (London, 1734) (New York: Garland, 1971).

27. All quotations from Young are from *The Poetical Works of Edward Young*, in 2 vols. (London: Bell and Daldy, 1858).

28. All quotations from Cowper are from *The Poems of William Cowper*, ed. John D. Baird and Charles Ryskamp, in 3 vols. (Oxford: Clarendon Press, 1980). By permission of Oxford University Press. See James Sambrook's discussion of Cowper's particularly vivid conviction of his own damnation (Introduction to The Task *and Selected Other Poems*, ed. James Sambrook [London: Longman, 1994], 3–10).

29. Cf. Pope's participation in the religious sublime in *Eloisa to Abelard* when Eloisa passionately articulates her longing for Abelard and God.

30. On an earlier example of a woman poet's use of the erotic in devotional poetry, see Helen Wilcox's discussion of the 1652 edition of "Eliza's Babes: or the Virgin's Offering. Being Divine Poems, and Meditations. written by a Lady, who onely desires to advance the glory of God, and not her own" ("My Hart is Full, My Soul Dos Ouer Flow": Women's Devotional Poetry in Seventeenth-Century England," in *Forging Connections: Women's Poetry from the Renaissance to Romanticism*, ed. Anne K. Mellor, Felicity Nussbaum, and Jonathan F. S. Post [San Marino, CA: Huntington Library, 2002), 31–33.

31. Rowe is omitted, notes Marshall, from David Morris's study on the religious sublime. See Marshall, *Poetry of Elizabeth Singer Rowe*, 72n.

32. Doody, "Women Poets," 223.

33. Yearsley's attention to sensibility and the sublime in this poem is extremely significant given that "Addressed to Sensibility" leads the second collection of her poems in which she announces her separation from the "patronage" of Hannah More.

34. Qtd. from Yearsley, *Poems on Various Subjects* (London, 1787).

35. Qtd. from *Original Poems. By a Lady....* (Edinburgh, 1786).

36. Albert R. Chandler, "The Nightingale in Greek and Latin Poetry," *Classical Journal* 30 (1934–35): 78. See Ann Messenger's discussion of Finch's unusual decision to have the nightingale win and her use of gendered pronouns for bird and poet (*His and Hers: Essays in Restoration and Eighteenth-Century Literature* [Lexington: University Press of Kentucky, 1986], 76–80).

37. Hinnant, *Poetry of Anne Finch*, 106.

38. Pipkin, "Material Sublime," 607.

39. All quotations from Seward are from *The Poetical Works* (1810) (New York: AMS, 1974).

40. James Usher, *Clio: or, a Discourse on Taste* (New York: Garland), 102–3.

41. John Dennis, "The Grounds of Criticism in Poetry," in *The Critical Works of John Dennis*, ed. Edward Niles Hooker, vol. 1 (Baltimore: Johns Hopkins Press, 1939), 359.

42. See Robert Markley, "Sentimentality as Performance: Shaftesbury, Sterne, and the Theatrics of Virtue," in *The New Eighteenth Century: Theory, Politics, English Literature*, ed. Felicity Nussbaum and Laura Brown (New York: Methuen, 1987).

43. Ashfield and de Bolla, *The Sublime*, 198.

44. Yearsley, *Poems on Several Occasions* (London: 1785).

45. Waldron, *Lactilla*, 14.

46. As Waldron explains: "The women who sold the milk appear to have been self-employed, with a respectable traditional position in their home villages." Thus Yearsley would have seen herself apart from farm laborers (*Lactilla*, 14).

47. Ibid., 116.

48. Cf. Jerome McGann, *The Poetics of Sensibility: A Revolution in Literary Style* (Oxford: Clarendon Press, 1996), 55, 59.

49. Yearsley, *Poems on Various Subjects, 1787* (Oxford: Woodstock Books, 1994).

50. See Ferguson on Yearsley's increasing attention to social love (*Eighteenth-Century Women Poets*, 55–56).

51. Waldron discusses Yearsley's increasing "impatience with organized religion" (*Lactilla*, 18).

52. Yearsley, *The Rural Lyre* (London: 1796).

53. Tim Burke, "Ann Yearsley and the Distribution of Genius in Early Romantic Culture," in *Early Romantics: Perspectives in British Poetry from Pope to Wordsworth*, ed. Thomas Woodman (Houndmills, UK: Macmillan, 1998), 228.

54. Price, "The Sublime Poem," 199.

55. Ibid., 196.

56. All quotations of Williams's poetry are from *Poems on Various Subjects* (London: 1823).

57. Lucinda Cole and Richard G. Swartz, "Why Should I Wish for Words?': Literacy, Articulation, and the Borders of Literary Culture," in *At the Limits of Romanticism: Essays in Cultural, Feminist, and Materialist Criticism*, ed. Mary A. Favret and Nicola J. Watson (Bloomington: Indiana University Press, 1994), 145.

58. Barbara Claire Freeman, "The Rise of the Sublime: Sacrifice and Misogyny in Eighteenth-Century Aesthetics," *Yale Journal of Criticism* 5, no. 3 (1992): 81–99, especially 84–85. "The interaction between the reason and the imagination in the sublime," argues Freeman, "is itself an allegory of gender relations within patriarchy" (85).

59. Pipkin, "Material Sublime," 598.

60. Peter de Bolla, *The Discourse of the Sublime: Readings in History, Aesthetics and the Subject* (Oxford: Basil Blackwell, 1989), 58.

61. de Bolla, *Discourse*, 293.

62. Ibid., 289.

63. See Nick Mansfield on how early modern and Enlightenment thought both articulates and critiques the autonomous self (*Subjectivity: Theories of the Self from Freud to Haraway* [New York: New York University Press, 2000], 14).

64. See Freeman's "The Rise" and Anne K. Mellor's *Romanticism and Gender* (New York and London: Routledge, 1993). Pipkin discusses both of these in his essay "Material Sublime" (598–600). My notion of horizontal rather than vertical transport resembles in part what Patricia Yaeger calls the "female sublime," although Yaeger describes this horizontal movement as a recent (twentieth-century) phenomenon practiced by women poets. See Yaeger, "Toward a Female Sublime," in *Gender and Theory: Dialogues on Feminist Criticism*, ed. Linda Kaufman (Oxford: Basil Blackwell, 1989).

65. In *Romanticism and Gender* Mellor analyzes a range of uses of the sublime. Pipkin's critique focuses on Mellor's discussion of those women writers who find "nature is a female friend, a sister, with whom they share their most intimate experiences" (97).

66. Pipkin, "Material Sublime," 599.

67. de Bolla, *Discourse*, 32, 39

68. Ashfield and de Bolla, *The Sublime*, 197.

69. de Bolla, *Discourse*, 33–34.

70. John Guillory, "The Ethical Practice of Modernity: The Example of Reading," in *The Turn to Ethics*, ed. Marjorie Garber, Beatrice Hanssen, and Rebecca L. Walkowitz (New York: Routledge, 2000), 39.

71. Charles Altieri, "The Literary and the Ethical: Difference as Definition," in *The Question of Literature: The Place of the Literary in Contemporary Theory*, ed. Elizabeth Beaumont Bissell (Manchester, UK: Manchester University Press, 2002), 43.

72. Ibid.

73. Derek Attridge, "Singular Events," in *The Question of Literature: The Place of the Literary in Contemporary Theory*, ed. Elizabeth Beaumont Bissell (Manchester, UK: Manchester University Press, 2002), 51.

74. Ibid.

Bibliography

Primary Sources

Adams, Jean. *Miscellany Poems. By Mrs Jane* [sic] *Adams*. 1734.

Addison, Joseph. *The Spectator*. Edited by Donald F. Bond. 5 vols. Oxford: Clarendon Press, 1965.

Baillie, John. *An Essay on the Sublime (1747)*. The Augustan Reprint Society, No. 4. Los Angeles: William Andrews Clark Memorial Library, 1953.

Behn, Aphra. *The Works of Aphra Behn. Poems*. Vol. 6. Edited by Montague Summers. London: W. Heinemann, 1915. New York: Phaeton Press, 1967. *The Works of Aphra Behn. The Plays 1682–1696*. Vol. 7. Edited by Janet Todd. Columbus: Ohio State University Press, 1996.

Blair, Hugh. *Lectures on Rhetoric and Belles Lettres*. Vol. 1. Edited by Harold F. Harding. Carbondale: Southern Illinois University Press, 1965.

Baillie, John. *An Essay on the Sublime (1747)*. The Augustan Reprint Society, No. 4. Los Angeles: William Andrews Clark Memorial Library, 1953.

Boswell, James. *Life of Johnson*. Edited by R. W. Chapman. Oxford: Oxford University Press, 1970.

Burke, Edmund. *A Philosophical Enquiry into the Origin of our Ideas of the Sublime and Beautiful*. Edited by Adam Phillips. Oxford: Oxford University Press, 1990.

Carstairs, Christian. *Original Poems. By a Lady, Dedicated to Miss Ann Henderson. A Tribute to Gratitude and Friendship*. 1786.

Collier, Mary. *The Woman's Labour* [and Stephen Duck, *The Thresher's Labour*]. Augustan Reprint Society, publication 230. Los Angeles: William Andrews Clark Memorial Library, 1985.

Collins, William. *Thomas Gray and William Collins: Poetical Works*. Edited by Roger Lonsdale. 1977. Reprint, Oxford: Oxford University Press, 1985.

Cowley, Abraham. *Poems: Miscellanies, The Mistress, Pindarique Odes, Davideis, Verses written on Several Occasions*. Edited by A. R. Waller. Cambridge: Cambridge University Press, 1905.

Cowper, William. *The Poems of William Cowper*. 3 vols. Edited by John D. Baird and Charles Ryskamp. Oxford: Clarendon Press, 1980.

Denham, Sir John. *Coopers Hill. Expans'd Hieroglyphicks: A Critical Edition of Sir John Denham's* Coopers Hill. Edited by Brendan O Hehir. Berkeley: University of California Press, 1969.

Dennis, John. *The Critical Works of John Dennis*. Vol. 1. Edited by Edward Niles Hooker. Baltimore: Johns Hopkins University Press, 1939.

Donne, John. *The Complete Poetry.* Edited by John T. Shawcross. New York: New York University Press, 1968.

Dryden, John. *The Works of John Dryden.* Vol. 1, *Poems 1649–1680.* Edited Edward Niles Hooker, H. T. Swedenberg, Jr., Vinton A. Dearing, et al. Berkeley, Los Angeles: University of California Press, 1956. The *Works of John Dryden.* Vol. 2, *Poems 1681–1684.* Edited by H. T. Swedenberg, Jr., and Vinton A. Dearing. Berkeley: University of California Press, 1972. *The Works of John Dryden.* Vol. 3, *Poems 1685–1692.* Edited by Earl Miner and Vinton Dearing. Berkeley: University of California Press, 1969.

Dyer, John. *Poems by John Dyer, L. L. B. Viz. I. Grongar Hill. II. The Ruins of Rome. III. The Fleece, in Four Books.* London, 1761.

Finch, Anne. *The Anne Finch Wellesley Manuscript Poems. A Critical Edition.* Edited by Barbara McGovern and Charles H. Hinnant. Athens: University of Georgia Press, 1998.

———. *The Poems of Anne Countess of Winchilsea.* Edited by Myra Reynolds. Chicago: University of Chicago Press, 1903.

Gray, Thomas. *Thomas Gray and William Collins: Poetical Works.* Edited by Roger Lonsdale. 1977. Reprint, Oxford: Oxford University Press, 1985.

Johnson, Samuel. *Lives of the Poets. A Selection.* London: J. M. Dent & Sons, 1975.

Killigrew, Anne. *Poems (1686) by Mrs. Anne Killigrew.* Gainesville, FL: Scholars' Facsimiles and Reprints, 1967.

Leapor, Mary. *Poems upon Several Occasions. By the late Mrs. Leapor.* 2 vols. London: 1748, 1751.

Milton, John. *Complete Poems and Major Prose.* Edited by Merritt Y. Hughes. New York: Macmillan, 1957.

Montagu, Lady Mary Wortley. *Essays and Poems and* Simplicity, a Comedy. Edited by Robert Halsband and Isobel Grundy. Oxford: Clarendon Press, 1993.

Ovid. *Metamorphoses.* Vol. 1. With an English translation by Frank Justus Miller. Loeb Classical Library. Cambridge, MA: Harvard University Press, 1984.

Philips, Katherine. *Poems.* London: 1667.

Pope, Alexander. *The Dunciad.* Edited by James Sutherland. Vol. 5, *The Poems of Alexander Pope.* London: Methuen; New Haven: Yale University Press, 1961.

———. *An Essay on Man.* Edited by Maynard Mack. Vol. 3, part 1. *The Poems of Alexander Pope.* London: Methuen; New Haven: Yale University Press, 1959.

———. *Pastoral Poetry and* An Essay on Criticism. Vol. 1. *The Poems of Alexander Pope.* Edited by E. Audra Williams and Aubrey Williams. London: Methuen; New Haven: Yale University Press, 1961.

Rowe, Elizabeth. *The Miscellaneous Works, in Prose and Verse, of Mrs. Elizabeth Rowe.* 2 vols. London: 1749.

Seward, Anna. *The Poetical Works* (1810). New York: AMS Press, 1974.

Shaftesbury, Anthony, Earl of. *Characteristics of Men, Manners, Opinions, Times*. Vols. 1 and 2. Edited by John M. Robertson. Indianapolis, IN: Bobbs-Merrill, 1964.

Sidney, Sir Philip. *The Poems*. Edited by William A. Ringler, Jr. Oxford: Clarendon Press, 1962.

Smith, Adam. *The Theory of Moral Sentiments*. Edited by Knud Haakonssen. Cambridge: Cambridge University Press, 2002.

Swift, Jonathan. *The Complete Poems*. Edited by Pat Rogers. New Haven: Yale University Press, 1983.

Thomson, James. *The Seasons and The Castle of Indolence*. Edited by James Sambrook. Oxford: Clarendon Press, 1972.

Usher, James. *Clio: or, a Discourse on Taste*. New York: Garland Press, 1970.

Warton, Joseph. "The Enthusiast." In *The Three Wartons: A Choice of Their Verse*, edited by Eric Partridge. London: Scholartis Press, 1927.

———. *An Essay on the Writings and Genius of Pope, 1756–1782*. 2 vols. Popeiana 18. New York: Garland Publishing, 1974.

Watts, Isaac. *Miscellaneous Thoughts in Prose and Verse, on Natural, Moral, and Divine Subjects....* (1734). New York: Garland Press, 1971.

Williams, Helen Maria. *Poems on Various Subjects*. London: 1823.

Yearsley, Ann. *Poems on Several Occasions*. London: 1785.

———. *Poems on Various Subjects. 1787*. Oxford: Woodstock Books, 1994.

———. *The Rural Lyre*. London: 1796.

Young, Edward. *The Poetical Works*. 2 vols. London: Bell and Daldy, 1858.

Secondary Sources

Abrams, M. H. *The Mirror and the Lamp: Romantic Theory and the Critical Tradition*. New York: Oxford University Press, 1953.

Altieri, Charles. "The Literary and the Ethical: Difference as Definition." In *The Question of Literature: The Place of the Literary in Contemporary Theory*, edited by Elizabeth Beaumont Bissell. Manchester, UK: Manchester University Press, 2002.

Andreadis, Harriette. "The Sapphic-Platonics of Katherine Philips, 1632–1664." *Signs* 15, no. 1 (Autumn 1989): 34–60.

Armstrong, Isobel, and Virginia Blain, eds. *Women's Poetry in the Enlightenment: The Making of a Canon, 1730–1820*. Houndmills: Macmillan, 1999.

Ashfield, Andrew, and Peter de Bolla, eds. *The Sublime: A Reader in British Eighteenth-Century Aesthetic Theory*. Cambridge: Cambridge University Press, 1996.

Attridge, Derek. "Singular Events." In *The Question of Literature: The Place of the Literary in Contemporary Theory*, edited by Elizabeth Beaumont Bissell. Manchester: Manchester University Press, 2002.

Aubin, Robert. *Topographical Poetry in XVIII-Century England*. New York: Modern Language Association, 1936.

Barash, Carole. *English Women's Poetry, 1649–1714: Politics, Community, and Linguistic Authority.* Oxford: Clarendon Press, 1996.

Barkan, Leonard. *The Gods Made Flesh: Metamorphosis and the Pursuit of Paganism.* New Haven: Yale University Press, 1986.

Barker-Benfield, G. J. *The Culture of Sensibility: Sex and Society in Eighteenth-Century Britain.* Chicago: University of Chicago Press, 1992.

Barrell, John. "'The Dangerous Goddess': Masculinity, Prestige, and the Aesthetic in Early Eighteenth-Century Britain." *Cultural Critique*, no. 12 (Spring 1989): 101–31.

———. *English Literature in History, 1730–80: An Equal, Wide Survey.* New York: St. Martin's Press, 1983.

———. *The Idea of Landscape and the Sense of Place, 1730–1840. An Approach to the Poetry of John Clare.* Cambridge: Cambridge University Press, 1972.

Bate, W. J. *The Burden of the Past and the English Poet.* Cambridge, MA: Harvard University Press, 1970.

———. *From Classic to Romantic: Premises of Taste in Eighteenth-Century England.* 1946. Reprint, New York: Harper, 1961.

Battersby, Christine. *Gender and Genius: Towards a Feminist Aesthetics.* Bloomington: Indiana University Press, 1989.

Bender, John. "A New History of the Enlightenment?" In *The Profession of Eighteenth-Century Literature: Reflections on an Institution*, edited by Leo Damrosch. Madison: University of Wisconsin Press, 1992.

Benedict, Barbara M. *Making the Modern Reader: Cultural Mediation in Early Modern Literary Anthologies.* Princeton: Princeton University Press, 1996.

Bermingham, Ann. "Elegant Females and Gentlemen Connoisseurs: The Commerce in Culture and Self-Image in Eighteenth-Century England." In *The Consumption of Culture, 1600–1800*, edited by Ann Bermingham and John Brewer. London: Routledge, 1995.

———. "System, Order, and Abstraction: The Politics of English Landscape Drawing around 1795." In *Landscape and Power*, edited by W. J. T. Mitchell. Chicago: University of Chicago Press, 1994.

Bloom, Harold. *The Anxiety of Influence: A Theory of Poetry.* New York: Oxford University Press, 1973.

Bogel, Fredric V. *Literature and Insubstantiality in Later Eighteenth–Century England.* Princeton: Princeton University Press, 1984.

Bonnell, Thomas F. "Collins, Lady Winchilsea, and the Pursuit of the Muse." In *Teaching Eighteenth-Century Poetry*, edited by Christopher Fox. New York: AMS Press, 1990.

Brissenden, R. F. *Virtue in Distress: Studies in the Novel of Sentiment from Richardson to Sade.* New York: Harper & Row, 1974.

Bronson, Bertrand H. "Personification Reconsidered." *ELH: A Journal of English Literary History* 14 (September 1947): 163–77.

Brower, Reuben A. "Lady Winchilsea and the Poetic Tradition of the Seventeenth Century." *Studies in Philology* 42 (January 1945): 61–80.

Brown, Laura. "The Feminization of Ideology: Form and the Female in the Long Eighteenth Century." In *Ideology and Form in Eighteenth-Century Literature*, edited by David Richter. Lubbock: Texas Tech University Press, 1999.

Brown, Marshall. *Preromanticism.* Stanford, CA: Stanford University Press, 1991.

Budick, Sanford. "The Demythological Mode in Augustan Verse." *ELH: A Journal of English Literary History* 37, no. 3 (September 1970): 389–414

———. *Poetry of Civilization: Mythopoeic Displacement in the Verse of Milton, Dryden, Pope, and Johnson.* New Haven: Yale University Press, 1974.

Burke, Tim. "Ann Yearsley and the Distribution of Genius in Early Romantic Culture." In *Early Romantics: Perspectives in British Poetry from Pope to Wordsworth,* edited by Thomas Woodman. Houndmills, UK: Macmillan, 1998.

Butler, Judith. *Bodies that Matter: On the Discursive Limits of "Sex."* New York: Routledge, 1993.

Burwick, Frederick. *Mimesis and Its Romantic Reflections.* University Park: Pennsylvania State University Press, 2001.

Campbell, Lily B. "The Christian Muse." *Huntington Library Bulletin* 8 (1935): 29–70.

Carretta, Vincent. *The Snarling Muse: Verbal and Visual Satire from Pope to Churchill.* Philadelphia: University of Pennsylvania Press, 1983.

Carruthers, Mary J. "The Re-Vision of the Muse: Adrienne Rich, Audre Lorde, Judy Grahn, Olga Broumas." *The Hudson Review* 36, no. 2 (1983): 293–322.

Cascardi, Anthony J. *Consequences of Enlightenment.* Cambridge: Cambridge University Press, 1999.

Cassirer, Ernst. *The Philosophy of the Enlightenment.* Translated by Fritz C. A. Koelln and James P. Pettegrove. 1951. Reprint, Princeton: Princeton University Press, 1979.

Cave, Terence. *The Cornucopian Text: Problems of Writing in the French Renaissance.* Oxford: Clarendon Press, 1979.

Chandler, Albert R. "The Nightingale in Greek and Latin Poetry." *Classical Journal* 30 (1934–35): 78–84.

Christmas, William J. *The Lab'ring Muses: Work, Writing, and the Social Order in English Plebeian Poetry, 1730–1830.* Newark: University of Delaware Press, 2001.

Cohen, Ralph. "The Augustan Mode in English Poetry." *Eighteenth-Century Studies* 1, no. 1 (September 1967): 3–32.

Cole, Lucinda, and Richard G. Swartz, "'Why Should I Wish for Words?': Literacy, Articulation, and the Borders of Literary Culture." In *At the Limits of Romanticism: Essays in Cultural, Feminist, and Materialist Criticism,* edited by Mary A. Favret and Nicola J. Watson. Bloomington: Indiana University Press, 1994.

Conroy, Mark. *Modernism and Authority: Strategies of Legitimation in Flaubert and Conrad.* Baltimore: Johns Hopkins University Press, 1985.

Crawford, Rachel. *Poetry, Enclosure, and the Vernacular Landscape, 1700–1830.* Cambridge: Cambridge University Press, 2002.

———. "Troping the Subject: Behn, Smith, Hemans and the Poetics of the Bower," *Studies in Romanticism* 38, no. 2 (Summer 1999): 249–79.

Culler, Jonathan. "Apostrophe." *Diacritics* 7, no. 4 (1977): 59–69.

Curran, Stuart. "Romantic Poetry: The I Altered." In *Romanticism and Feminism*, edited by Anne K. Mellor. Bloomington: Indiana University Press, 1988.

Curtius, Ernst. *European Literature and the Latin Middle Ages*. New York: Pantheon, 1953.

D'Alessandro, Jean Ellis. "Anne Countess of Winchilsea and the Whole Duty of Woman: Socio-Cultural Inference in a Reading of 'The Introduction.'" *Lingue del Mondo* 52, no. 5/6 (1988): 9–15.

Deane, C. V. *Aspects of Eighteenth-Century Nature Poetry*. Oxford: Basil Blackwood, 1935.

de Beauvoir, Simone. *The Second Sex*. Translated and edited by H. M. Parshley. New York: Vintage, 1980.

de Bolla, Peter. *The Discourse of the Sublime: Readings in History, Aesthetics and the Subject*. Oxford: Basil Blackwell, 1989.

DeJean, Joan. *Fictions of Sappho, 1546–1937*. Chicago: University of Chicago Press, 1989.

de Man, Paul. *The Rhetoric of Romanticism*. New York: Columbia University Press, 1984.

De Shazer, Mary K. *Inspiring Women: Reimagining the Muse*. New York: Pergamon, 1986.

Deutsch, Helen. *Resemblance & Disgrace: Alexander Pope and the Deformation of Culture*. Cambridge, MA: Harvard University Press, 1996.

Diehl, Joanne Feit. "'Come Slowly—Eden': An Exploration of Women Poets and Their Muse." *Signs* 3, no. 3 (1978): 572–87.

Di Pesa, Pamela. "The Imperious Muse: Some Observations on Women, Nature, and the Poetic Tradition." In *Feminist Criticism: Essays on Theory, Poetry, and Prose*, edited by Cheryl L. Brown and Karen Olson. Metuchen, NJ: Scarecrow Press, 1978.

Dobrée. Bonamy. *English Literature in the Early Eighteenth Century, 1700–1740*. Oxford: Clarendon Press, 1959.

Doody, Margaret Anne. *The Daring Muse: Augustan Poetry Reconsidered*. Cambridge: Cambridge University Press, 1985.

———. "Sensuousness in the Poetry of Eighteenth-Century Women Poets." In *Women's Poetry in the Enlightenment: The Making of a Canon, 1730–1820*, edited by Isobel Armstrong and Virginia Blain. Houndmills, UK: Macmillan, 1999.

———. "Women Poets of the Eighteenth Century." In *Women and Literature in Britain, 1700–1800*, edited by Viven Jones. Cambridge: Cambridge University Press, 2000.

Dubrow, Heather. "Guess Who's Coming to Dinner? Reinterpreting Formalism and the Country House Poem." *Modern Language Quarterly* 61, no. 1 (2000): 59–77.

Eagleton, Terry. *The Ideology of the Aesthetic*. Oxford: Basil Blackwell, 1990.

Ellis, Frank H. "Gray's *Elegy*: The Biographical Problem in Literary Criticism." In *Twentieth-Century Interpretations of Gray's Elegy: A Collection of Critical Essays*, edited by Herbert W. Starr. Englewood Cliffs, NJ: Prentice-Hall, 1968.

Ellison, Julie. *Cato's Tears and the Making of Anglo-American Emotion.* Chicago: University of Chicago Press, 1999.

Empson, William. *Some Versions of Pastoral.* London: Chatto & Windus, 1935.

Erickson, Robert A. *The Language of the Heart, 1600–1750.* Philadelphia: University of Pennsylvania Press, 1997.

Erskine-Hill, Howard. *The Augustan Idea in English Literature.* London: E. Arnold, 1983.

Ezell, Margaret J. M. "The Posthumous Publication of Women's Manuscripts and the History of Authorship." In *Women's Writing and the Circulation of Ideas: Manuscript Publication in England, 1500–1800,* edited by George L. Justice and Nathan Tinker. Cambridge: Cambridge University Press, 2002.

———. *Writing Women's Literary History.* Baltimore: Johns Hopkins University Press, 1993.

Fabricant, Carole. "The Aesthetics and Politics of Landscape in the Eighteenth Century." In *Studies in Eighteenth-Century British Art and Aesthetics,* edited by Ralph Cohen. Berkeley: University of California Press, 1985.

———. "Binding and Dressing Nature's Loose Tresses: The Ideology of Augustan Landscape Design." In *Studies in Eighteenth-Century Culture,* vol. 8, edited by Roseann Runte. Madison: University of Wisconsin Press, 1979.

———. "Defining Self and Others: Pope and Eighteenth-Century Gender Ideology." *Criticism* 39, no. 4 (1997): 503–29.

———. *Swift's Landscape.* Baltimore: Johns Hopkins University Press, 1982.

Fairer, David. *English Poetry of the Eighteenth Century, 1700–1789.* London: Longman, 2003.

———. *Pope's Imagination.* Manchester, UK: Manchester University Press, 1984.

Fairer, David, and Christine Gerrard, eds. *Eighteenth-Century Poetry: An Annotated Anthology.* Oxford: Blackwell, 1999.

Favret, Mary A, and Nicola J. Watson, eds. *At the Limits of Romanticism: Essays in Cultural, Feminist, and Materialist Criticism.* Bloomington: Indiana University Press, 1994.

Feingold, Richard. *Moralized Song: The Character of Augustan Lyricism.* New Brunswick, NJ: Rutgers University Press, 1989.

Ferguson, Moira. *Eighteenth-Century Women Poets: Nation, Class, and Gender.* Albany, NY: SUNY Press, 1995.

Flinker, Noam. "Courting Urania: The Narrator of *Paradise Lost* Invokes His Muse." In *Milton and the Idea of Woman,* edited by Julia M. Walker. Urbana: University of Illinois Press, 1988.

Fontanier, Pierre. *Les Figures du Discours.* Introduction by Gérard Genette. Paris: Flammarion, 1977.

Freadman, Anne. "Poeta (1st dec., n., fem.)." *Australian Journal of French Studies* 16, no. 2 (1972): 152–65.

Freeman, Barbara Claire. "The Rise of the Sublime: Sacrifice and Misogyny in Eighteenth-Century Aesthetics." *Yale Journal of Criticism* 5, no. 3 (1992): 81–99.

Frieden, Ken. *Genius and Monologue.* Ithaca: Cornell University Press, 1985.

Frye, Northrop. "Towards Defining an Age of Sensibility." In *Eighteenth-Century English Literature: Modern Essays in Criticism*, edited by James L. Clifford. New York: Oxford University Press, 1959.

Fulford, Tim. *Landscape, Liberty and Authority: Poetry, Criticism and Politics from Thomson to Wordsworth*. Cambridge: Cambridge University Press, 1996.

Fullard, Joyce. Introduction to *British Women Poets, 1660–1800: An Anthology*. Edited by Joyce Fullard. Troy, NY: Whitston, 1990.

Fuss, Diana. *Identification Papers*. New York: Routledge, 1995.

Gallagher, Catherine. "Embracing the Absolute: The Politics of the Female Subject in Seventeenth-Century England." *Genders* 1 (Spring 1988): 24–39.

Gebauer, Gunter, and Christoph Wulf. *Mimesis: Culture, Art, Society*. Translated by Don Reneau. Berkeley: University of California Press, 1992.

Gentili, Bruno. *Poetry and Its Public in Ancient Greece: From Homer to the Fifth Century*. Baltimore: Johns Hopkins University Press, 1988.

Gilbert, Pamela K. "The 'Other' Anne Finch: Lady Conway's 'Duelogue' of Textual Selves." *Essays in Arts and Sciences* 26 (October 1997): 15–26.

Gilbert, Sandra, and Susan Gubar. "'But Oh! That Deep Romantic Chasm'": The Engendering of Periodization." *The Kenyon Review* 13, no. 3 (Summer 1991): 74–81.

———. *The Madwoman in the Attic: The Woman Writer and the Nineteenth-Century Literary Imagination*. New Haven: Yale University Press, 1979.

Gleckner, Robert. *Gray Agonistes: Thomas Gray and Masculine Friendship*. Baltimore: Johns Hopkins University Press, 1997.

Greene, Richard. *Mary Leapor: A Study in Eighteenth-Century Women's Poetry*. New York: Oxford University Press, 1993.

Greer, Germaine. "Wordsworth and Winchilsea: The Progress of an Error." In *The Nature of Identity*, edited by William Weathers. Tulsa, OK: University of Tulsa, 1981.

Greer, Germaine, Susan Hastings, Jeslyn Medoff, Melinda Sansone, eds. *Kissing the Rod: An Anthology of Seventeenth-Century Women's Verse*. New York: Farrar Straus Giroux, 1988.

Griffin, Dustin. *Patriotism and Poetry in Eighteenth-Century Britain*. Cambridge: Cambridge University Press, 2002.

———. "The Visionary Scene: Vision and Allegory in the Poetry of Pope." In *Enlightening Allegory: Theory, Practice, and Contexts of Allegory in the Late Seventeenth and Eighteenth Centuries*, edited by Kevin L. Cope. New York: AMS Press, 1993.

Grundy, Isobel, "Lady Mary Wortley Montagu and Her Daughter: The Changing Use of Manuscripts." In *Women's Writing and the Circulation of Ideas: Manuscript Publication in England, 1500–1800*, edited by George L. Justice and Nathan Tinker. Cambridge: Cambridge University Press, 2002.

Guillory, John. *Cultural Capital: The Problem of Literary Canon Formation*. Chicago: University of Chicago Press, 1993.

———. "The Ethical Practice of Modernity: The Example of Reading." In *The Turn to Ethics*, edited by Marjorie Garber, Beatrice Hanssen, and Rebecca L. Walkowitz. New York: Routledge, 2000.

———. *Poetic Authority: Spenser, Milton, and Literary History.* New York: Columbia University Press, 1983.

Hagstrum, Jean H. *The Sister Arts: The Tradition of Literary Pictorialism and English Poetry from Dryden to Gray.* Chicago: University of Chicago Press, 1958.

Hammond, Brean S. *Pope and Bolingbroke: A Study of Friendship and Influence.* Columbia: University of Missouri Press, 1984.

Hartman, Geoffrey. *Beyond Formalism.* New Haven: Yale University Press, 1970.

Hinnant, Charles H. *The Poetry of Anne Finch: An Essay in Interpretation.* Newark: University of Delaware Press, 1994.

Hobby, Elaine. *Virtue of Necessity: English Women's Writing, 1649–88.* Ann Arbor: University of Michigan Press, 1989.

Hoffman, Arthur W. *John Dryden's Imagery.* Gainesville: University of Florida Press, 1962.

Hope, A. D. "Anne Killigrew, or the Art of Modulating." In *Dryden's Mind and Art*, edited by Bruce King. Edinburgh: Oliver and Boyd, 1969.

Hughes, Helen Sard. *The Gentle Hertford: Her Life and Letters.* New York: Macmillan, 1940.

Huhn, Tom. "Burke's Sympathy for Taste." *Eighteenth-Century Studies* 35, no. 3 (2002): 379–93.

Hunt, John Dixon. *The Figure in the Landscape: Poetry, Painting, and Gardening During the Eighteenth Century.* Baltimore: Johns Hopkins University Press, 1976.

Hutchings, W. B. "'Can Pure Description Hold the Place of Sense?': Thomson's Landscape Poetry." In *James Thomson: Essays for the Tercentenary*, edited by Richard Terry. Liverpool: Liverpool University Press, 2000.

Ingrassia, Catherine. *Authorship, Commerce, and Gender in Early Eighteenth-Century England: A Culture of Paper Credit.* Cambridge: Cambridge University Press, 1998.

Jackson, Wallace. *Immediacy: The Development of a Critical Concept from Addison to Coleridge.* Amsterdam: Rodopi, 1973.

Jaffe, Nora Crow. *The Poet Swift.* Hanover, NH: University Press of New England, 1977.

Johnson, Claudia L. *Equivocal Beings: Politics, Gender, and Sentimentality in the 1790s, Wollstonecraft, Radcliffe, Burney, Austen.* Chicago: University of Chicago Press, 1995.

Jones, Robert W. *Gender and the Formation of Taste in Eighteenth-Century Britain: The Analysis of Beauty.* Cambridge: Cambridge University Press, 1998.

Justice, George L., and Nathan Tinker, ed. *Women's Writing and the Circulation of Ideas: Manuscript Publication in England, 1550–1800.* Cambridge: Cambridge University Press, 2002.

Kairoff, Claudia Thomas. "Eighteenth-Century Women Poets and Readers." In *The Cambridge Companion to Eighteenth-Century Poetry*, edited by John Sitter. Cambridge: Cambridge University Press, 2001.

Kaul, Suvir. *Thomas Gray and Literary Authority: A Study in Ideology and Poetics.* Stanford, CA: Stanford University Press, 1992.

King, Kathryn R. "Elizabeth Singer Rowe's Tactical Use of Print and Manuscript." In *Women's Writing and the Circulation of Ideas: Manuscript Publication in England, 1550–1800*, edited by George L. Justice and Nathan Tinker. Cambridge: Cambridge University Press, 2002.

———. "Jane Barker, *Poetical Recreations*, and the Sociable Text." *ELH: A Journal of English Literary History* 61, no. 3 (1994): 551–70.

Knapp, Steven. *Personification and the Sublime: Milton to Coleridge*. Cambridge, MA: Harvard University Press, 1985.

Kolodny, Annette. *The Lay of the Land: Metaphor as Experience and History in American Life and Letters*. Chapel Hill: University of North Carolina Press, 1975.

Korshin, Paul J. *Typologies in England, 1650–1820*. Princeton: Princeton University Press, 1982.

Kramer, David Bruce. *The Imperial Dryden: The Poetics of Appropriation in Seventeenth-Century England*. Athens: University of Georgia Press, 1994.

Krieger, Murray. "Presentation and Representation in the Renaissance Lyric: The Net of Words and the Escape of the Gods." In *Mimesis: From Mirror to Method, Augustine to Descartes*, edited by John D. Lyons and Stephen G. Nichols, Jr. Hanover, NH: University Press of New England, 1982.

Labbe, Jacqueline. *Romantic Visualities: Landscape, Gender, and Romanticism*. New York: St. Martin's Press, 1998.

Landry, Donna. *The Muses of Resistance: Laboring-Class Women's Poetry in Britain, 1739–1796*. Cambridge: Cambridge University Press, 1990.

———. "The Traffic in Women Poets." *The Eighteenth Century: Theory and Interpretation* 32 (1991): 180–92.

Levinas, Emmanuel. *Entre Nous: On Thinking-of-the-Other*. Translated by Michael B. Smith and Barbara Harshav. New York: Columbia University Press, 1998.

Limbert, Claudia A. "Katherine Philips: Controlling a Life and Reputation." *South Atlantic Review* 56, no. 2 (1991): 27–42.

Lipking, Lawrence. "The Gods of Poetry: Mythology and the Eighteenth-Century Tradition." In *Augustan Subjects: Essays in Honor of Martin C. Battestin*, edited by Albert J. Rivero. Newark: University of Delaware Press, 1997.

Lonsdale, Roger. Introduction to *Eighteenth-Century Women Poets: An Oxford Anthology*. Edited by Roger Lonsdale. Oxford: Oxford University Press, 1989.

Loscocco, Paula. "'Manly Sweetness': Katherine Philips among the Neoclassicals." *The Huntington Library Quarterly* 56, no. 3 (Summer 1993): 259–79.

Lovejoy, Arthur O. "'Nature' as Aesthetic Norm." In *Essays in the History of Ideas*. Baltimore: Johns Hopkins University Press, 1948.

Low, Anthony. *The Georgic Revolution*. Princeton: Princeton University Press, 1985.

Mack, Maynard. *The Garden and the City: Retirement and Politics in the Later Poetry of Pope, 1731–43*. Toronto: University of Toronto Press, 1969.

———. "The Muse of Satire." In *Collected in Himself: Essays Critical, Biographical and Bibliographical on Pope and Some of His Contemporaries*. Newark: University of Delaware Press, 1982.

Mack, Robert L. *Thomas Gray: A Life.* New Haven: Yale University Press, 2000.

Mahoney, John L. *The Whole Internal Universe: Imitation and the New Defense of Poetry in British Criticism, 1660–1830.* New York: Fordham University Press, 1985.

Mallinson, Jean. "Anne Finch: A Woman Poet and the Tradition." In *Gender at Work: Four Women Writers of the Eighteenth Century*, edited by Ann Messenger. Detroit: Wayne State University Press, 1990.

Mandell, Laura. *Misogynous Economies: The Business of Literature in Eighteenth-Century Britain.* Lexington: University Press of Kentucky, 1999.

———. "'Those Limbs Disjointed of Gigantic Power': Barbauld's Personifications and the (Mis)Attribution of Political Agency." *Studies in Romanticism* 37 (Spring 1998): 27–41.

Mansfield, Nick. *Subjectivity: Theories of the Self from Freud to Haraway.* New York: New York University Press, 2000.

Markley, Robert. "Sentimentality as Performance: Shaftesbury, Sterne, and the Theatrics of Virtue." In *The New Eighteenth Century: Theory, Politics, English Literature*, edited by Felicity Nussbaum and Laura Brown. New York: Methuen, 1987.

Marshall, Madeleine Forell. Introduction to *The Poetry of Elizabeth Singer Rowe, 1674–1737*. Edited by Madeleine Forell Marshall. Studies in Women and Religion, vol. 25. Lewiston, NY: Edwin Mellen Press, 1987.

Martin, Roberta C. "'Beauteous Wonder of a Different Kind': Aphra Behn's Destabilization of Sexual Categories." *College English* 61, no. 2 (November 1998): 192–210.

Maruca, Lisa. "Political Propriety and Feminine Property: Women in the Eighteenth-Century Text Trades." *Studies in the Literary Imagination* 34, no. 1 (Spring 2001): 79–99.

McDowell, Paula. *The Women of Grub Street: Press, Politics, and Gender in the London Literary Marketplace, 1678–1730.* Oxford: Clarendon Press, 1998.

McGann, Jerome. *The Poetics of Sensibility: A Revolution in Literary Style.* Oxford: Clarendon Press, 1996.

———. *The Romantic Ideology: A Critical Investigation.* Chicago: University of Chicago Press, 1983.

McGovern. Barbara. *Anne Finch and Her Poetry: A Critical Biography.* Athens: University of Georgia Press, 1992.

———. "Finch, Pope, and Swift: The Bond of Displacement." In *Pope, Swift, and Women Writers*, edited by Donald C. Mell. Newark: University of Delaware Press, 1996.

McGovern, Barbara, and Charles H. Hinnant, eds. *The Anne Finch Wellesley Manuscript Poems: A Critical Edition.* Athens: University of Georgia Press, 1998.

McKillop, Alan Dugald. *The Background of Thomson's* Seasons. Minneapolis: University of Minnesota Press, 1942.

Melberg, Arne. *Theories of Mimesis.* Cambridge: Cambridge University Press, 1995.

Mell, Donald C., ed. *Pope, Swift, and Women Writers*. Newark: University of Delaware Press, 1996.

Mellor, Anne K., ed. *Romanticism and Feminism*. Bloomington: Indiana University Press, 1988.

———. *Romanticism and Gender*. New York: Routledge, 1993.

Merchant, Carolyn. *The Death of Nature: Women, Ecology, and the Scientific Revolution*. New York: Harper and Row, 1983.

Mermin, Dorothy. "Women Becoming Poets: Katherine Philips, Aphra Behn, Anne Finch." *ELH: A Journal of English Literary History* 57 (1990): 335–55.

Messenger, Ann. *His and Hers: Essays in Restoration and Eighteenth-Century Literature*. Lexington: University Press of Kentucky, 1986.

———. "Publishing without Perishing: Lady Winchilsea's *Miscellany Poems* of 1713." *Restoration* 5 (1981): 27–37.

Mitchell, W. J. T. Introduction to *Landscape and Power*, edited by W. J. T. Mitchell. Chicago: University of Chicago Press, 1994.

Morris, David B. *Alexander Pope: The Genius of Sense*. Cambridge, MA: Harvard University Press, 1984.

———. *The Religious Sublime: Christian Poetry and Critical Tradition in 18th-Century England*. Lexington: University Press of Kentucky, 1972.

Morse, David. *The Age of Virtue: British Culture from the Restoration to Romanticism*. Houndmills: Macmillan, 2000.

Nicolson, Marjorie Hope. *Newton Demands the Muse: Newton's Opticks and the Eighteenth Century Poets*. Princeton: Princeton University Press, 1946.

Novak, Maximillian E. "Shaping the Augustan Myth: John Dryden and the Politics of Restoration Augustanism." In *Greene Centennial Studies: Essays Presented to Donald Greene in the Centennial Year of the University of Southern California*, edited by Paul J. Korshin and Robert R. Allen. Charlottesville: University Press of Virginia, 1984.

O Hehir, Brendan. *Expans'd Hieroglyphicks: A Critical Edition of Sir John Denham's Coopers Hill*. Berkeley: University of California Press, 1969.

Ortner, Sherry B. "Is Female to Male as Nature Is to Culture?" In *Woman, Culture, and Society*, edited by Michelle Zimbalist Rosaldo and Louise Lamphere. Stanford, CA: Stanford University Press, 1974.

Parker, Blanford. *The Triumph of Augustan Poetics: English Literary Culture from Butler to Johnson*. Cambridge: Cambridge University Press, 1998.

Paxson, James J. *The Poetics of Personification*. Cambridge: Cambridge University Press, 1994.

Peckham, Morse. "Gray's 'Epitaph' Revisited." In *Twentieth-Century Interpretations of Gray's Elegy: A Collection of Critical Essays*, edited by Herbert W. Starr. Englewood Cliffs, NJ: Prentice-Hall, 1968.

Pipkin, John G. "The Material Sublime of Women Romantic Poets." *SEL: Studies in English Literature* 38 (1998): 597–619.

Pollak, Ellen. *The Poetics of Sexual Myth: Gender and Ideology in the Verse of Swift and Pope*. Chicago: University of Chicago Press, 1985.

Poovey, Mary. "Aesthetics and Political Economy in the Eighteenth Century: The Place of Gender in the Social Constitution of Knowledge." In *Aesthetics and Ideology*, edited by George Levine. New Brunswick, NJ: Rutgers University Press, 1994.

Prescott, Sarah, and David E. Shuttleton, eds. *Women and Poetry, 1660–1750*. Houndmills, UK: Palgrave, 2003.

Price, Martin. "The Sublime Poem: Pictures and Powers." *The Yale Review* 58 (1968): 194–213.

Revard, Stella P. "The Seventeenth-Century Religious Ode and Its Classical Models." In *"Bright Shootes of Everlastingnesse": The Seventeenth-Century Religious Lyric*, Essays in Seventeenth-Century Literature, vol. 2, edited by Claude J. Summers and Ted-Larry Pebworth. Columbia: University of Missouri Press, 1987.

Reynolds, Myra. Introduction to *The Poems of Anne Countess of Winchilsea*. Chicago: University of Chicago Press, 1903.

Riede, David G. *Oracles and Hierophants: Constructions of Romantic Authority*. Ithaca: Cornell University Press, 1991.

Riffaterre, Michael. "Prosopopeia." *Yale French Studies* 69 (1985): 107–23.

Rooney, Ellen. "Form and Contentment." *Modern Language Quarterly* 61, no. 1 (2000): 17–40.

Rose, Mark. *Authors and Owners: The Invention of Copyright*. Cambridge, MA: Harvard University Press, 1993.

Ross, Marlon B. "Authority and Authenticity: Scribbling Authors and the Genius of Print in Eighteenth-Century England." In *The Construction of Authorship: Textual Appropriation in Law and Literature*, edited by Martha Woodmansee and Peter Jaszi. Durham, NC: Duke University Press, 1994.

———. *The Contours of Masculine Desire: Romanticism and the Rise of Women's Poetry*. New York: Oxford University Press, 1989.

Rosset, Clément. *L'anti-nature: Éléments pour une philosophie tragique*. Paris: Presses universitaires de France, 1973.

Rothstein, Eric. *Restoration and Eighteenth-Century Poetry, 1660–1780*. Boston: Routledge & Kegan Paul, 1981.

Rumbold, Valerie. *Women's Place in Pope's World*. Cambridge: Cambridge University Press, 1989.

Runge, Laura L. *Gender and Language in British Literary Criticism, 1660–1790*. Cambridge: Cambridge University Press, 1997.

Salvaggio, Ruth. *Englightened Absence: Neoclassical Configurations of the Feminine*. Urbana: University of Illinois Press, 1988.

Salzman, Paul. "Aphra Behn: Poetry and Masquerade." In *Aphra Behn Studies*, edited by Janet Todd. Cambridge: Cambridge University Press, 1996.

Sambrook, James. Introduction to *James Thomson's The Seasons and The Castle of Indolence*. Edited by James Sambrook. Oxford: Clarendon Press, 1972.

———. Introduction. William Cowper. The Task *and Selected Other Poems*. Edited by James Sambrook. London: Longman, 1994.

———. *James Thomson, 1700–1748: A Life*. Oxford: Clarendon Press, 1991.

Scarry, Elaine. *On Beauty and Being Just*. Princeton: Princeton University Press, 1999.

Schiebinger, Londa. *Nature's Body: Gender in the Making of Modern Science.* Boston: Beacon Press, 1993.

Schindler, Walter. *Voice and Crisis: Invocation in Milton's Poetry.* Hamden, CT: Archon Books, 1984.

Sessions, William A. "Abandonment and the English Religious Lyric in the Seventeenth Century." In *"Bright Shootes of Everlastingnesse": The Seventeenth-Century Religious Lyric*, Essays in Seventeenth-Century Literature, vol. 2, edited by Claude J. Summers and Ted-Larry Pebworth. Columbia: University of Missouri Press, 1987.

Shawcross, John T. "The Metaphor of Inspiration in *Paradise Lost.*" In *Th'upright Heart and Pure; Essays on John Milton Commemorating the Tercentenary of the Publication of* Paradise Lost, edited by Amadeus P. Fiore. Pittsburgh: Duquesne University Press, 1967.

Sherburn, George, and Donald F. Bond, *The Restoration and Eighteenth Century, 1660–1789. A Literary History of England.* Vol. 3. Edited by Albert C. Baugh. 2nd ed. London: Routledge & Kegan Paul, 1967.

Sherwin, Paul. *Precious Bane: Collins and the Miltonic Legacy.* Austin: University of Texas Press, 1977.

Shevelow, Kathryn. *Women and Print Culture: The Construction of Femininity in the Early Periodical.* London: Routledge, 1989.

Siskin, Clifford. "Personification and Community: Literary Change in the Mid- and Late- Eighteenth Century" *Eighteenth-Century Studies* 15, no. 4 (Summer 1982): 371–401.

Sitter, John. *Literary Loneliness in Mid-Eighteenth-Century England.* Ithaca: Cornell University Press, 1982.

Skinner, Gillian. "Women's Status as Legal and Civil Subjects: 'A Worse Condition than Slavery Itself'?" In *Women and Literature in Britain, 1700–1800*, edited by Vivien Jones. Cambridge: Cambridge University Press, 2000.

Snider, Alvin. "Cartesian Bodies." *Modern Philology* 98, no. 2 (November 2000): 299–319.

Solomon, Harry M. *The Rape of the Text: Reading and Misreading Pope's* Essay on Man. Tuscaloosa: University of Alabama Press, 1993.

Soper, Kate. *What Is Nature? Culture, Politics and the Non-human.* Oxford: Blackwell, 1995.

Spacks, Patricia Meyer. *An Argument of Images: The Poetry of Alexander Pope.* Cambridge, MA: Harvard University Press, 1971.

———. *The Poetry of Vision: Five Eighteenth-Century Poets.* Cambridge, MA: Harvard University Press, 1967.

Starr, Herbert W. "'A Youth to Fortune and to Fame Unknown': A Re-estimation." In *Twentieth-Century Interpretations of Gray's* Elegy: *A Collection of Critical Essays*, edited by Herbert W. Starr. Englewood Cliffs, NJ: Prentice-Hall, 1968.

Staves, Susan. *Married Women's Separate Property in England, 1660–1833.* Cambridge, MA: Harvard University Press, 1990.

———. *Players' Scepters: Fictions of Authority in the Restoration.* Lincoln: University of Nebraska Press, 1979.

Stiebel, Arlene. "Subversive Sexuality: Masking the Erotic in Poems by Katherine Philips and Aphra Behn." In *Renaissance Discourses of Desire*, edited by Claude J. Summers and Ted-Larry Pebworth. Columbia: University of Missouri Press, 1993.

Straub, Kristina. "Indecent Liberties with a Poet: Audience and the Metaphor of Rape in Killigrew's 'Upon the Saying that My Verses' and Pope's *Arbuthnot*." *Tulsa Studies in Women's Literature* 6 (1987): 27–45.

Sutherland, John H. "The Stonecutter in Gray's 'Elegy.'" In *Twentieth-Century Interpretations of Gray's* Elegy: *A Collection of Critical Essays*, edited by Herbert W. Starr. Englewood Cliffs, NJ: Prentice-Hall, 1968.

Teague, Frances. "Early Modern Women and 'the muses ffemall.'" In *"The Muses Females Are": Mary Moulsworth and Other Women Writers of the English Renaissance*, edited by Robert C. Evans and Anne C. Little. West Cornwall, CT: Locust Hill Press, 1995.

Terry, Richard. *Poetry and the Making of the English Literary Past, 1660–1781.* Oxford: Oxford University Press, 2001.

Thomas, Claudia N. *Alexander Pope and His Eighteenth-Century Women Readers.* Carbondale: Southern Illinois University Press, 1994.

Todd, Janet. *Sensibility: An Introduction.* London: Methuen, 1986.

Trickett, Rachel. "The Augustan Pantheon: Mythology and Personification in Eighteenth-Century Poetry." *Essays and Studies* 6 (1953): 71–86.

Turner, James. *The Politics of Landscape: Rural Scenery and Society in English Poetry 1630–1660*. Cambridge, MA: Harvard University Press, 1979.

Van Doren, Mark. *The Poetry of John Dryden.* New York: Harcourt, Brace, 1920.

Vieth, David M. "Irony in Dryden's Ode to Anne Killigrew." *Studies in Philology* 62 (1965): 91–100.

Waldron, Mary. *Lactilla, Milkwoman of Clifton: The Life and Writings of Ann Yearsley, 1753–1806*. Athens: University of Georgia Press, 1996.

Wasserman, Earl R. "Collins' 'Ode on the Poetic Character.'" *ELH: A Journal of English Literary History* 34 (1967): 92–115.

———. "The Inherent Values of Eighteenth-Century Personification." *PMLA* 65, part 2 (1950): 435–63.

———. *The Subtler Language: Critical Readings of Neoclassic and Romantic Poems*. Baltimore: Johns Hopkins Press, 1959.

Weinbrot, Howard D. *Augustus Caesar in "Augustan" England: The Decline of a Classical Norm*. Princeton: Princeton University Press, 1978.

Weinfield, Henry. *The Poet without a Name: Gray's* Elegy *and the Problem of History*. Carbondale: Southern Illinois University Press, 1991.

Weiskel, Thomas. *The Romantic Sublime: Studies in the Structure and Psychology of Transcendence.* Baltimore: Johns Hopkins University Press, 1976.

Wesling, Donald. "Augustan Form: Justification and Breakup of a Period Style." *Texas Studies in Literature and Language* 22, no. 3 (Fall 1980): 394–428.

Wilcox, Helen. "My Hart is Full, My Soul Dos Ouer Flow": Women's Devotional Poetry in Seventeenth-Century England." In *Forging Connections: Women's Poetry from the Renaissance to Romanticism*, edited by Anne K. Mellor, Felicity Nussbaum, and Jonathan F. S. Post. San Marino, CA: Huntington Library, 2002.

Willey, Basil. *The Eighteenth-Century Background: Studies on the Idea of Nature in the Thought of the Period.* London: Chatto & Windus, 1940.

Williams, Raymond. "Nature." In *Keywords: A Vocabulary of Culture and Society*, revised edition. New York: Oxford University Press, 1983.

Wilson, Penelope. "Engendering the Reader: 'Wit and Poetry and Pope' Once More." In *The Enduring Legacy: Alexander Pope Tercentenary Essays*, edited by G. S. Rousseau and Pat Rogers. Cambridge: Cambridge University Press, 1988.

Winn, James Anderson. "Pope Plays the Rake: His Letters to Ladies and the Making of the *Eloisa*." In *The Art of Alexander Pope*, edited by Howard Erskine-Hill and Anne Smith. New York: Barnes & Noble, 1979.

———. *"When Beauty Fires the Blood": Love and the Arts in the Age of Dryden.* Ann Arbor: University of Michigan Press, 1992.

Wolfson, Susan J. "Reading for Form." *Modern Language Quarterly* 61, no. 1 (March 2000): 1–16.

Woodman, Thomas, ed. *Early Romantics: Perspectives in British Poetry from Pope to Wordsworth.* Houndmills, UK: Macmillan, 1998.

Woodmansee, Martha. *The Author, Art, and the Market: Rereading the History of Aesthetics.* New York: Columbia University Press, 1994.

———. "The Genius and the Copyright: Economic and Legal Conditions of the Emergence of the 'Author.'" *Eighteenth-Century Studies* 17, no. 4 (Summer 1984): 425–48.

Yaeger, Patricia. "Toward a Female Sublime." In *Gender and Theory: Dialogues on Feminist Criticism*, edited by Linda Kaufman. Oxford: Basil Blackwell, 1989.

Young, Elizabeth V. "Aphra Behn, Gender, and Pastoral." *SEL: Studies in English Literature* 33, no. 3 (1993): 523–43.

Zionkowski, Linda. *Men's Work: Gender, Class, and the Professionalism of Poetry, 1660–1784.* New York: Palgrave, 2001.

Zwicker, Steven N. *Lines of Authority: Politics and English Literary Culture, 1649–1689.* Ithaca: Cornell University Press, 1993.

———. *Politics and Language in Dryden's Poetry: The Arts of Disguise.* Princeton: Princeton University Press, 1984.

Index

Abrams, M. H., 24
Adams, Jean, 89–90, 93
Addison, Joseph: "Ode," 86–88; *Spectator*, 86, 89, 111, 188 n. 21
Adorno, Theodor, 24
Alpheus, 65, 191 n. 63
Altieri, Charles, 165–66
Andreadis, Harriette, 180 n. 12
Anne, Queen of England, 101–3, 105, 191 n. 62
antislavery poetry, 163–64
Apollo, 44, 49, 58, 62–64, 67–68, 71, 78, 103, 104, 127, 129, 137
Arethusa, 65–66, 191 n. 63
art as imitation of nature, 14, 46, 63, 98
Ashfield, Andrew, 144, 157–58, 200 n. 22, 202 n. 68
Attridge, Derek, 166, 203 n. 74
Aubin, Roger, 186 n. 2
Augustan. *See* periodization
authority, poetic: and gender, 12–13, 31–39, 45–47, 54–72; and morality (*see* virtue); and political authority, 31–35, 39–40, 75–76, 102; and prophecy, 64, 77; and religious authority, 35–37, 77–78

Baillie, John, 143
Barash, Carol, 75–76, 167 n. 1, 180 n. 9, 180 n. 13, 181 n. 21, 181 n. 25, 182 n. 29, 182 n. 32, 182 n. 33, 184 n. 52
Barkan, Leonard, 174 n. 13

Barker-Benfield, G. J., 141, 199 n. 5, 199 n. 6
Barrell, John, 22, 186 n. 3, 188 n. 23, 191–92 n. 69, 193 n. 80
Bate, Walter Jackson, 170 n. 35, 172 n. 57
Battersby, Christine, 19, 193 n. 80
Beattie, James, 143
Behn, Aphra: "On a Juniper-Tree, cut down to make Busks," 95–100; "To the fair Clarinda," 99
Bender, John, 169 n. 19
Benedict, Barbara, 194 n. 18
Bermingham, Ann, 170 n. 31
Blair, Hugh, 142, 143, 145, 172 n. 56
Bloom, Harold, 34
Bogel, Fredric, 135, 138, 196–97 n. 37, 197 n. 42, 198 n. 58
Bolingbroke, Henry St. John, Viscount, 105–9, 191–92 n. 69
Bond, Donald, 197 n. 38
Bonnell, Thomas, 183 n. 36
Boyer, James, 31
Brissenden, R.F., 200 n. 13
Bronson, Bertrand, 171 n. 50
Brower, Reuben, 194 n. 13
Brown, Laura, 17–18
Brown, Marshall, 168 n. 17
Budick, Sanford, 174 n. 13
Burke, Edmund, 142, 143, 144
Burke, Tim, 162
Burwick, Frederick, 22
Butler, Judith, 85, 171 n. 42

Campbell, Lily, 176 n. 28
Carretta, Vincent, 191 n. 62, 191 n. 65
Carruthers, Mary, 180 n. 11
Carstairs, Christian: "Nightingale," 150–151
Cassandra, 64
Cassirer, Ernst, 171 n. 49, 193 n. 2
Chandler, Albert, 201 n. 36
Charles I, King of England, 83–85, 187 n. 14
Charles II, King of England, 32, 39–41
class and representation, 93–94, 116, 119, 121, 131, 157–61. *See also* labor
Cole, Lucinda, 164
Coleridge, Samuel T., 30
Collier, Mary: "The Woman's Labour," 93–94
Collins, William: "Ode to Evening," 126–29; "Ode on the Poetical Character," 129–31
commodification, 23–24, 97, 119, 133–34. *See also* marketplace, literary
Conroy, Mark, 30
Cowley, Abraham, 35–36
Cowper, William: "Hatred and Vengeance, My Eternal Portion," 147–48; "The Castaway," 148
Crawford, Rachel, 82, 186 n. 3, 190 n. 51
Culler, Jonathan, 171 n. 50
Curran, Stuart, 169 n. 25
Curtius, Ernst, 173 n. 2, 176 n. 28

D'Alessandro, Jean Ellis, 183 n. 36, 194 n. 12
Daphne, 58, 62–65, 93, 95, 103
Deane, C. V., 187 n. 9
de Beauvoir, Simone, 179 n. 3
de Bolla, Peter, 144, 157–58, 164, 165, 200 n. 22, 202 n. 68
DeJean, Joan, 180 n. 4
de Man, Paul, 186 n. 8
Denham, John: *Cooper's Hill*, 82–85, 88, 90
De Shazer, Mary, 179 n. 4

desire: for the divine, 77–78, 146–49; and representation, 84–85, 126–28, 156; and sexual reputation, 98–100
Deutsch, Helen, 45, 100, 169 n. 20, 172 n. 58, 178 n. 61, 190 n. 56, 191 n. 57
Diehl, Joanne Feit, 179 n. 4
Di Pesa, Pamela, 179 n. 4
divine, the, 35–37, 61–62, 77–78, 86–88, 146–49
Dobrée, Bonamy, 37, 175 n. 18
Donne, John, 72
Doody, Margaret Anne, 16, 32, 138, 149, 169 n. 22, 172 n. 58, 175 n. 18
Dryden, John: *Absalom and Achitophel*, 39, 190 n. 54; "Anne Killigrew," 41–42, 64–66; *Annus Mirabilis*, 38; *Astraea Redux*, 190 n. 54; *Eleonora*, 42–44; *Mac Flecknoe*, 38; *Threnodia Augustalis*, 38, 40
Dubrow, Heather, 171 n. 48
Dunton, John, 76, 171 n. 37
Dyer, John: "Grongar Hill," 119–20

Eagleton, Terry, 172 n. 54
Ellis, Frank, 198 n. 51
Ellison, Julie, 199 n. 6
empirical representation: and fancy, 83–84; and the feminine, 22, 87, 100, 109, 121, 127; and feminine nature, 81–82; and myth, 37–38, 43
Empson, William, 197 n. 49, 198 n. 53
Erickson, Robert, 189 n. 35, 196 n. 33
Erskine-Hill, Howard, 174 n. 7
ethics and aesthetics, 152, 165–66
Eusden, Laurence, 194 n. 18
Exclusion Crisis, the, 40
Ezell, Margaret, 29, 173 n. 61

Fabricant, Carole, 80, 94, 168 n. 9, 178 n. 59, 189 n. 39
Fairer, David, 11, 16, 45, 195 n. 20
fancy. *See* imagination
feminine, the: functions of 17, 81–83, 85–88, 100–110, 111–12; as "je ne

sais quoi," 19; as restrictive to women writers, 62–63, 66, 88–90. *See also* muse; personification
Ferguson, Moira, 160, 167 n. 1
Finch, Anne: "An Epistle. From Ardelia to Mrs. Randolph in Answer to her Poem upon Her Verses," 72–74; "Friendship between Ephelia and Ardelia," 74–75; "The Introduction," 68–69; "A Letter to the Same Person," 71–72; "From the Muses, at Parnassus," 69–70; "A Nocturnal Reverie," 113–15; "Preface," 67–68, 88–89; "To Mr. F. Now Earl of W.," 70–71; "To the Nightingale," 151–53; "To the Right Honourable Frances Countess of Hartford who engaged Mr Eusden . . . ," 116–19
Flinker, Noam, 175 n. 27
Flora, 102
Fontanier, Pierre, 193 n. 1
Freadman, Anne, 179 n. 2, 180 n. 4
Freeman, Barbara Claire, 26, 164, 165, 202 n. 58, 202 n. 64
Frieden, Ken, 192–93 n. 80
friendship: and authority, 40; and mimesis, 53, 54–56, 72–74
Frye, Northrop, 168 n. 17
Fulford, Tim, 82
Fuss, Diana, 26, 172 n. 52

Gallagher, Catherine, 53
Gebauer, Gunter, 53, 184 n. 60
gendered structure of representation: 13–14, 18, 44, 80–83, 164–65; "de-gendered," 98. *See also* representation; subject-object relations
genius, 85, 108, 192–93 n. 80
Gentili, Bruno, 179–80 n. 4
Gerard, Alexander, 143
Gerrard, Christine, 195 n. 20
Gilbert, Pamela, 194 n. 11
Gilbert, Sandra, 13, 169 n. 25
Gleckner, Robert, 134, 169 n. 20, 197 n. 50, 198 n. 58
graveyard poetry, 197 n. 38

Gray, Thomas: "The Bard," 145–46; *Elegy*, 131–35, 145; "The Progress of Poesy," 198 n. 57
Greene, Richard, 169 n. 25
Greer, Germaine, 76, 171 n. 37, 184 n. 62, 195 n. 23
Griffin, Dustin, 16, 179 n. 64
Gubar, Susan, 13, 169 n. 25
Guillory, John, 133, 135, 165, 174 n. 11, 198 n. 55

Hagstrum, Jean, 177 n. 47, 193 n. 4, 193 n. 6, 196 n. 29
Hammond, Brean, 108, 191 n. 68, 192 n. 79
heart: landscape of the, 92–93; writing on the, 189 n. 35
Hertford, Countess of, 116, 120, 121
Hinnant, Charles H., 11, 52, 152, 182 n. 36, 184 n. 48, 184 n. 50, 184 n. 56, 194 n. 14, 194 n. 16, 194 n. 18
Hobby, Elaine, 180 n. 15, 181 n. 25, 182 n. 32
Hoffman, Arthur, 177 n. 43, 177 n. 47
Home, Henry, 193 n. 6
Hope, A. D., 177 n. 45
Hughes, Helen Sard, 195 n. 23
Huhn, Tom, 199–200 n. 10
Hunt, John Dixon, 191 n. 66, 192 n. 78
Hutchings, W.B., 195 n. 24, 196 n. 31

identification: 67, 70, 75, 113–18, 165; and female friendship, 56; and sensibility, 142; symbolic violence of, 26
imagination, or fancy, 84, 86, 129, 147, 149
Ingrassia, Catherine, 45, 178 n. 62, 179 n. 71, 190 n. 56
inspiration, 34–37, 44, 51

Jackson, Wallace, 193–94 n. 6
Jaffe, Nora Crow, 168 n. 6
James II, King of England, 32, 40–41

Johnson, Claudia, 199 n. 6
Jones, Robert, 170 n. 35

Kairoff, Claudia Thomas, 13. *See also* Thomas, Claudia N.
Kaul, Suvir, 133, 135, 194 n. 8, 197 n. 49, 197–98 n. 50
Keats, John, 28
Killigrew, Anne: "Alexandreis," 59–60; "To the Queen," 60–61; represented by Dryden, 41–42, 64–66; "Upon the saying that my Verses were made by another," 61–66
King, Kathryn, 185 n. 69, 190 n. 50
Korshin, Paul, 174 n. 13
Kramer, David Bruce, 178 n. 56
Krieger, Murray, 75

Labbe, Jacqueline, 80, 188 n. 29
labor: internalized, 133–34; and laboring class, 78, 131–33, 135–38, 159; poetic, 111–12, 125–26, 135–38. *See also* class
Landry, Donna, 167 n. 1, 170 n. 30
landscape. *See* nature, property; prospect
language, limits of, 67, 71–75, 115, 117–18, 124–25, 151–53. *See also* representation
Leapor, Mary: "Crumble-Hall," 93; "The Muses Embassy" 78; "The Proposal," 78; "The Sacrifice. An Epistle to Celia," 78; "On Winter," 135–38
Levinas, Emmanuel, 138–39, 199 n. 69
Lipking, Lawrence, 33, 81, 138, 172 n. 51, 187 n. 10, 193 n. 3
Locke, Mary, 143–44
Longinus, 143
Lonsdale, Roger, 18–19, 185 n. 70, 188 n. 26, 200 n. 20
Loscocco, Paula, 181 n. 19, 181 n. 20, 182 n. 34
Lovejoy, Arthur O., 14–15
Low, Anthony, 186 n. 3

Mack, Maynard, 178 n. 57, 192 n. 72, 193 n. 80

Mahoney, John, 171 n. 38, 171 n. 39, 180 n. 6, 180 n. 7
Mallinson, Jean, 183 n. 36, 194 n. 9
Mandell, Laura, 167 n. 1, 168 n. 15, 171 n. 43
Mansfield, Nick, 202 n. 63
manuscript circulation, 29, 76
marketplace, literary, 19, 23–24. *See also* commodification
Markley, Robert, 201 n. 42
Marshall, Madeleine Forell, 201 n. 31
Martin, Roberta, 189 n. 45
Maruca, Lisa, 168 n. 4
Mary of Modena, 59–61, 181 n. 23
masculinity: and incorporation of the feminine, 20, 21, 46–47, 100–110, 131–33; and the muse, 30–50; and poetic subjectivity, 16, 19, 20, 44, 120; and virtue, 144–46
McDowell, Paula, 168 n. 4, 170 n. 33
McGann, Jerome, 159, 169 n. 19
McGovern, Barbara, 75, 182–83 n. 36, 183 n. 43, 194 n. 18, 195 n. 23
McKillop, Alan, 196 n. 30
Melberg, Arne, 14
Mellor, Anne, 165, 169 n. 25, 202 n. 64, 202 n. 65
Merchant, Carolyn, 113, 168 n. 8, 186 n. 4, 194 n. 11
Mermin, Dorothy, 51
Messenger, Ann, 183 n. 36, 201 n. 36
Milton, John, 36–37, 176 n. 31
mimesis: anti-mimetic, 67; and marriage, 71–72; as ontological emulation, 22, 24, 55–57, 73, 106–10; and personification, 117–19, 128–30; politics of, 53; transformative function of, 14; violence of, 58, 62–63, 65. *See also* representation
Montagu, Lady Mary Wortley: "Epistle to Bathurst," 90–93
More, Hannah, 159
Morris, David B., 27, 140, 190 n. 58, 199 n. 9, 201 n. 31
Morse, David, 184 n. 64
muse(s): as defining authority and representation, 30–50; and subject-object relations, 51–79

myth(s), uses of, 18, 38, 61, 65–66, 103–4. *See also names of individual mythological characters.*

Narcissus, 84, 191 n. 66
nature: art as imitation of, 14, 46, 63, 98; as feminine, 14–15, 62–63, 66; as form or order, 14–15, 24, 193 n. 2; immanence with, 22, 112–15, 122–23; and vitalism, 113. *See also* property; prospect
Nicolson, Marjorie Hope, 175 n. 26
nightingale, 150–53
Novak, Maximillian, 174 n. 7

O Hehir, Brendan, 187 n. 13, 187 n. 16
Ortner, Sherry, 168 n. 8
Ovid, 62, 103

Pan, 102, 103, 191 n. 63
Parker, Blanford, 169–70 n. 27
pastoral: 91–93, 94–98, 102, 104; and laborer's perspective, 137
Paxson, James, 171 n. 50
Peace of Utrecht, 191 n. 64
Peckham, Morse, 198 n. 51
periodization, 11, 15–17
personification, 95–97, 111–38, 193 n. 1, 193 n. 3
Philips, Katherine: 55–59; "Friendship's Mystery, To my dearest Lucasia," 56; "To my Excellent Lucasia, on our Friendship," 55–56; "To the Excellent Mrs. Anne Owen, upon her receiving the name of Lucasia," 56–57
Philo-Philippa [pseudonym]: "To the Excellent Orinda," 58–59
Phoebus. *See* Apollo
Piper, William Bowman, 173 n. 5
Pipkin, John G., 26, 153, 164, 165, 200 n. 21, 202 n. 65
poetic kinds, hierarchy of, 12–13, 45, 73, 153
Pollak, Ellen, 49, 170–71 n. 36, 179 n. 74
Poovey, Mary, 18, 188 n. 20

Pope, Alexander: *Dunciad*, 48–49; *Eloisa to Abelard*, 178 n. 58; *Essay on Criticism*, 47–48; *Essay on Man*, 105–110; "Messiah," 178 n. 58; *Pastorals*, 45–47; *Windsor Forest*, 101–5
Price, Martin, 197 n. 45
Priestley, Joseph, 196 n. 32
property: 82–84, 88–90, 93, 100; self as, 64, 190 n. 56, 194 n. 8; and women's sexual reputations, 95–99. *See also* nature; prospect
prospect: 80–110, 119; governmental politics of, 83–85, 101–5

representation: 51–53, 57; as gendered structure, 13–14, 18. *See also* mimesis; subject-object relations
Revard, Stella P., 175 n. 23
rhetorical conventions, gender and, 12–13. *See also* authority; muse(s); personification
Riede, David, 169 n. 24
Riffaterre, Michael, 196 n. 34
Rogers, Pat, 135, 183 n. 41, 198 n. 58
Rooney, Ellen, 171 n. 47
Rose, Mark, 167 n. 4
Ross, Marlon, 169 n. 25, 172 n. 58
Rosset, Clément, 186 n. 7, 191 n. 60
Rothstein, Eric, 16
Rowe, Elizabeth Singer: 76–78; (blank verse) soliloquy 7, 77, 148–49; (blank verse) soliloquy 8, 77–78, 149, 185 n. 68; "The Vision," 77
Rumbold, Valerie, 45, 190 n. 56
Runge, Laura, 19, 26, 164

Salvaggio, Ruth, 194 n. 12
Salzman, Paul, 190 n. 52
Sambrook, James, 195 n. 23, 196 n. 36, 200 n. 28
satire, 91, 92, 172 n. 59
Schiebinger, Londa, 168 n. 9
Schindler, Walter, 176 n. 29, 179 n. 65
sensibility, 140–42, 149–53. *See also* sublime
Sessions, William A., 141, 199 n. 8

Seward, Anna: "Address to Woman," 153; "Sonnet 10. To Honora Sneyd," 156–57; "Sonnet 71, To the Poppy," 155–56; "Sonnet 82," 153–54; "Sonnet 88," 154; "Sonnet 89," 154–55; "Sonnet 90," 154–55
Shaftesbury, Anthony Ashley Cooper, 3rd Earl of, 28, 31, 173 n. 3
Shawcross, John, 175 n. 27
Sherburn, George, 197 n. 38
Sherwin, Paul, 127, 197 n. 40, 197 n. 41
Shevelow, Kathryn, 167 n. 4, 174 n. 17
Sidney, Sir Philip, 71, 75
Siskin, Clifford, 31, 138, 171 n. 50
Sitter, John, 146, 168 n. 17, 194 n. 7, 195 n. 22
Skinner, Gillian, 188 n. 30
Smith, Adam, 144–45
Snider, Alvin, 189 n. 42, 189 n. 43
Solomon, Harry, 192 n. 76
Soper, Kate, 168 n. 8
Spacks, Patricia Meyer, 48, 106, 179 n. 69, 179 n. 70, 196 n. 27
Starr, Herbert, 198 n. 51
Staves, Susan, 88, 177 n. 42, 188 n. 30
Steele, Richard, 18–19
Stiebel, Arlene, 180 n. 12
Straub, Kristina, 182 n. 31
Stuart court, 53, 76, 102
subjectivity, poetic: annihilation or surrender of, 28, 56, 93; as "deep self," 23, 110, 134–35, 140; elusiveness of, 99–100; and ethics, 165–66; and feminine virtue, 47, 61, 93
subject-object relations: assertion of the object, 91–93, 94, 98, 116; and personification, 24–25, 113–19, 121–39; and revisions of the muse, 51, 71–79. *See also* mimesis; representation
sublime, the: female, 202 n. 64; gendered structure of 164–65; and obscurity, 146, 151, 154, 156–60, 162; religious sublime, 140–41, 146–49; and sensibility, or sentimental sublime, 140–65

Sutherland, John, 198 n. 51
Swartz, Richard G., 164
Swift, Jonathan: "Apollo Outwitted. To the Honourable Mrs Finch," 68; *Cadenus and Vanessa*, 50; "The Dean's Reasons for Not Building at Drapier's Hill," 94; "Drapier's Hill," 94; "Stella's Birthday (1723), 49–50; "Verses Wrote in a Lady's Ivory Table-Book," 189 n. 34

Teague, Francis, 181 n. 27
Terry, Richard, 172 n. 60
Thomas, Claudia N., 167 n. 1, 168 n. 7, 192 n. 71. *See also* Kairoff, Claudia Thomas
Thomson, James: *The Seasons*, 120–26
Todd, Janet, 199 n. 7
topographical poetry. *See* prospect
Trickett, Rachel, 189 n. 33
Turner, James, 186 n. 3, 186 n. 6, 188 n. 23

Usher, James, 154

Van Doren, Mark, 38
Vieth, David, 177 n. 45
Virgil, 44, 73
virtue: and masculinity, 144–46; and poetic authority, 41–43, 47–48, 59–61, 65, 93, 158; and sublimity, 42–43, 142–45, 164
vitalism, 113

Waldron, Mary, 158, 198–99 n. 65, 201 n. 45, 201 n. 46, 202 n. 51
Warton, Joseph, 141–42, 195 n. 22
Wasserman, Earl, 171 n. 50, 187 n. 16, 191 n. 64, 191 n. 67, 197 n. 46
Watts, Isaac: "The Hurry of the Spirits," 146–47
Weinbrot, Howard, 174 n. 7
Weinfield, Henry, 131–32
Weiskel, Thomas, 197 n. 44, 200 n. 11
Wesling, Donald, 173 n. 5
Wilcox, Helen, 201 n. 30

Williams, Helen Maria: "On the Bill . . . Regulating the Slave-Trade," 163–64
Williams, Raymond, 14
Wilson, Penelope, 174 n. 10
Winn, James Anderson, 38–39, 40, 41, 58, 176 n. 36, 176–77 n. 41, 177 n. 46
Wolfson, Susan, 168 n. 14, 168 n. 16
Woodmansee, Martha, 167–68 n. 4, 185 n. 1
Wordsworth, William, 18–19
Wulf, Christian, 53, 184 n. 60

Yaeger, Patricia, 202 n. 64

Yearsley, Ann: "Addressed to Sensibility," 149–50; "To Mrs. V———N," 158; "Remonstrance in the Platonic Shade," 160–63; "To Those Who Accuse the Author of Ingratitude," 159–60
Young, Edward: *The Last Day*, 147
Young, Elizabeth, 189 n. 40, 189 n. 45

Zionkowski, Linda, 23–24, 167 n. 1
Zwicker, Steven, 32, 35, 39, 174 n. 8, 175 n. 21, 175 n. 22, 176 n. 38, 176 n. 39